Rails Across London

John Glover

crecy.co.uk

First published 2018

ISBN 978 0 86093 690 9

Printed by Opolgraf in Poland

Crécy Publishing Ltd
1a Ringway Trading Estate, Shadowmoss Rd, Manchester M22 5LH
www.crecy.co.uk

Front cover:
A southbound Thameslink train arrives at Kentish Town on 4 April 2017, formed of eight-car unit No 700009. There is a first-class yellow band at the top of the leading side of the first vehicle, but this can be quite difficult to see. *John Glover*

Back cover, top:
Freight traffic along the North London line may, as here, be making south west, though Feltham Yard has long since gone. No 66058 is seen here heading west through South Acton station towards Feltham on 4 June 2013. *John Glover*

Back cover, middle:
At Bourne End on 6 November 1998, the Marlow branch train formed of 165001 waits in what appears to be an ordinary wayside station, until one notices that the line is truncated at the far end. This was the former continuation to High Wycombe, but there is a road beyond the stops and housing beyond that. The platform on the right can take five cars, but it is not possible to proceed from there towards Marlow. *John Glover*

Back cover, bottom:
On the Hertford East branch, unit 315849 arrives at the terminus in September 2001, with its tail lights already lit for the return journey. It sports the colourless (undercoat?) livery which was at the time common on such services. Signalling was still locally controlled from the Great Eastern box, seen here, with a searchlight-style colour-light starting signal on the right. *John Glover*

Contents

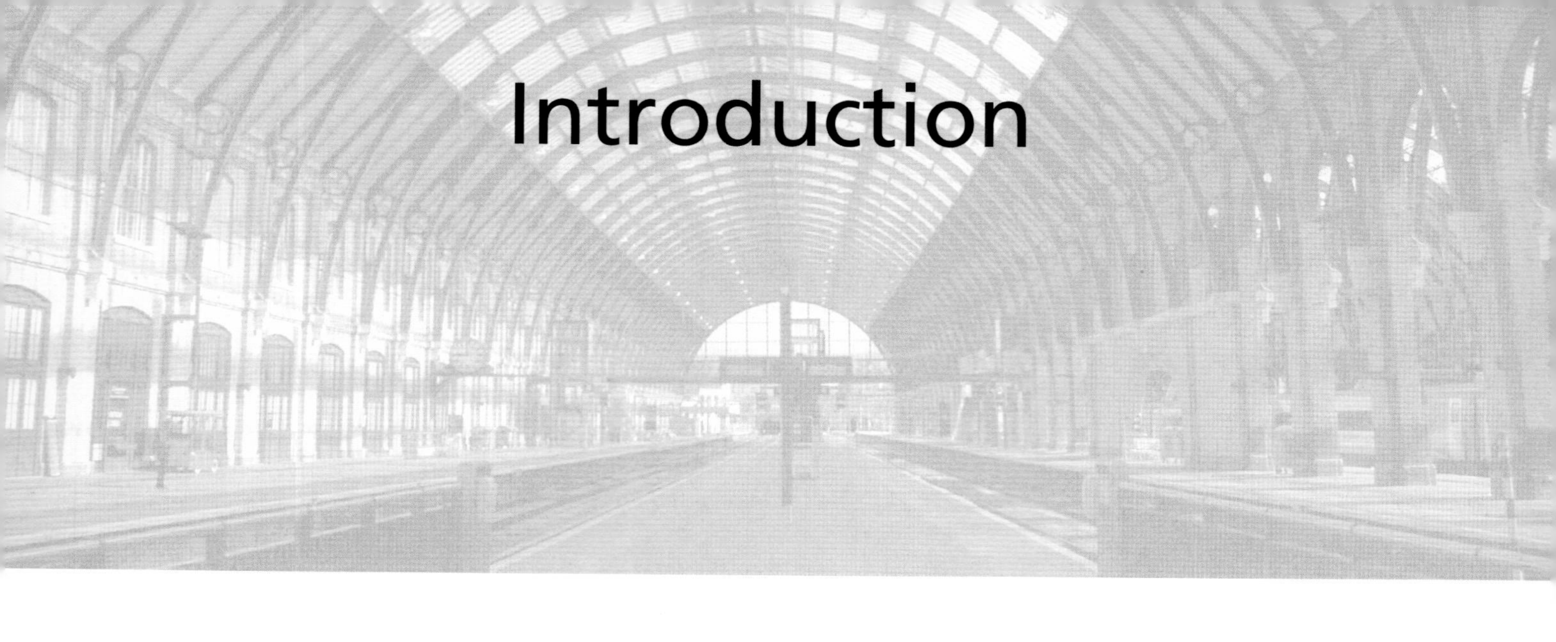

Introduction

This volume explores and discusses the three biggest developments in London's railways for many years. These are the east–west Crossrail (Elizabeth) line, the Thameslink north-south large scale upgrade, and what may become Crossrail 2. All are aimed at meeting the growing travel market in the London area by providing extra capacity and relieving many railway routes of the severe congestion problems with which they are faced.

As so often with matters railway, the gestation period goes back many years. This book traces their origins and their development, through to the fruition – or nearly so – of two of them. These are large scale schemes by any measure and they are not achieved quickly, certainly not within the timespan of one General Election to the next.

In the 1930s the Government kick-started an investment programme with cheap money, but this was cut short by World War 2. Times change, as do political priorities; one of the most striking themes of post-war planning was the concerted push to rid the London scene of the ugly railway bridges across the Thames. This would have had severe consequences for the network and its users, which the book explores.

This representation of an early Metropolitan Railway train may be found at the base of the History Sundial outside Tower Hill station (which is on the District line). Tunnels filled with smoke and the lack of protection for the locomotive crew are both authentic, though the coach doors do not have the rounded tops that became an unofficial trademark. *John Glover*

In reality, apart from some electrification works, the financial realities of post-war Britain meant that very little happened at all. The Victoria line, identified as a prime requirement in 1949, opened over 20 years later.

This was not purely a matter for what is now termed National Railways. How does (or should) London Underground fit in? The distribution of large numbers arriving at the London termini, nearly all some distance from the centre was an obvious task, but could the Underground cope? It had its own business of carrying people from the many suburbs it served directly.

In all of this, the seeds of the present cross-London projects can be identified.

This book draws together the various themes and approaches used over the years. It records the many successful ventures in modernising the system, but also some of the underlying threats.

It concludes with a tentative look into the future. It should perhaps be stated that the emphasis is on urban, suburban and London Underground railways and matters specific to London and the South East.

John Glover
Worcester Park, Surrey
December 2017

On a Saturday morning, the main line platforms at King's Cross are rarely as empty as this. The view is down Platforms 6 and 7 on 2 July 2016, showing the fine station building at its best. *John Glover*

1 Networks Become Established

Reaching London from north, west and east, the railways for the most part touch, but do not cross, this semi-circle; and the southern lines, with one exception, are content if they can deliver their passengers on the northern bank of the river. Charles Booth, 1892

This book is about the development of London's railways after the early years had passed. The story thus starts in the inter-war years of 1918–1939, continuing to the present day and beyond.

There are however a number of events in the earlier history which proved to have long term effects on what has happened subsequently. These are:

- The 1846 Royal Commission on London Termini, which determined where the termini should, or more precisely should not, be built.
- The 1892 Joint Select Committee (House of Commons, House of Lords) on Electric and Cable Railways. Their findings largely determined the quite restricted tunnel dimensions of London's future tube railways, and
- The different wishes and expectations of local authorities, compared with the essentially commercial approach of the main line railway companies such as the Great Northern and the London & South Western railways. This had a considerable effect in the approach of those railways which were later to become part of what today is London Underground.

These are now discussed separately.

Royal Commission

The coming of the real railway age started with the opening of the Liverpool & Manchester Railway in 1830. This had been followed by a period of massive railway construction works, to the extent that by 1851 the network had grown to 6,800 miles and showed little sign of stopping.

That was in many ways a good thing, but it was uncoordinated growth which would give rise to several route duplications. But what would happen in the capital? Would the companies want to build a massive terminus (the low land on a north/south axis between Farringdon and the Thames had been mentioned), or should these noisy and land-hungry companies be kept at bay as far as possible?

From the railway companies' point of view, London was already more built up than many other cities, and that caused its own problems. If they wanted to penetrate the central area, somewhere near the Strand, perhaps, this would mean much demolition and very expensive land acquisition. In exchange they would gain benefits in terms of revenue generation from passenger traffic, but in the early years the extent of this was far from certain.

Thus, when Euston was opened in 1837 it was situated a little to the north of the Euston Road which forms a substantial highway along the north side of the central area. But there was still public concern, and this saw the setting up of the Royal Commission on London termini, which reported in 1846.

London Termini without the Underground.

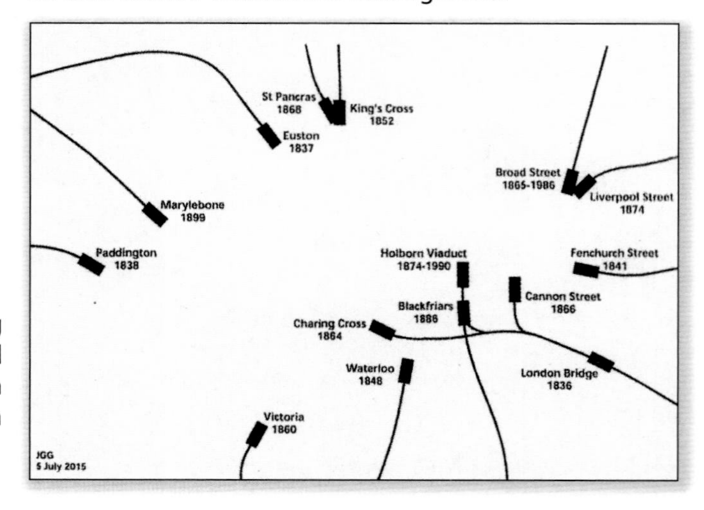

This set the outer limits of railway building as Euston Road with its extensions in the north, London Bridge in the east, Hyde Park Corner in the west and the River Thames in the south. Other railway companies followed the Euston Road example, with King's Cross in 1852, and Paddington in 1854, for instance.

With a few exceptions, this is what happened. The main incursions were those by the Southern companies, which took place across the Thames. This saw the minimal penetration north of the river of Charing Cross and Cannon Street, and the rather more substantial length of two routes (the Chatham and the Brighton lines) to Victoria. Blackfriars and its onward routes (to Holborn Viaduct and to Farringdon) was a special case, discussed later.

One result was that in many cases some additional transport was needed for people to reach their destinations. It was just too far, or took too long, to walk. That can be seen in today's commuter traffic in which there is large scale transfer to London Underground at the main termini, but the problem was real enough in the 19th century.

Less obviously, the 1846 Royal Commission in effect stopped any main line company from providing a through service from one side of central London to the other. The 'no go' area in the centre of the capital was some four miles from east to west and one and a half miles from north to south. It not merely distorted directly the pattern of railway building, but also exercised an arbitrary and indirect influence upon the conditions of competition between companies[1].

This, together with the cost of necessary land acquisition, was enough to make sure that the Royal Commission's intentions were fulfilled.

Subsurface underground

The original part of what was to become London Underground was opened on 10 January 1863 between Paddington and Farringdon Street. This was the first stage of the Metropolitan Railway. Construction was by the cut-and-cover method, ie dig a deep trench, shore up the sides, provide drainage, lay the ballast and the track, then roof it all over (or provide bridging points).

A second company, the Metropolitan District (today's District line), soon appeared, and between them these two companies constructed a large network around the edges of central London but extending outwards and mostly above ground to destinations such as Harrow, Uxbridge, Hounslow, Wimbledon and Barking.

Rather later there was the little matter of electric trains replacing steam. The reasons were succinctly put by Lord Banbury of Southam, in 1933: 'One is the atmosphere and the other is that it was necessary to run as many trains as possible.'

Via Blackfriars

The establishment of the Metropolitan Railway east of King's Cross was followed quickly with the double track over the section thence to Moorgate being increased to four tracks. Physical connections were made with the Great Northern and (later) the Midland Railway. This section was known as the Widened Lines. The Great Western was already connected at Paddington.

The primary reason was to serve goods yards, themselves intended to give access to the various wholesale food markets. But it also allowed the running of main line suburban trains through to the City destination of Moorgate.

From Great Portland Street station looking west, the tunnels seem to be unnecessarily wide. This is a throwback to the early years of the Metropolitan, which was laid with mixed gauge track. The first operator was the Great Western Railway with its 7ft 0¼in broad gauge. After the GW's withdrawal, the platforms were extended outwards. The date is 2 January 2015. ***John Glover***

In the early days when the coaches of the Metropolitan had slam doors, as did other companies, there was the problem of the top edge of the doors hitting the tunnel walls if they were opened in a tunnel section. The company devised an elegant solution by fitting the doors with rounded tops, as seen here at North Weald on 29 June 2013, to lessen the chance of such contact. *John Glover*

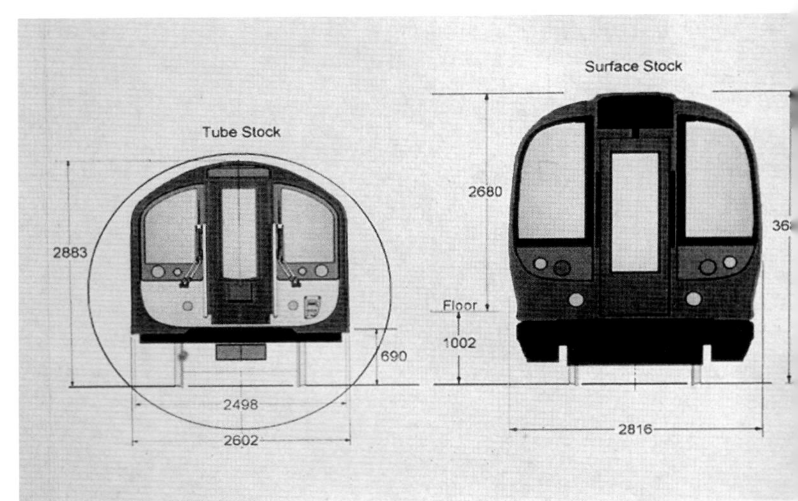

The relative sizes of modern tube and subsurface stock are illustrated by this diagram, which shows how much less excavation (and less soil disposal) is needed when building a tunnel for tube trains rather than subsurface stock. Of particular note is the floor height above rail level, which varies by 312mm or approximately one foot. Ideally, platform heights are adjusted accordingly and the sharing of any one platform by both types of stock is avoided wherever possible.

Why not trains from south of the river as well? The wholesale food markets still needed to be reached. Thus the London, Chatham & Dover Railway was permitted to build a new bridge across the Thames for their Blackfriars station and thence via the Snow Hill tunnel to reach the Widened Lines of the Metropolitan at Farringdon, just short of the platforms.

There was also a link from Blackfriars to a city terminus at Holborn Viaduct. This was on the approximate site of the present City Thameslink station, but with the track at a much higher level.

Passenger services over the link across the Thames did not survive World War 1, though freight and parcels traffic remained. They slowly withered away and all traffic had ceased by 1969. The line was closed and the track lifted in 1971.

The track bed however remained available, to be resurrected a couple of decades later in 1988 as part of what was to become the Thameslink network. This was also the cue for the closure of the now redundant Holborn Viaduct passenger terminus, with the last train running on 26 January 1990.

Tube construction

The City & South London Railway (originally King William Street to Stockwell and now part of the Northern line) might have been worked by cable railway or electrically powered. The latter was chosen. It did, however, have a major drawback in that by common consent, the diameter of the original running tunnels at 10ft 2in was too small. Parliament intervened, and the Committee considering Electric and Cable Railways in 1892 decided that tunnels for tube construction would in future be not less that 11ft 6in wide.

And so it came to pass, with later tube railways that were to fill a very considerable gap in the centre of London constructed to something close to this minimum dimension. This was in spite of the London County Council arguing for 16ft so that they could take full size trains (or nearly so) like the Metropolitan and the District railways, but to no avail.

In this, they may have been right in terms of the freedom that this would have given for inter-running, but making a financial case for constructing what would later become the Central line and a little later the Bakerloo, Northern and Piccadilly lines was difficult enough already. For the central London sections of the latter lines, we have largely the intervention of the American financier Charles Tyson Yerkes to thank.

That produced two distinct Underground railway systems, the subsurface and the tube lines, which for the most part have to be treated separately.

Outlook and ownership

All the tube railways and the District Railway were to come under the aegis of the Underground Electric Railways Company of London (UERL). Formed in 1902, the UERL eventually acquired bus and tram interests as well. A programme of route expansion took the Underground into newly created suburbs of the capital, serving the areas that the main line railways missed. Thus Hounslow West was reached in 1884, Wimbledon in 1889, Barking in 1902, Ealing Broadway (by Central line) 1920, Edgware in 1924, Morden in 1926, and Cockfosters in 1933.

The UERL did not include the Metropolitan Railway, which maintained a separate but also expanding existence until the creation of the London Passenger Transport Board (LPTB) in 1933.

The status of the LPTB was that of a public corporation. It was not nationalised, but it had the statutory duty[2] of 'securing the provision of an adequate and properly co-ordinated system of passenger transport ... and to take such steps as they consider necessary for extending and improving the facilities for passenger transport ... in such manner as to provide most efficiently and conveniently for the needs (of the area concerned)'. The Board was also entreated to break even financially.

A major problem for the newly created London Transport was the distribution within central London of passengers arriving at the main line terminals, in addition to the traffic which the Underground itself was carrying from the suburbs to the centre. This was to lead to a rethink of which organisations should be doing what.

The main line railways of the Great Western (GWR), Southern (SR), London Midland & Scottish (LMSR) and London & North Eastern (LNER), were private companies run for profit until they, together with the LPTB, were nationalised on 1 January 1948.

Peripherals

Outside the central London area and apart from the radial routes of the main line railways, there were four peripheral parts of that system of note. All of these now have passenger services, mostly provided by London Overground:

- The West London line provides a link from Willesden Junction to Clapham Junction. This was used mainly for freight between locations north and south of the river. It uses Chelsea Bridge to cross the Thames. Passenger train service provision has been intermittent.
- The North London line runs from Willesden Junction to Stratford; its main purpose was to give the London & North Western Railway access to London's docklands. A western extension from Willesden Junction provides a route to Richmond. At Gospel Oak the Tottenham & Hampstead line diverges to give a direct route from the North London to Barking and north Thames-side.
- The East London line between Whitechapel and New Cross/New Cross Gate has had a chequered history. The Thames Tunnel was built by the Brunels, father and son, for horse-drawn vehicles, but it was never used as such as no access ramps were built. It was converted to railway use in 1869 and latterly saw a passenger service run by London Underground.
- In South London there are a series of links allowing access between Clapham Junction and all four major railway companies south of the Thames.

The Leslie Green stations on London Underground, many of which remain, are unmistakeable. They are well known for their ox-blood tiles and half-moon windows at first floor level. This is Belsize Park, photographed on 7 May 2008. *John Glover*

System development

That, very briefly, was the situation in London's rail transport by the early 1930s. Nearly all the Underground was now electrified, although steam traction was still operating passenger services on the Metropolitan line north of Rickmansworth. All freight, and some engineering trains, were also steam hauled.

On the national system, the Southern Railway was already making extensive use of electric traction, particularly in the inner suburban areas, as was the London District of the LMS Railway.

All other operations, including the longer distance passenger services, were provided by steam traction.

Next steps

A scourge of the inter-war period was the economic depression and the persistent high levels of unemployment. This created misery for individuals, but it also depressed the earnings of companies. The transport industry was no exception. Transport was that much less able to indulge in capital schemes, which in the long term would bring added prosperity to the areas served.

The inter-war period on the subsurface lines of the Underground saw large-scale construction of cars of this general type. This is Q23-stock Driving Motor Car, No 4248, now resident in the London Transport Museum. It was built by Gloucester Carriage & Wagon Co in 1923. The end bays next to the cab seen here were comfortable seating areas for four, away from the ever moving crowds nearer the doors. *John Glover*

Action by the newly elected Labour government in 1929 saw the passing of the Development (Loan Guarantees and Grants) Act, 1929. This subsidised local authorities and public utilities to undertake capital development work and thus create new jobs on, it was hoped, a national scale.

As a result, the Underground companies were able to fund the extension of the Piccadilly line north from Finsbury Park to Cockfosters and paralleling the District line west from Hammersmith to Northfields. The Metropolitan Railway built the branch from Wembley Park to Stanmore and was able to quadruple the section north to Harrow-on-the-Hill. Station reconstruction was also made possible, sometimes on a considerable scale such as the merger of Holborn (Piccadilly line) and British Museum (Central line) into today's single station and the rebuilding of Piccadilly Circus station.

Creation of the Board

The Bill to create the London Passenger Transport Board (LPTB) originated in late 1930, but it had an extended gestation period. This spanned the 1931 general election. The National Government which succeeded Labour in 1931 was Conservative dominated, and different ideas came to the fore.

Ideas for reorganisation were nothing new, though this far they had had little result.

There was however a common thread:

- The transport services of London could not be administered effectively by any existing organisation of central or local government;
- As far as possible, they ought to be placed under the control of a single authority;
- That single authority ought to be a small and expert body; and
- That body should be empowered to control and coordinate in the public interest all passenger transport interests in London.

This was quite a tall order, since in the early 1930s ownership in what was to become the London Passenger Transport Area was distributed between 17 railway undertakings, 17 tramways and 63 omnibus undertakings, as well as numbers of small bus operators. There were also several motor coach undertakings, such as Green Line.

Ideas of securing a coordinated service were in vogue and competition was seen as wasteful. The answer was to be a system of unified ownership and management, which would cut out overlapping and uneconomic services. The public would benefit from through services, through bookings and easy interchange, which was ripe for development.

The London Passenger Transport Bill was reworked and taken forward; the LPTB came into existence on 1 July 1933.

Ownership

There was thus to be compulsory transfer of ownership to the LPTB, based on the Underground Railways of London (UERL), known as the Combine. That included the Metropolitan Railway (which had escaped the Railway Grouping of 1923), all the local authority tramways in the area, and most local buses.

The LPTB thus created was to be a public utility corporation, freed from political control and run on business lines. It was neither a nationalised nor a municipalised undertaking (and as a result that much more acceptable on a cross-party basis).

Main line railways

The situation with the main line railways was much more difficult; then, as now, their interests stretched far beyond any geographical area in which a newly created LPTB could reasonably claim any interest.

It was agreed on all sides that there were insuperable difficulties in attempting to separate the suburban services from the rest of the system, and that the main lines should be left out of any scheme of common ownership.

Instead, Standing Joint Committees would be created, consisting of four persons representing the Board and one from each of the four main line companies (the Great Western, the Southern, the London Midland & Scottish and the London & North Eastern railways). The Committee would be charged with considering and reporting on proposals for cooperation in the provision and working of services, including matters such as through bookings, running powers, the inter-availability of tickets and (most importantly) the apportionment of receipts.

More uniformity in the matter of fares and charges would be overseen by a reconstituted Railway Rates Tribunal.

The London & North Western Railway purchased third-rail EMUs for their London suburban services from Metro-Cammell/Oerlikon. Driving Motor Brake Third Open No 28249 survives in the National Railway Museum at York. It was built in 1915. These and similar vehicles were withdrawn with the delivery of what were described as the London District three-car sets. Later Class 501, they were built at Eastleigh from 1957. ***John Glover***

Agreements

The Standing Joint Committee reports would form the basis of agreements between the LPTB and the company(ies) concerned, Such agreements could run to the application of funds for the provision of facilities and any of them might assist the others financially in so doing.

That would enable the main line companies to embark on the further electrification of their suburban lines and to carry out other long overdue improvements.

The physical area concerned was to be known as the London Passenger Transport Area. For railways, that would extend to Baldock in the north and Horsham in the south, but rather closer in to Slough in the west and Gravesend in the east (slightly more restrictive for buses).

Pooling Scheme

A compulsory Pooling Scheme would be created to cover all the local passenger transport undertakings in the London Traffic Area. This would entail the pooling of fares revenues of all concerned (buses and trams as well as rail), then redistributing it on an agreed basis between the participants. The problems for the Main Line railways of separating their revenues between those earned inside the area and outside the area will be apparent.

Importantly, each company was able to set operating expenses against that revenue before it was pooled. These were the costs which varied with the mileage run, not the total costs attributable. Additional allowances might be made where services were expanded or new infrastructure constructed.

As originally constituted, this was to result in the allocations shown in Table 1.1 (overleaf), expressed as percentages. The need to extend these to five decimal points is perhaps an indication of the hard bargaining involved, which continued for the first two years of the Board's existence. This was in the days before calculators, let alone computers.

A revision was then agreed for the year to 30 June 1935, which increased the Board's proportion by 0.1% and reduced that of the Main Line railways by a similar amount. The very substantial proportion which accrued to the Southern Railway, much of whose inner suburban

Table 1.1: London Passenger Pooling Scheme, 18 June 1935

London Passenger Transport Board	62.00473%
Main Line Railways	
Great Western Railway	1.33541%
Southern Railway	25.55158%
London Midland & Scottish Railway	5.09340%
London & North Eastern Railway	6.01488%
Total, Main Line Railways	37.99527%
	100%

Source: LPTB Annual Report and Accounts 1935

network was already electrified, will be apparent.

The scheme did not survive the onset of World War 2; it was abandoned after the financial year 1938–39.

It may be of interest to review the then volume of traffic on each of the various undertakings, which are shown in Table 1.2 for the year ended 30 June 1938 as, probably, the most representative year.

Table 1.2 shows that the Main Line companies were carrying substantially more passengers than the Board's railways and probably for rather longer distances too. However, the total volume of rail travel was much less than the passenger journeys made on road based transport, even though those journeys were likely to have been relatively short.

Emphasising the difficulty of making meaningful financial comparisons over a long period of time, the average fare paid per passenger journey was recorded at 2.341 (old) pence. That is very marginally less than 1p in today's coinage.

Table 1.2 Originating passenger journeys recorded in the pooling scheme for the year ended 30 June 1938.

Originating on the LPTB system, passenger journeys, millions	
Railways	488
Buses & Coaches	2,167
Trams	701
Trolleybuses	368
Total LPTB	

Lord Ashfield

It was clear by the 1930s that operational problems meant that the railway system could not continue to cope with growing traffic without some major attention.

The Chairman of the London Passenger Transport Board, Lord Ashfield, suggested in the House of Lords[3] that merely electrifying main line suburban services was not enough. They would still deposit their commuting passengers at the various main line railway termini, who then resorted to the Underground for the last part of the journey to work.

What was needed was for the Underground to take over some main line branch railways, building their own new lines to connect with them, and then to operate the whole. This is broadly what was to happen with the eastern extension of the Underground's Central line from Liverpool Street to Stratford and beyond.

But the core Underground network was also becoming overloaded, and his key to that was the construction of a new high-speed line parallel to the existing line, such as could be found in New York and which was at least contemplated on the Charing Cross route of the Northern. 'The further out that people live, the more the need for speed.'

Finding the optimum balance between the Outer Suburban and Inner Suburban businesses and the means of distributing passengers in central London, taking all available modes of transport into consideration, remains a major question today.

New Works Programme

Chief among the new approach was the New Works Programme 1935/40. This was announced in the House of Commons by the Chancellor of the Exchequer, Neville Chamberlain, on 5 June 1935.

The New Works Programme was a large-scale £40 million scheme (1935 prices), which would involve the Underground, the Great Western and the London & North Eastern companies.

The prime purpose was to relieve the main line railways of short distance local traffic, which it was felt could be served more effectively by the Underground. This also freed up capacity on the main line railways for longer distance travel to and from central London.

It was also to help alleviate certain known areas of congestion, to afford fresh outlets for the population, and to assist in solving the housing problem. Financing of the scheme was the subject of the London Passenger Transport (Agreement) Act, 1935, under which HM Treasury would guarantee both the principal and the interest of a finance company loan. This would be divided in the proportions LPTB 70%, GWR 5% and LNER 25%.

As announced initially, the main works were as shown in Table 1.3. It is interesting in the sense of 'who does what?' Change of ownership, such as might later be agreed, was not disclosed on the original agenda.

Table 1.3: New Works Programme 1935/40[4]

1. The LNER will electrify their main line to Shenfield and their Loughton and Grange Hill branches. The Board will construct an extension of their Central line to come to the surface at Stratford, continue in tunnel to Leyton and a junction with the LNER and thence in tunnel to Newbury Park. The existing Central line would see new rolling stock and platform lengthening.
2. The LNER will electrify their Edgware, High Barnet and Alexandra Palace branches and double the line to Edgware. The Board will extend their Archway tube to a physical junction at East Finchley, and their Northern City line from Moorgate to a physical junction with the electrified suburban line north of Finsbury Park. Through services will be operated from all branches to the City and from the Edgware and High Barnet lines to the west central area.
3. The GWR will construct and electrify two additional surface tracks alongside their line from North Acton to Ruislip. The Central line trains terminating at Wood Lane will be projected over this line.
4. The Board will construct a tube railway from a junction with the Bakerloo at Baker Street to Finchley Road, and rearrange, realign and resignal the tracks of the Metropolitan northwards to eliminate conflicts between the express and local lines.
5. The Board will reconstruct the Aldgate junctions and Aldgate East station to increase capacity.
6. The Board will substitute trolleybuses for trams.
7. The Board will rebuild King's Cross, Post Office (St Paul's from 1937) and many other stations in the central Area.
8. The electric power supply will be enlarged and improved (no details).

The programme involves the building of about 12 miles of new tube railways, the electrification of approximately 44 miles of suburban railway, the doubling and electrification of about 12½ miles of further suburban railways, and the substitution of trolleybuses for tramcars on 148 route miles.

World War 2

In the event, World War 2 overtook much of the necessary works that followed. Northern line Underground trains reached High Barnet via Archway in 1940 and Mill Hill East (for the barracks there) in 1941. After the war, work on the Central line was resumed and it was extended at each end. In the east it took over the former Great Eastern branch to Epping and Ongar, and that from Newbury Park to Woodford. (The short section of about one mile from Ilford to Newbury Park was abandoned for passenger purposes). In the west, the Central line was extended from North Acton to West Ruislip. All this work was completed by 1949, though electric trains did not reach Ongar until 1957.

The further extensions of the Central line were not included in the original New Works Programme (above), neither was the four tracking of the Metropolitan line north of Harrow-on-the-Hill to (as it turned out) Watford South Junction, and electrification from Rickmansworth to Amersham and Chesham. This was opened in 1960 and coincided with the stations beyond Amersham to Aylesbury being served solely by the Marylebone services of British Railways.

Cancelled

Other areas were less fortunate. The proposed extension of Northern line services from Mill Hill East to Edgware over LNER tracks and new construction northwards from Edgware to Bushey Heath was abandoned in the 1950s, as was the electrification of the LNER branch from Finsbury Park to Alexandra Palace and the connection to what was now the Northern line at East Finchley. The main cause was the implementation of Green Belt policies, but in any event there was little money available for large scale capital works by what were now nationalised industries.

On the edge of Clapham Common, near Clapham South Underground station, this unprepossessing building may be found. It is seen here on 3 March 2013. This is an entrance (one of two) to a World War 2 tunnelled air raid shelter. It is one of a series constructed on the possible alignment of an express Northern line, which might just have been built after the end of hostilities. *John Glover*

Green Belt

The inter-war period saw outward moves by the population to the new suburbs that were springing up in all directions from central London. For the railways, this was a time of change and their responses varied. Thus the Metropolitan Railway, through its wholly owned estates company, had been able to develop land around its stations very much to that railway's commercial advantage. Elsewhere, the Underground was ceasing to be merely an urban phenomenon, as it extended its tentacles into the new suburbs.

Of these, the extension of the Piccadilly line already mentioned was a prime example, but there were others. Thus the Northern went south to Morden in 1926, the District east to the huge London County Council estate at Becontree and the Metropolitan north to Stanmore, both in 1932. The Southern Railway did their bit too, with their line to Chessington South completed as far as it ever was to go in 1939, and continued generally with their electrification schemes.

So far, so good, or so it seemed. But others were less certain. Was it really so clever to cover all the available land in what seemed to be an ever-increasing radius of the capital with terraced or semi-detached houses? Where were the open spaces for sport and recreation that those living in these houses could enjoy?

Good idea or not, there was no future in building new railways, or extensions to those already existing, if the population projections were not going to be fulfilled. The Metropolitan Green Belt is a designated statutory area around London that was first proposed in 1935.

The subsequent Greater London Plan by Abercrombie published in 1945 made further suggestions of what might happen. This was to be the era of decentralisation, with new housing built way beyond what was called the inner urban ring, the suburban area ring and a Green Belt area outside that. Abercrombie proposed that the Green Belt should be up to six miles wide.

Beyond that would be the outer-county ring, stretching from Baldock (Herts) in the north to Horley (Surrey) in the south, High Wycombe (Bucks) in the west and Tilbury (Essex) in the east.

The Town & Country Planning Act 1947 with its provisions for compensation allowed local authorities to include Green Belt policies in their development plans, though this took some time.

New trains

The network expansions and their electrification required new trains to run them. Thus British Railways Eastern Region would introduce 92 three-car DC electric units for working the Liverpool Street–Shenfield services, a scheme which was completed in 1949. This was overhead electrification at 1,500v DC, which in 1956 would be converted to AC.

These trains were fitted with sliding doors, in contrast to the situation on the Southern Region where slam door rolling stock would continue to be built for all services (apart from the Waterloo & City) until the early 1970s. The Shenfield vehicles were thus more akin to the trains introduced by the LMS on their newly electrified Wirral services in 1938.

The Bakerloo and the Northern tube services shared what turned out to be a huge build of the 1938 tube stock, the prototype cars of which were the first of their type to banish all electrical and other equipment to underfloor locations, or in some cases hidden under the seating. This made all the space available for passengers apart from driving cabs and a modest space for the Guard. Trains were made up to seven cars, those on the Bakerloo incorporating an earlier (1927) trailer car.

Overall, 1,288 cars of this very successful build were to become part of the 1938 stock fleet and their 1949 derivatives. They had a clean general internal design, which was to see little change for the ensuing 40 years. It was also acknowledged generally that they were extremely comfortable. The majority were constructed either before the outbreak of war or in its early years, the remainder post-war.

The extent of the commitment by the LNER can be judged by their agreement to own (and therefore fund) some of the vehicles of the 1938 tube stock to operate on the newly extended Northern line. These were the cars that were to run 'their' services in the future. A total of 289 cars thus carried solebar plates 'Property of LNER'. In all other respects, these cars were identical to those owned by London Transport, who maintained the whole fleet.

The ownership plates remained in place until the general withdrawal of the 1938 stock cars in the 1970s, though six of the ex-LNER cars themselves remain in passenger service today in the Isle of Wight as Class 483 units Nos 483006/7/8.

There were substantial builds of new stock for the District too, both before and after the War. The fleet of R stock extended eventually to the best part of 400 vehicles, in six-car or eight-car formations. These were supplemented by O and P stock.

Objectives

In the cases mentioned above, the intended effect was to extend or cement the influence of the Underground across an extending area into the new suburbs, whilst also providing through rail links from north to south of the capital (Northern line) and east to west (Central line). This also avoided the need for such services to finish at costly London terminal stations on British Railways. These were, together with their approach tracks, freed up to be used for other purposes.

However, other forces were also at play, as will be demonstrated.

2

Planning the Post-War World

Building a railway, particularly underground, represents a long term commitment, which cannot soon be abandoned without an intolerable waste of social effort. F. A. A. Menzler, Chief Development and Research Officer, LTE

This era was characterised by large amounts of planning activity, but seemingly rather little of it for the benefit of the railways or their passengers.

COUNTY OF LONDON PLAN, 1943

The County of London Plan was prepared for the London County Council by John Henry Forshaw and (Sir) Patrick Abercrombie. It was published in 1943, shortly after the mid-point of World War 2, a period which was described carefully by its authors as 'during a pause in the development of our ancient capital'. This large document formed a wide-ranging and ambitious plan to set out a vision for the future.

It should be mentioned here that what was then the County of London became what are now known as the Inner London Boroughs in 1965. The Plan's findings need to be read in that context. The County of London was subsumed into the geographically much larger Greater London Council (GLC), which absorbed nearly the whole of Middlesex and parts of Hertfordshire, Essex, Kent and Surrey.

The GLC itself was abolished in 1986. Virtually the same area is now that of the Greater London Authority (GLA), set up in 2000 with an elected Mayor.

Roads

It is perhaps worth noting that this Plan was first and foremost one made by town planners. Transport was not a major feature, apart from the pressing need for the tackling of road congestion.

The proposed remedies entailed the construction of a major fast traffic Ring Road (the B road), at between 2½ and 3 miles from central London. Of railway interest, the western side was to run parallel with the West London line. There were sections both north and south of the Thames. In between, the B Ring Road would be divided by a main North–South and a main East–West road. These would meet together in a jolly flyover complex, somewhere in the vicinity of the north end of Waterloo bridge. Tunnelling would be used where necessary.

Within the B road, there would be an A Ring Road about two miles from central London, aimed at central London traffic and joining up the main railway termini. This would be for the most part an adaptation of existing roads; it too would continue south of the river.

Beyond the B Ring Road would be 10 radial roads connecting to the trunk roads of the country, but also of note was the C Ring Road. This would in essence be improvements to the North and South Circular roads and the connections between them.

Only limited sections of the proposed roads were built, such as the A102(M) in East London and Westway, the A40(M) link. Beyond that, the much later construction of the M25 Motorway would provide a route round rather than through the capital. Most of the M25 is in the surrounding counties rather than Greater London.

Railways

The authors were kind to the London Passenger Transport Board, created only 10 years earlier in 1933, describing it as 'a heroic endeavour to harmonise and rationalise the system, with a large measure of success'. The main line railways too were praised and the whole was said to work amazingly well. Then came the 'but'.

The perceived shortcoming was that the transport system had never been replanned as a whole as an integral part of a plan for London. Forshaw and Abercrombie aimed to put this right.

There were five main areas of interest:

- **Economy in working.** Where possible, suburban and main line traffic should be separated for operational benefits. The amount of land then occupied by the railway, including sidings, depots and yards, was excessive. Main line terminal stations should be rebuilt at separate levels. Suburban lines would need to go underground, main lines at ground level (and at first floor level if necessary), with a roof deck over the station for air landings.

A separate section of the Plan noted the difficulty in getting between aerodromes and central London. One suggestion received had been the use of taxi-plane services, which might land on the roofs of railway stations. The main line railways were said to have been approached on this issue but their reactions, even if printable, were not stated.

- **Electrification**. Main line railways should be electrified generally, at least on a regional basis, with low level interchanges between suburban services and the tube network.
- **Cross-river bridges and viaducts.** By 1900 London had railways at four levels – on viaduct, on the surface, subsurface and tube. Some of the viaduct level stations were in East London, on the Tilbury and Great Eastern lines, but most were on the South Bank, with elevated stations and cross river bridges. They had to be placed at such a height that they would not obstruct river traffic, but also to give access to suitable terminal station sites on the generally rather higher North Bank. They included today's Charing Cross and Cannon Street, though Blackfriars which straddles the valley of the River Fleet was rather different. Other large elevated stations were London Bridge, Fenchurch Street and St Pancras.

Within three miles of Waterloo, there was over 20 miles of track on viaducts. These, said the Plan, had the effect of stifling much needed development sites on the South Bank, as well as obstructing passage on the river.

- **Co-ordination of services**. Electrification of all suburban services north of the river and tunnelled approaches to deep level interchanges would allow the proper coordination of services and relieve the existing Underground lines in the north and north west.

Charing Cross is indeed in the centre of London as this photograph of October 2011 taken from the London Eye demonstrates. It is central to the extent that road distances are measured from here as a datum point. Two Class 465 units are seen in the station throat. *John Glover*

- **Goods distribution**. Could small goods yards be replaced by fewer large ones with better north/south connections, especially near the docks?

What, then, was proposed? A major objective was the elimination of at least some of the approach viaducts in the inner areas, the railway bridges across the river and the terminal stations at surface level on the north bank. The alternative suggestion was to construct two separate railway routes from the existing approach lines on the south side, at deep level, both operating on the terminal loop principle and affording interchange facilities at stations on the route. There would be an independent north–south tunnel connection between existing surface systems.

The four routes are shown in Map 2.1.

North bank (A)

A new deep level 8-mile north bank link to run in tunnel from Battersea (with connections from the South Western), then with stations at Victoria, Charing Cross, Blackfriars, Cannon Street and along the north bank of the Thames to Wapping. The line would then turn south and run parallel to the East London line, with stations at Shadwell and Surrey Quays. The line would surface and join the South Eastern in the New Cross/Deptford area (8 miles).

South East, City and West End Loop (B)

A new deep-level bi-directional 6-mile loop connecting new underground stations at London Bridge and Waterloo East on the south bank, Charing Cross and Cannon Street on the north. (Whether or not a station at Blackfriars would be included on this loop was unclear.) This loop would be continued in tunnel, rising in the Surrey Canal area with connections to both the South Eastern and Brighton lines.

These two schemes were intended to dispense with the need for the present high-level stations at Charing Cross, Cannon Street, London Bridge and Waterloo East, together with their bridge and viaduct connections.

County of London Plan 1943, proposed new cross-river rail routes. Abercrombie and Forshaw's County of London Plan of 1943 provided this illustration of how their ideas of non-terminal passenger loops from the South Eastern network might work. The importance of goods traffic is indicated by the goods rings, in which the West London and North London lines both feature. The lack of detail and various approximations no doubt reflect that this was in the middle of World War 2.

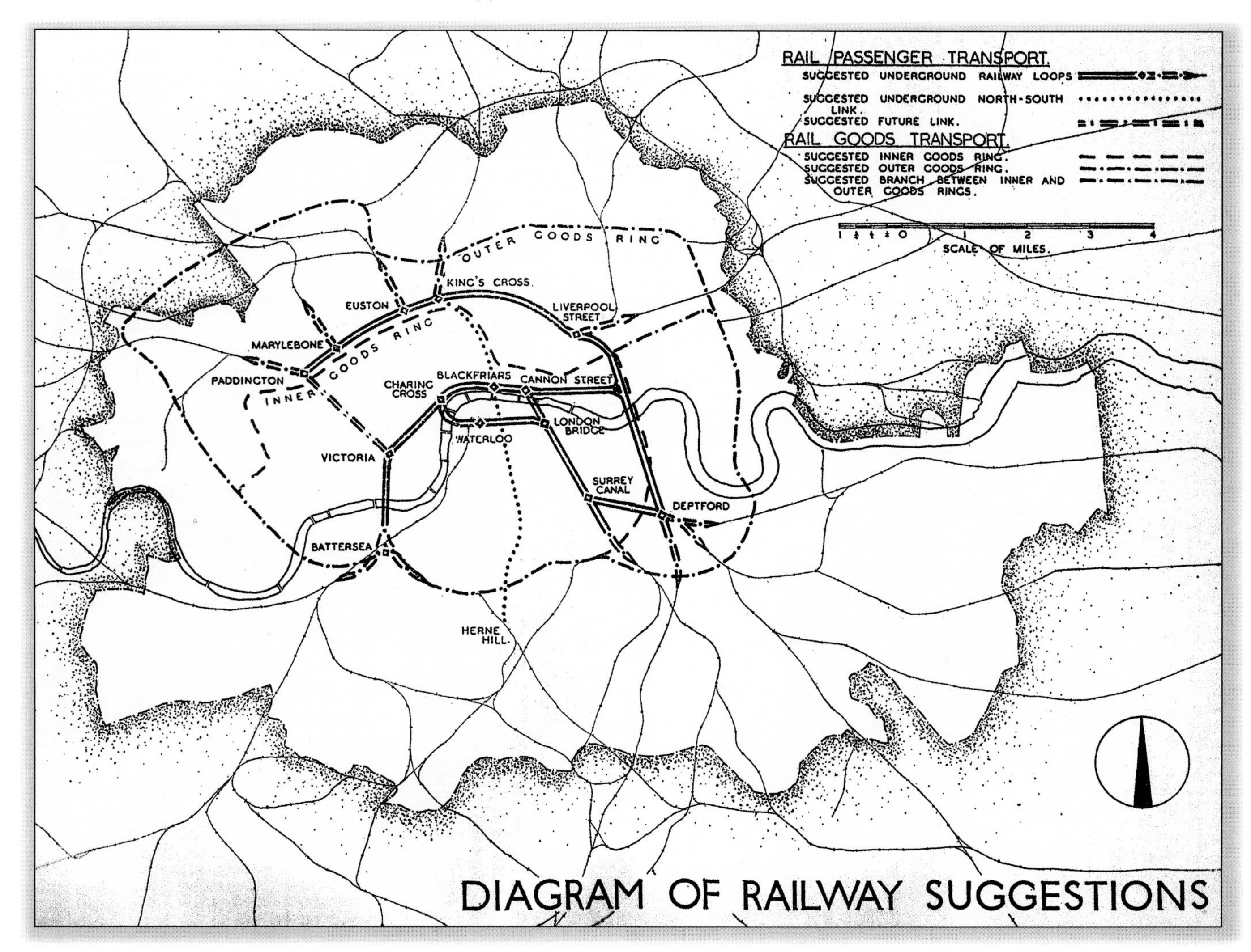

North–South Tunnel (C)

This was to be an underground link between King's Cross and Loughborough Junction, which would include replacing the then existing viaduct from south of Snow Hill (City Thameslink area) to Loughborough Junction with a tunnel. Stations at low level would replace those at high level at Blackfriars and Elephant & Castle.

Northern Arc Passenger Route (D)

Another requirement was the improvement of the northern terminals at Paddington, Marylebone, Euston, King's Cross and Liverpool Street, all of which would remain. The rerouting of St Pancras traffic into Euston was seen as possible, but no details were given.

Separately, the provision of a northern arc underground suburban passenger route was suggested. This would run from Victoria (with connections in both directions to Route A), passing under Hyde Park to Paddington and with platforms below the main line stations listed above. From Liverpool Street there would be links to Cannon Street and to Wapping, both on Route A.

Victoria station and the associated Grosvenor Bridge over the Thames were deemed suitable to stay, but Waterloo was less fortunate. 'We visualise Waterloo station remaining for a considerable time until a new station, south of the present site [is built]. This would give facilities for a separate low level connection with London Bridge.'

Goods traffic

For goods, the use of the north side of the Underground's Circle line for the distribution of goods traffic in the central area, using existing connections to the main line railways, was anticipated. This goods ring would be continued on the south side.

Supplementing this would be an outer goods circuit, near the County of London boundary, with a new cross-river tunnel at Greenwich. Most of the rest of this route was to be made up from the existing North London, West London and South London lines.

A view of the Cannon Street railway bridge over the Thames from the north bank on 19 June 2016 with Southeastern's 376012 approaching. Was the bridge really so disfiguring to the landscape that serious propositions should be made to bury the railway underground, with all the problems that would bring, plus a huge charge to the public finances? ***John Glover***

Peckham Rye station consists of two separated sets of lines, all elevated above street level. This scene of 15 April 2010 looks north from the island platform used by South London line trains towards the Catford loop lines, where a train can be seen in the platform before departing westwards towards Denmark Hill. ***John Glover***

Critique

This abbreviated summary of the 1943 conclusions does indicate some rather different ideas on how the railway systems might be updated. Proposals for the Underground railways of London Transport are noticeable by their absence. Indeed, they are hardly mentioned.

There are also substantial gaps in the proposals made for the national system. New low-level loops around parts of central London to replace the main line terminal stations are all very well, but would they be up to the task of carrying the large passenger loads which are implied as a result? Would the station stop times be short enough to enable a sufficient throughput of trains?

The gaps are also a little disconcerting. What would happen to the suburban services into St Pancras if that station ceased to exist, or how would trains from the south London areas actually proceed?

Details are lacking, as are their quantification, understandably so as this was after all in a time of war. Also of relevance was the continuing decline in the population of the County of London, due to the attraction of the extensive inter-war building in what became the new suburbs and the result of people moving house, but also to the widespread bomb damage in the centre.

It is, though, difficult to avoid the impression that the proposals were driven first and foremost by a wish to get rid of the cross-river railway bridges and the viaducts which fed them. This had been a (very) long-standing desire amongst artistic circles, with Hungerford Bridge (the Charing Cross railway bridge) being a prime target. In fairness, by no stretch of the imagination could Hungerford Bridge be called beautiful, but it did serve a very useful purpose.

This had been a recurring problem. The Southern's General Manager Sir Herbert Walker was recorded as speaking to his despondent officers trying to work out how they could possibly cope without Charing Cross. 'Do not worry,' he said. 'Charing Cross bridge will still be there, long after I have left the scene'[5]. And so it is, nearly 70 years after his death in 1949.

Missing

What does seem to be missing from Forshaw and Abercrombie's 1943 Plan is any consideration of the wishes and needs of the vast numbers of passengers who would be affected. What benefits and/or disbenefits might result? Or was it more a case of 'we know what is good for you'?

Practicality issues surrounding the alternative provisions, such as they were, also seem to be largely ignored. The removal of the river bridges and approach viaducts were a way of achieving an end that was thought desirable at the time, but at tremendous cost. Would not the extensive road plans contained in that same Plan have a similarly deleterious effect on the environment?

London Bridge station would not have escaped demolition. Class 415/1 4-EPB no 5202 arrives to a well-filled platform on 27 April 1990. Whatever else might be said against them, slam door stock like this was adept at mopping up the crowds. *John Glover*

Also missing was any consideration of the inevitable disruption during construction, which would also have been prolonged. Would all the existing facilities have remained open while the work was in progress? The cross-river proposals were all in tunnel, none bridges, and no new rail bridges have been built across the Thames since then.

GREATER LONDON PLAN, 1944

Abercrombie's Greater London Plan 1944 was published in the following year. This introduced the concept of satellite towns, for which he suggested a number of locations, though many of these sites were later discarded. They were given the name of New Towns,

The New Towns Act 1946 established an ambitious programme. It gave the government powers to designate areas of land for new town developments administered by New Town Development Corporations. These would find homes for those living in poor or bombed-out housing, for the returning servicemen and for what became known as the baby boomers, as well as those attempting to escape the urban sprawl generally.

Typically, the New Towns had a target population of 80,000 each. The objective was to make them as self-contained as possible in terms of employment and economic life. It was not the intention that they would become dormitories for people commuting to London, though not all their future residents would agree.

Table 2.1 shows the New Towns that were actually built within a 50-mile radius of the capital, together with the year in which they were so designated and their distance from central London termini.

Table 2.1: Designated New Towns, year of designation and distance from London rail termini

Stevenage, Hertfordshire	1946	27½ miles	King's Cross
Crawley, West Sussex	1947	30¾ miles	Victoria
Hemel Hempstead, Hertfordshire	1947	24½ miles	Euston
Harlow, Essex	1947	22¾ miles	Liverpool Street
Welwyn Garden City, Hertfordshire	1948	20¼ miles	King's Cross
Hatfield, Hertfordshire	1948	17¾ miles	King's Cross
Basildon, Essex	1949	24¼ miles	Fenchurch Street
Bracknell, Berkshire	1949	32¼ miles	Waterloo
Milton Keynes, Buckinghamshire	1967	49¾ miles	Euston

Electric Underground railways need a source of power, and for much of the system this was to be provided by this power station, owned by the group, at Lots Road, Chelsea. With fuel supplied by shipping, it is seen here on 22 April 2009. The station was decommissioned in 2002 and the building awaits its fate. *John Glover*

Abercrombie estimated that his original list of 10 locations could accommodate around half a million people as New Town residents, and a further 200,000 by the expansion of existing towns such as Ashford (Kent), Aylesbury, Basingstoke, Chelmsford and Didcot.

Rail electrification

Some changes to the provision of railway services would be needed. The earlier wish to see all railways electrified was apparently to be construed as all railways that actually entered London. Thus steam traction was likely to be used in the area further out than the traction changeover points, which were identified as being Chelmsford, Bishop's Stortford, Hitchin, Luton, Watford, Aylesbury, Princes Risborough, Didcot, and Basingstoke. It was considered (more or less correctly) that the rest of the Southern Railway routes were likely to be electrified throughout, anyway.

Furthermore, all branch lines in the Greater London area should be electrified and alternatives to steam traction found for goods traffic 'making for cleanliness and reducing the pollution of the atmosphere'. Many years later, it is quite difficult to envisage the extent to which large numbers of steam locomotives contributed to poor air quality.

Main line trains on the Metropolitan beyond Rickmansworth had to be hauled by steam traction provided by British Railways before 1960, when the fourth rail was extended to Amersham and Chesham. For this task, a fleet of 20 Bo-Bo locomotives was built for the Metropolitan Railway, of which this one, No 12 *Sarah Siddons,* survives in working order. It (she?) is seen at an Open Day at Old Oak Common, with not a conductor rail in sight. *John Glover*

Steam to electric changeover points would have been established at key locations, to keep the capital free of smoke, or at least more nearly so. Aylesbury, now only an outer-suburban terminus and no more an intermediate calling point on the last main line to the north, sees 165.013 in the former up main platform on 13 March 2010. *John Glover*

Clapham cutting on the South Western sees Class 416/2 2-EPB two-car unit No 5793 approaching with a Waterloo to Shepperton service. This was one of 15 units transferred from South Tyneside on the de-electrification of that system. Very similar to the Southern units, they could be distinguished by their larger than usual luggage space (for taking prams to the seaside), 10 fewer seats as a consequence, and the slightly smaller route indicator panel. *John Glover*

New provision

An interesting proposal was to join up some existing non-radial lines with new trackwork as a result of the redistribution of population and industry. This, it was thought, could be done at modest cost. The example given (see Map 2.2) was Watford to Chelmsford via Hemel Hempstead, Harpenden, Welwyn Garden City, Hertford, Ware, Hoddesdon (rather than Broxbourne), North Weald, Ongar and Margaretting (on the Great Eastern main line, south west of Chelmsford). As can be seen, this was a good fit for the five satellite towns then intended in the area.

Relatively little new formation work would (then) have been needed, the main sections being south east of Hoddesdon until the Epping–Ongar branch was reached, then again east of Ongar. Whether the main lines would be crossed by flat junctions, flyovers or diveunders was not even mentioned, let alone discussed.

Below: Proposed Orbital Rail Route, Watford to Chelmsford, Greater London Plan, 1944.

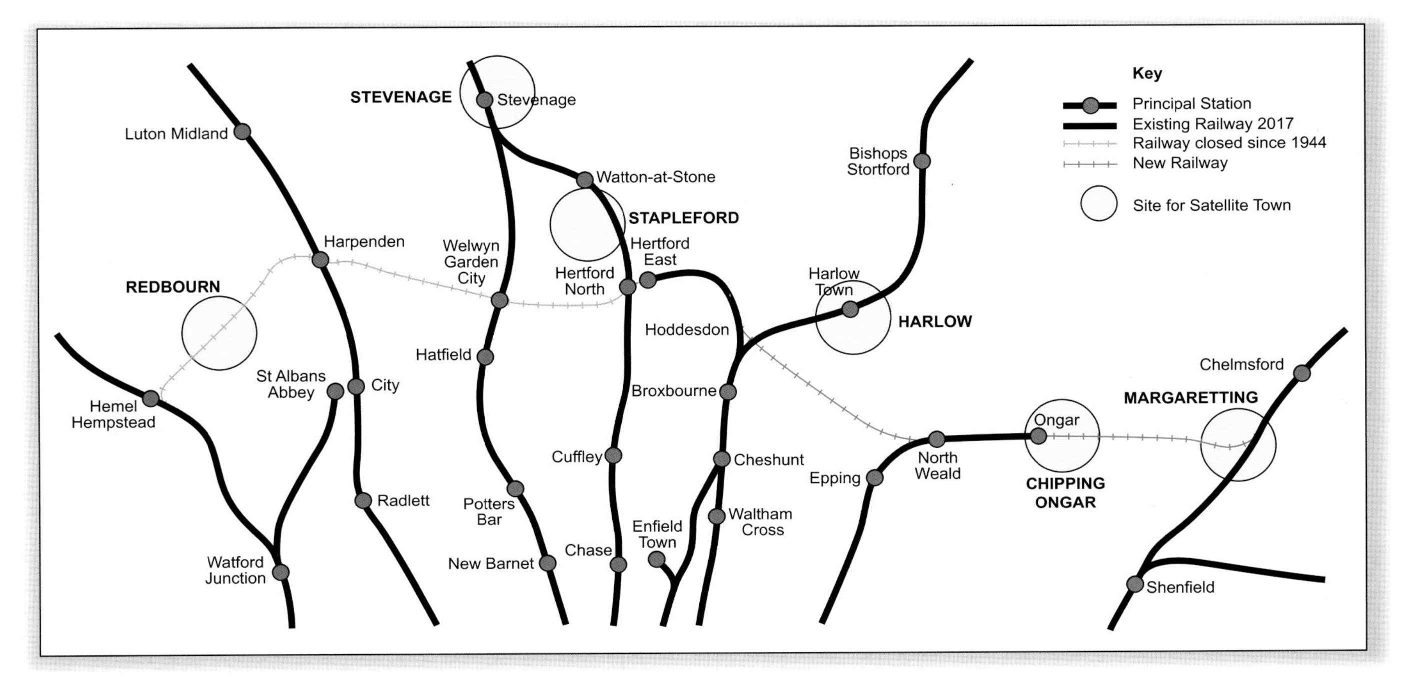

The station at Harlow Town was equipped with double island platforms to include two loops, with the Bishop's Stortford electrification and its becoming the main station for the New Town here. Sadly, it is not near anything much other than the River Stort Navigation, as the surrounding greenery suggests. A Stansted Express service with 317729 calls on the down main. *John Glover*

Stations

In reality, the New Towns tended not to be well served by rail. Thus 15 years later a spanking new station was built at Harlow Town on the Cambridge main line. Unsurprisingly, this was on the existing railway route in the river valley and hence a bus ride away from the town centre. At Crawley the station was resited, with a large bus station placed outside, but that was not until 1968 or 21 years after designation.

Similarly, a station for Basildon was deemed unnecessary by British Railways Eastern Region. 'What's wrong with Laindon or Pitsea stations, a couple of miles either side?' they growled. The railway finally gave in and opened a station at Basildon in 1974. In the year 2016/17, the total passengers using Basildon was estimated by the Office of Rail & Road (ORR) as 3.18 million, compared with 2.20 million at Laindon and 1.23 million at Pitsea.

By now, Heathrow Airport had become a reality and the new plan declared flatly that 'a rail link from Feltham is required' for London passengers. Some matters advance only slowly, but today we have at least got as far as a bus service link between the two.

This is supplemented elsewhere by Heathrow Express, Heathrow Connect (in future the Elizabeth line) and the Underground's Piccadilly.

Next stage

As with the previous 1943 Plan, the authors felt that their suggestions might need to be deliberated on by a body appointed for the purpose and indeed this was to come about. The Railway (London Plan) Committee 1944 was set up to examine the technical and operational issues, and to suggest modifications and alternatives that they felt desirable. The Committee reported to the Minister of Transport in two stages, on 21 January 1946 and with a Final Report on 3 March 1948.

These are considered in turn, both in respect of the then priorities and how they might match those of today. Most of the grand ideas remain unfulfilled. The reality was that the parts of the 1935–40 New Works programme already started would not be completed until 1949 (or later) and other parts would be abandoned altogether. A major cause of this was the restriction on housing development by the implementation of Green Belt policies 'to provide a lung for the overcrowded capital'. By 1962 the primary aim was to prevent urban sprawl.

The other problem was that in the immediate (and indeed not so immediate) post-war years, the nation was broke.

Harlow Town station is very much a late 1950s construction, but none the worse for that. This 2001 street view shows some of the towers for lifts used in the days of parcels traffic being conveyed in quantity, now used only for providing disabled access. *John Glover*

Wimbledon station in Southern inter-war style has a modest forecourt in relation to its passenger numbers. It is used by the Underground's District line, Thameslink and London Tramlink as well as the principal operator, then South West Trains. It is 15 April 2010. *John Glover*

Election

During the war, railways had been under the control of HM Government; what would happen after the end of the conflict in 1945?

There was the little matter of the 1945 General Election, which was won by Labour. Under the heading 'Industry in the Service of the Nation' their manifesto included the following:

> 'Public ownership of inland transport. Co-ordination of transport services by rail, road, air and canal cannot be achieved without unification. And unification without public ownership means a steady struggle with sectional interests or the enthronement of a private monopoly, which would be a menace to the rest of industry.'

The outcome was the Transport Act, 1947, which established the British Transport Commission. The Railways Executive and the London Transport Executive were two of its subsidiaries.

Vesting day was 1 January 1948.

RAILWAY (LONDON PLAN) COMMITTEE 1944, REPORT 1946

The Railway (London Plan) Committee was chaired by Prof Sir Charles Inglis, a distinguished civil engineer, supported by luminaries from various disciplines on the main line railways, London Transport, the Railway Inspectorate and a technical adviser.

Given that one of the principal features of the 1943 Plan was the effective closure of most of the existing Southern termini, the Committee provided some useful statistical data. Reproduced below in Table 2.2 are the numbers of people arriving at all the termini during the busiest 60-minute period in the morning peak. This was for an unspecified pre-war year, probably 1938.

The figures refer to all passengers, not just those using suburban services.

Such tables will be familiar to many and the overwhelming importance of the Southern Railway terminals plus those of Liverpool Street and Fenchurch Street is most noticeable. Conversely, those stations served by the LMSR and GWR accounted for less than 10% of the total passengers between them.

This illustrates indirectly how important passenger revenues were to the Southern companies and those serving East Anglia. The companies with longer distance routes serving the Midlands, the North and the West had more diverse portfolios, which enabled them to profit more from the carriage of goods, particularly coal. London suburban traffic was not ignored, but neither was it unduly sought after.

The result was the expansion of the Underground and the Metropolitan Railway to north, north-west and west London. Elsewhere the main line companies but particularly the Southern Railway resisted such incursions into what they considered to be 'their' territory, with considerable success.

The number of passenger rail journeys made in the London Passenger Transport Area was also given. In 1938, of a total of 1.1 billion journeys, 0.6 billion were on the main line railways (54%) and 0.5 billion (46%) on London Transport railways.

Table 2.2 Total passengers arriving during the maximum morning peak hour c1938

Railway	Terminal Station	Passengers	Company totals	%
GWR	Paddington	4,800	4,800	2.4
LMSR	Euston	5,800		
	St Pancras	2,100		
	Broad Street	6,000	13,900	7.0
LNER	King's Cross	9,000		
	Marylebone	3,900		
	Liverpool Street	34,700		
	Fenchurch Street#	10,500	58,100	29.4
SR	Waterloo	24,300		
	Victoria	16,400		
	Charing Cross	17,000		
	Blackfriars plus Holborn Viaduct	13,700		
	Cannon Street	18,100		
	London Bridge*	31,300	120,700	61.1
Totals			197,500	100

#Fenchurch Street was an LMS/LNER joint station, but has been allocated here to the LNER to reflect later boundary changes under British Railways.

*10% of passengers arriving at London Bridge interchanged and then proceeded to other terminals.

Source: Railway (London Plan) Committee, 1946 report

On the Right Lines?

The Working Party asked two fundamental questions. First, is a large scale development plan for London railways needed, or could the present system be adapted to meet public needs with comparatively minor adjustments?

Second, would the coming decades see a rise or fall in the volume of rail traffic? It followed that if the then network was reasonably satisfactory and traffic levels were either constant or declining, it would be very difficult to justify large scale expenditure.

The Committee's approach was that the railway system should remain substantially as it then existed, modernised where necessary, but adapted to meet town planning requirements. They would also impose certain new railways designed to strengthen what existed and add new facilities of lasting value. On future passenger volumes, they felt that these would continue to increase.

They were however completely opposed to the idea of underground loop working which the 1943 Plan championed. This would result in extremely complex junctions and conflicting movements, which would seriously affect line capacity. Some of them would be as awkward as the triple set of double junctions that afflict London Underground operations in the Aldgate area, which are still there today.

There was however an interesting and prophetic caveat. If the 1943 Report considered loop working right and proper for trains of the Southern Railway, would not logic suggest that it should be applied also to suburban trains using the northern terminals? 'Perhaps', said the Working Party, 'but a series of loops in the north and another series in the south would be no substitute for through north to south working'. This is what the Working Party recommended, a theme which would be taken up seriously many years later.

All these suburban trains would need to be both powered by electricity and fitted with sliding doors.

Long distance services

There were also the long-distance services to be considered, for which accommodation would need to be made. It is of interest why the Committee felt that it would be impractical to cater for them at deep level and what they would need:

- An efficient means of transfer between street and train for passengers and a vast amount of luggage, mails, newspapers and general parcels traffic, including fish and fruit,
- The provision of an ample concourse close to the trains to allow the regulation of passengers to various destinations, especially at peak periods and in the holiday seasons,
- Ancillary passenger amenities, as near the trains as possible, including waiting and refreshment rooms, cloakrooms, bookstalls, booking and information offices, telephones and lavatories,
- Sufficient platforms to allow trains for the longer distances to remain in the station an appreciable time for loading and unloading of passengers, luggage and parcels, and for seat reservation procedures,
- Servicing of trains, including routine inspection, cleaning of incoming trains forming outgoing services, replenishing of lavatory vehicles and restocking of refreshment cars, etc.'

It is interesting to contemplate how many of these 'requirements' would still hold good in today's circumstances, with perhaps some new ones added?

Queuing for tickets can be a time-consuming process and those waiting to be served plus those accompanying them can take up a considerable amount of space. This is Victoria on 15 August 2003. *John Glover*

So while three of the proposed new railways were discarded, both on technical grounds and for their effects on passengers, the Committee were impressed with the North–South link through Blackfriars which 'appears to be feasible both from the operational and the engineering points of view, and also offers some possible gain as regards gradients'.

Thus did the upgrading and improvement of what was much, much, later to become the foundation of Thameslink, gain support. This line would have progressed under the river, rather than over it, though on a very different route from that in use today, as would be suggested by the later 1949 Working Party.

Charing Cross and Cannon Street

However, none of this had any effect regarding Charing Cross and Cannon Street stations, with their bridge approaches over the Thames and lengthy viaducts on the south bank.

The Working Party estimated that around 75,000 suburban passengers in the peak hour would be affected by the closure of these stations, to cope with which it would be necessary to provide no fewer than five new double-track railways across, or rather more specifically beneath, the Thames.

This would include the closure of the present London Bridge station and its reconstruction half a mile further south east. This was identified as being on a new site adjacent to Tower Bridge Road and below ground level. Here, substantial interchange between the various routes was to be expected. Services from both the South Eastern and Brighton lines would proceed variously as follows:

Proposed New Railways in Tunnel, Railway (London Plan) Committee, 1944.

Route 1 to Alexandra Palace (on the then branch from Highgate) and Enfield Town with new central area stations at Fenchurch St and Moorgate.

Route 2 to Watford Junction with new central area stations at Bank, Holborn and Euston.

Route 3 to High Wycombe and Aylesbury with new central area stations at Bank, Holborn, Tottenham Court Road, Bond Street and Marylebone.

Route 4 to St Albans and Harpenden with new central area stations at Cannon Street, Blackfriars, Aldwych, Piccadilly Circus, Marble Arch and Paddington.

Route 5 to Slough, Windsor and Maidenhead with new central area stations at Waterloo, Charing Cross, Piccadilly Circus, Marble Arch and Paddington.

All trains on all lines would call at Tower Bridge Road.

The southern tunnel portals were to be at New Cross Gate, South Bermondsey, North Kent East Junction, Lewisham and Hither Green.

Main line services which would otherwise have terminated at London Bridge, Cannon Street, Holborn Viaduct or Charing Cross stations would proceed from the Tower Bridge Road station on a new viaduct to terminate at Waterloo East (which would have lost all its other services). It would pass further away from Southwark Cathedral than the existing line and Waterloo East platforms were at least nearer the West End than Tower Bridge Road.

Even so, it could hardly compete with Charing Cross for passenger convenience. The arrangement would also make transfer to/from South Western services at Waterloo main station relatively easy.

Routes 1-5 above would also convey longer distance passengers whose trains would otherwise take them to Waterloo East.

Routes with higher numbers (Routes 6–12) were seen as being required for congestion relief; Route 8 bears a resemblance to what would later be built as the Victoria line, while Route 9 has some similarities to later proposals for the Chelsea–Hackney line, later Crossrail 2,

RAILWAY (LONDON PLAN) COMMITTEE 1944, FINAL REPORT 1948

Having disposed of the Southern terminals problem as best they could, given their terms of reference, the Committee turned their attention elsewhere. Much of this related to the terminals serving the main lines of the other Big Four companies.

The Northern terminals

The proposed reconstruction of Fenchurch Street on a new ground level site perhaps as much as three miles further east was deemed impractical. The approach viaduct would have to remain for goods depot access, and passengers would demand bus replacement services. Forthcoming housing development in South Essex would result in additional patronage and what was wanted was additional tracks and electrification. 'So there!' was the unwritten response.

The Committee was similarly forthright about the proposed reconstruction of Liverpool Street station on the Bishopsgate goods depot site half a mile further east. 'Bishopsgate had been abandoned as unsuitable over seventy years ago', was their caustic comment. The volume of peak traffic at Liverpool Street was greater than at any other London terminus, and although a fair number of passengers interchanged with the Underground or buses, the majority worked within a short radius of the station.

They also noted that no alternative locations were suggested for the goods traffic then using Bishopsgate.

Their conclusions on the high-level station at Broad Street, which the 1943 Plan wanted amalgamated with low-level Liverpool Street, were that the cost would be formidable. Again, the viaduct would need to be retained for goods traffic, so what might usefully be achieved?

In 1935 the LMS had considered combining the stations of Euston and St Pancras with a new station on what might be called an extended terminal loop. This would be broadly parallel to the Euston Road. Investigation showed that it would require 55 acres of land for the 22 platforms required (!), carriage sidings would be needed at each end of the station, and that there would be fundamental but unspecified problems in operating trains from Crewe to Leeds (the example given). The whole station would be on a continuous curve, with heavy approach gradients.

An alternative scheme of extending Euston to accommodate St Pancras trains as well met with similar difficulties.

A revised reconstruction scheme which in 1948 was before the Minister for decision 'will effect much needed improvement for handling mails and parcels traffic, with better facilities for passengers and a larger concourse while retaining the Great Hall and the Doric Arch.'

That scheme, which was supported by the Committee, never progressed. Both Hall and Arch were demolished in the 1960s rebuilding for the Euston electrification.

The frontage of Paddington, the Plan recommended, should be brought forward about 200 yards from Praed Street to reach the A4209 Sussex Gardens, thereby improving road access. The station might also acquire four extra platform faces. The Committee felt this to be a good idea and noted that it might be done without altering the level of the Circle line station over which it would need to pass.

London freight exchange

The Committee were hesitant in making firm proposals for the creation of new freight facilities and felt that much more work needed to be done before conclusions could be reached. Of considerable interest was the then extent of the exchange of wagons between the various railways.

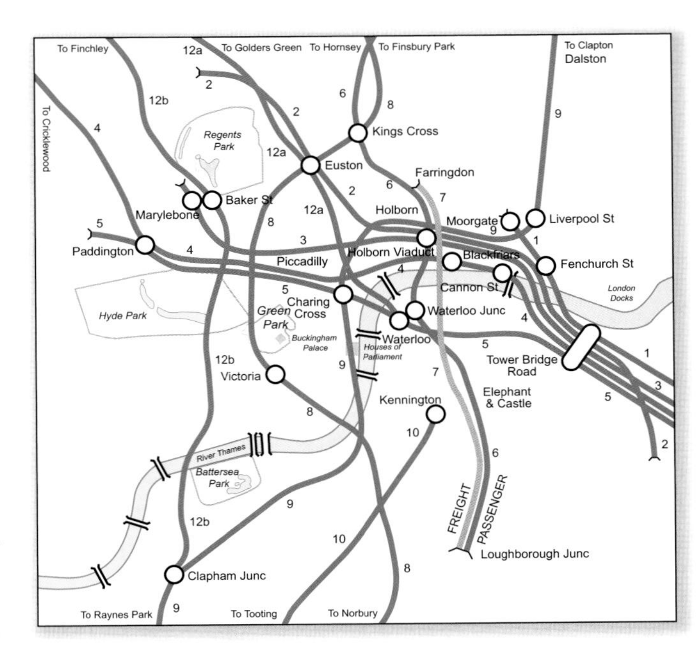

Proposed New Railways in Tunnel, Railway (London Plan) Committee, 1944.

The main flows were between the northern companies, LMS and LNE, and the Southern, with a secondary flow between the east and the west (LNE and GW). These were set out in some detail as shown in Table 2.3. This was before the days of block trains in any volume; these will nearly all be wagon load movements. Their magnitude, in addition to all passenger services, is quite remarkable, even given that many movements would be at night.

Given the often restricted length of freight trains in cross-London services due to a combination of steep gradients and limited haulage power, plus the length of signalling sections and the ability or otherwise to recess them to let other trains pass, this amounted to a lot of trains.

Table 2.3: Normal Daily Exchange of Wagons via London Junctions

	North to South	South to North
LMS (Midland) and SR		
SE&C via Widened Lines	400	400
LBSC via Widened Lines	80	75
LBSC via Barnes	185	190
LSW via Feltham	530	450
Total wagons LMS (Mid) and SR	**1,395**	**1,315**
LMS (LNW) and SR		
SE&C via West London Extension	230	220
LBSC via West London Extension	215	270
LSW via Kew	450	400
Total wagons LMS (LNW) and SR	**895**	**890**
LNE (GN) and SR		
Via Widened Lines	786	652
LNE (GE) and SR		
Via East London Line	153	224
LNE (GC) and SR (LSW)		
Via Neasden and Feltham	120	120
Total wagons LNE and SR	**1,059**	**996**

	South West to South East	South East to South West
GWR and SR		
Via Old Oak Common and Norwood	120	120
Via Old Oak Common and Hither Green	120	120
Total wagons, South West and South East	**240**	**240**
	East to West	West to East
LNE (GE) and GWR		
Temple Mills and Acton	306	258
LNE (GN) and SR		
Ferme Park and Acton	137	–
LMS and LNE (GE)		
Via Willesden and Temple Mills	150	150
GWR and LMS (LTS)		
Via Acton and Plaistow	100	100
Total wagons East and West	**693**	**508**
Grand total	**4,282**	**3,949**

Source: Railway (London Plan) Committee, final report, 1948

The appearance of Hungerford Bridge which carries the four-track railway out of Charing Cross and across the Thames has been much improved by the installation of a new footbridge on each side, seen here from the bottom of Northumberland Avenue on 12 September 2011. Would a similar construction in the 1930s have warded off the criticism? *John Glover*

Above: Wimbledon A box at the Waterloo end of the station still stands, though it has long been superseded by the Area Signalling Centre way beyond the country end of the platforms. This Odeon style box was a hallmark of the Southern Railway style, though their numbers are fast diminishing. This photograph was taken in May 2004. *John Glover*

It was not all by rail, though, with goods cartage used between London terminals. An intriguing idea of the Committee was to build an underground railway of small dimensions and with automatic working. This was seen as similar to the then Post Office Railway and thought worthy of investigation (but without result).

The railways and their freight depots used a lot of land in central London because of the multiplicity of depots. Their concentration into fewer and larger sites might reduce this. But it would give rise to greater road traffic volumes, since the average distance by road to and from the depots would increase.

This would cause a difficulty, as a lot of horse-drawn vehicles would need to be replaced by motor vehicles. The reason given was that some of the longer routes would be more than the horses could manage.

Another consideration was proposals for the decentralisation of the main wholesale markets, which did eventually take place. By then, though, the railway's role in supplying them was much diminished.

The two reports of the Railway (London Plan) Committee 1944 were reviewed by the newly set up British Transport Commission (BTC), whose London Plan Working Party Report was published in 1949 (next Chapter). Representing the nationalised transport industries, the BTC had a rather wider remit.

Importantly, they did not have to accept the proposed removal of the river bridges as a planning requirement, and they were also able to draw upon the evolving post-war situation in coming to their conclusions.

IDEAS FROM OUTSIDE

Meanwhile, other interests were putting forward their proposals for post-war reconstruction. One such wanted to reduce the London termini to four only. These were to be:

- Paddington, little change
- Euston, St Pancras and King's Cross, combined in one two-level structure
- Broad Street and Liverpool Street, similar treatment
- A Southern terminus combining Victoria, Waterloo, Charing Cross, Holborn Viaduct, Blackfriars, Cannon Street and London Bridge.

This was all very well, but at that time the Southern's terminals had about 80 platforms between them, with 30 or so running lines on the approaches. Flying and burrowing junctions would take up vast areas to bring them all into one terminal. Where could it be situated, on which side of the river, and how would vast volumes of passengers get to and from their ultimate destinations? Victoria and London Bridge are in a straight-line distance of around three miles apart.

Passengers would still have to get from home to work and back again, and they deserved some say in the matter.

Many years later, in 1976, Sir Peter Parker as the incoming Chairman of British Rail was to remark that he had 55 million people to help him; everybody seems to be an expert on railways and ready with instant advice.[6]

3

Nationalised British Railways

It is not possible to say how quickly the expenditure made under the Modernisation Plan will fructify. British Transport Commission, 1959

BRITISH TRANSPORT COMMISSION LONDON PLAN WORKING PARTY REPORT, 1949

Traffic requirements

As this Working Party pointed out, unenthusiastically, the huge infrastructure investment programme which would result from the closure and removal of the Southern stations and river bridges was all to be carried out to satisfy planning interests. There was no good railway traffic reason for any of it.

There were two exceptions relating to the route via Blackfriars, which was looked upon reasonably favourably. The routes referred to by letters (Route A etc) were devised originally by the earlier Committee. Those described here are the amended versions from this Working Party.

> **Route A** would run in full size tunnel from the Loughborough Junction/Herne Hill area via Elephant & Castle, Ludgate Circus, Chancery Lane, Russell Square, Euston and then to both the Midland and Great Northern main lines. These would both be electrified in the suburban area. This railway would be of particular value to the New Town developments.
>
> **Route B** was to be a freight route, again in a main-line-sized tunnel, replacing the route via Blackfriars, but crossing under the Thames at Greenwich on a new alignment.

As the justification for both Route A and Route B was attributable primarily to planning interests, the Working Party suggested hopefully that the planning budgets would pay for at least part of the costs.

In the Working Party's opinion, there were three main railway requirements for London in post-war Britain. These were the relief of overcrowding on existing lines, the provision of new railway routes where there was already an acknowledged deficiency, and the provision of new facilities for new traffic.

The Working Party then launched into what they considered to be the essentials of a practical railway plan. They are repeated here in full as they are no less relevant today:

- There are two types of urban services. First are high-frequency services with frequent stops. These trains have plenty of doors and ample standing room, and are used on routes extending 10–12 miles from the centre.
- There are also the outer suburban services, whose main purpose is the rapid movement of people in bulk to and from the outer suburbs. Such trains need high seating capacity with relatively infrequent stops, but at lower frequencies.
- The two types of service do not mix well for line capacity reasons and this should be avoided where possible. Interchange between the two service types is important for passengers, with the urban services performing a distribution function.
- Cross platform interchange is ideal but not always possible, especially if three (or more) underground lines meet at a single point. There is a limit to the space available in central London, which poses its own constraints on line curvature, line gradients and the distance between the street and the platforms.
- Precision operation of high frequency urban services requires them to be self-contained wherever possible and not to share tracks with freight or long-distance passenger services.

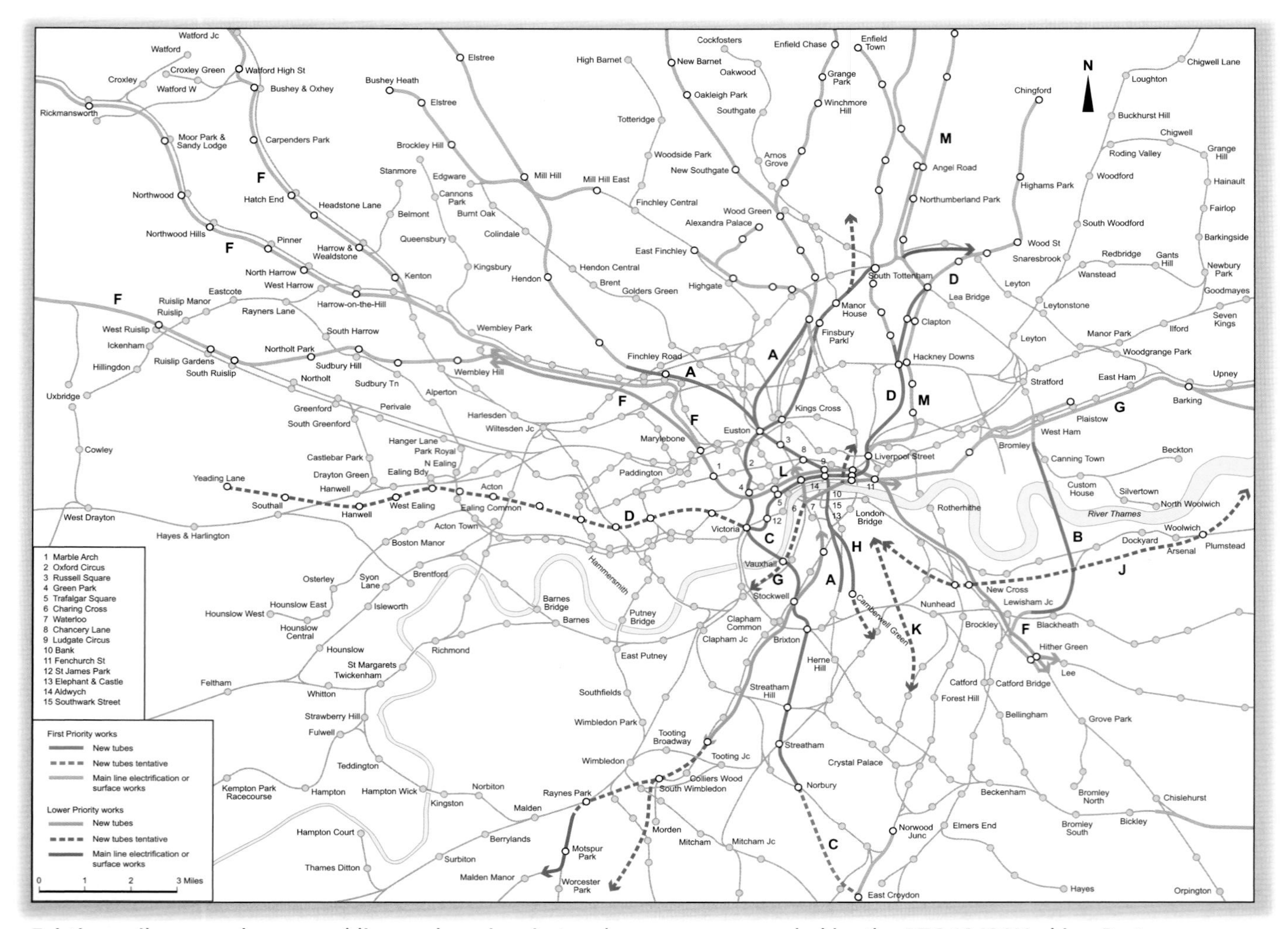

Existing railways and proposed line and services in London, as recommended by the BTC 1949 Working Party.

- New railways expensively constructed in tunnel should have reasonable prospects for off-peak as well as peak traffic. They can assist with the relief of road congestion, and confer a marked benefit on the travelling public.
- New urban railways should be on new alignments so they can make a contribution to traffic distribution, rather than duplicate existing lines. Outside the central area, parallel express operation may be useful, as with the Metropolitan line to Wembley Park and Harrow-on-the-Hill.

Consequently, the Working Party produced their own list of priorities for new lines.

Route C would be a new passenger route from East Croydon via Norbury, Streatham, Streatham Hill, Brixton, Stockwell, Vauxhall, Victoria, Green Park, Oxford Circus, Euston, King's Cross, Finsbury Park, Manor House, Seven Sisters and Angel Road. There might be a branch from Seven Sisters to Tottenham and Walthamstow. Notably, this would have to be a line for tube stock, due to the restricted space at Oxford Circus. It was a service very much in the urban category.

There in essence is the Victoria line. After prolonged delays, construction was to start in 1962 and it was opened in sections 1968–71. The sections south of Brixton or that to Angel Road were never built.

Route D was an attempt to provide a new connection between the West End and the City, running from Enfield Town/Chingford with an underground junction at Hackney Downs, via Liverpool Street, Bank, Ludgate Circus and Aldwych to Trafalgar Square and Victoria, thence possibly via High Street Kensington and the Uxbridge Road to Yeading.

The list of possible new lines continued, though later ideas clearly had much more development work needed. **Route E** was to relieve the southern part of the Underground's Northern line with a duplicate service from Kennington to Tooting Broadway (fast, or maybe non-stop), calling at the same stations to South Wimbledon, then branch into a route to Chessington South (using existing surface alignments beyond Motspur Park) and another to Morden and North Cheam.

Even if the proposed cross river station closures were abandoned, congestion on South Eastern services was still going to be a problem. Lengthening of suburban trains to 10 cars was later carried out. (This was in preference to double-deck trains, an eight-car set of which was designed by O. V. S. Bulleid of the Southern and ran experimentally for 22 years between 1949 and 1971.)

Route F was devised to fill a gap. The recommendation was a new tube railway of main line dimensions, running from Hither Green via Fenchurch Street, Bank, Ludgate Circus and Trafalgar Square (in part as Route D). At the southern end, it was proposed that it should be connected to the Gillingham services via Dartford, and those from Sevenoaks.

At the other end, it would continue to Marble Arch and Marylebone, thence to Neasden, High Wycombe and Aylesbury. A branch would use a new connection from the Great Central (GC) to the LNW lines at Kenton to continue to Berkhamsted and Tring. The lines north of London would need to be electrified.

The essence of **Route G** was the construction of flyovers at Barking and the electrification of the London, Tilbury & Southend (LT&S) section, which formed the basis of work carried out under the British Railways 1955 Modernisation Plan and completed in 1961–62.

Route H was changes that might be made to the Bakerloo line. The Working Party noted that Parliamentary powers had been obtained for its extension from Elephant & Castle to Camberwell Green in 1931 and these had been kept alive. The inadequacy of the terminal arrangements at Elephant limited the service to 32 trains per hour (tph); this could be raised to 40tph (for which the signalling already allowed) with the extension. Quite how practical 40tph might have been (a train every 90 seconds) was not discussed.

The line might be taken further, to Herne Hill or beyond.

If Route F was constructed, it was proposed that the northern section of the Bakerloo might be cut back from Watford Junction to Harrow & Wealdstone (which has been the situation since 1984, but without Route F).

A further proposal was to create a new line to run between Baker Street, Bond Street and Green Park and thus relieve the Bakerloo, but what would happen at each end? No satisfactory ideas were forthcoming, though coupled to the Stanmore branch of the Bakerloo this would much later form Stage 1 of the Jubilee line to Charing Cross, opened in 1979.

Other schemes included the provision of tube railways in south east London, what could usefully be done with the Holborn–Aldwych shuttle (closed 1994), electrification to Bishops Stortford (achieved in 1960) and making a case for extending trains on the South Eastern section from eight cars to ten cars. This was done and resulted in a major building programme for two-car units, plus platform extensions, signalling alterations, greater depot accommodation and so on.

Engineering

Preliminary investigations showed that the proposals would result in three passenger tube lines of main-line size with a total length of 34 route miles, five tube lines of conventional size totalling 63¼ route miles, and one freight route of main-line size, 5½ miles. That summed to 102¾ route miles, of which just under one half was classified as first priority works. The total cost for all works below ground (only) was put at £238 million at 1949 prices.

For tubes of main line size, running tunnels would be of 17ft internal diameter and station tunnels 26ft. Platform lengths of 650ft on main line tubes would be needed to accommodate 10-car trains, others generally 450ft for eight cars. For the main line tubes it would be necessary to design special rolling stock with high seating capacity and sliding doors.

Considerable lengths of tube tunnel would need to be driven using compressed air, due to the presence of water-bearing gravel rather than London clay.

Line curvature should not exceed 20 chains (¼ mile), except perhaps at the entrance and exits to/from some station tunnels. Only in exceptional circumstances would gradients need to exceed 1 in 50.

Additional electricity generation would be needed for power requirements, whether provided by the National Grid or the British Transport Commission, together with substations, distribution plant, cables and equipment.

For comparison, the Piccadilly line platforms at Holborn on London Underground are 135ft below street level; the deepest on the proposed new construction was 120ft, for which two banks of escalators would be needed for access.

There was thus much to be done, but was it all well founded? Sixteen years on, the 1965 Railway Plan for London (see later) was critical, averring that the proposals made in 1949 were designed to modernise, integrate and expand the rail services, but were not required to have particular regard to the economic and financial consequences.

COUNTY OF LONDON DEVELOPMENT PLAN, 1951

This series of reports led, in time, to the County of London Development Plan in 1951, where the County of London gave their views on what had been presented to them.

The Council agreed that the removal of Charing Cross station and Hungerford Bridge should remain in abeyance for a period not exceeding 25 years (until 1976) and that Cannon Street, which was seen as a less important case, might remain for up to 30 years (1981).

And no, the Council would not be able to make any contribution to the cost of the Route A proposals for Blackfriars bridge and station, and invited HM Government so to do. The City Corporation was equally forthright, in that 'it would not wish to press for the railway works to be carried out if it involved any substantial financial contribution from the[ir] planning funds'.

What was apparent was the shift of attention from Blackfriars bridge over the Thames to the railway bridge on the same route over the road at Ludgate Circus. This was crossed between Blackfriars and Farringdon and in doing so obstructed the view of St Paul's Cathedral from Fleet Street. Much later, demolishing that bridge and its replacement by a railway in tunnel did turn out to be negotiable.

While the Council had in effect to accept the recommendation that the main schemes relating to the removal of the Thames railway bridges and their associated stations was not going to happen, they did have further views on the viaducts and the use of the arches underneath. Thus 'many of those used for industrial or commercial purposes are in a deplorable condition' and blight whole neighbourhoods. Could they not be set up as playgrounds, or open spaces, instead?

Again, that would seem to have been more of a matter for local authority budgets, given also that the renting out of these spaces presumably resulted in some income for the railway.

More recently, the South London viaducts despised by some have been praised by others. Thus the continuous viaduct of nearly 3½ miles between London Bridge and Deptford underpinned London's first railway, the London & Greenwich. There are 851 semi-circular arches, interrupted only by 27 bridges over the intervening streets. This is one of the oldest and longest viaducts in the world.

There are other viaducts of a similar nature, and it is of interest that the reasons given for their original construction included the housing that was already in existence and the avoidance of the need to build those wretched level crossings.

MODERNISATION PLAN 1955

By the mid-1950s, national transport planning priorities had switched to catering for the private car and heavy goods vehicles; the first section of motorway in Britain, the Preston by-pass, was to be opened on 5 December 1958. The railway system at best stagnated and passenger numbers fell.

The British Railways Modernisation Plan[7] had five main components, shown here at contemporary prices:

1. Renewal and updating of track, signalling and structures. £210 million
2. The elimination of steam traction, coupled with electrification were justified, otherwise dieselisation. £345 million
3. Replacement of passenger rolling stock, notably by multiple-units, with passenger stations and parcels depots modernised. £285 million

The idea of sliding door stock for suburban services never really caught on in the Modernisation years. Thus the 1949 Shenfield stock for the Eastern Region (later Class 306) remained one of the few examples to be found in the London area, apart that is from London Underground, through to the 1970s. This is the preserved set 017. ***John Glover***

One of the early Class 302s, No 221 is seen on the up fast line approaching Gidea Park. This unit was loaned from the LT&S line. In the foreground is one of the original DC gantries, delete masts for the 1949 inner suburban electrification. *John Glover*

4. No fewer than 55 freight marshalling yards were to be built or reconstructed and continuous brakes would become standard on all goods wagons [though these would still be vacuum, rather than air]. Wagon stocks would be renewed, with 750,000 larger wagons replacing the then total of about 1,100,000. £365 million

5. Sundry items, including development and research work, railway packet port improvements, staff welfare and offices. £35m million

The total bill came to £1,240 million, which the Commission airily rounded down to £1.200 million. It was a 15-year programme, though as it turned out that timescale was rather nominal.

Noticeable are the huge amounts which would be dedicated to updating the fleet, both traction and rolling stock, while the proportion allocated to infrastructure seems decidedly modest. It was certainly not enough to contemplate even vaguely the major works proposed by Abercrombie and others in central London.

Ideas for new construction or a rethink of what the railways should really be doing were completely absent. Old pre-war plans were rehashed, but there were vague threats to unremunerative services ... which are little used by the public and ... should be largely handed over to road transport[8].

All this was for the railways of Britain as a whole. Specifics were few and far between and related mostly to electrification. Some of these were foreseen in the 1940s reports already discussed. The extensions from Shenfield to Chelmsford and to Southend Victoria were already under way, albeit as DC schemes. Others affecting the South East were:

- London, Tilbury & Southend.
- Great Eastern to Clacton, Ipswich and Felixstowe, though the latter remains non-electrified.
- Chingford/Enfield Town/Bishop's Stortford and Hertford East. This group was known as the CHENFORD scheme.
- Kent Coast, essentially work left unfinished by the Southern Railway.
- Great Northern suburban from Moorgate/King's Cross to Letchworth, in the event, to Royston.

Main line electrification was to be:

- Euston/Birmingham/Manchester/Liverpool (EBML), but not then north of Crewe.
- King's Cross–Doncaster-Leeds, plus perhaps York. This was the last of all these works to make progress and was completed (to Scotland) nearly 36 years later, in 1991.

A Southern look-alike that isn't. A Class 501 unit is about to leave South Acton station with a North London line service from Broad Street to Richmond in May 1978. These trains were built for this route by BR Eastleigh and were fitted with destination blinds, something then unknown on Southern territory. The open land to the left of the shelter is the site of the station for the District line branch from South Acton, closed in 1959. *John Glover*

Re-appraisal of the Modernisation Plan

The focus of this book is on passenger services, but they are by no means everything. It needs to be remembered that the railway was founded on freight traffic and this was for long the main revenue earner.

The importance that management attached to freight was therefore very substantial. In 1957, British Railways earned almost as much from the carriage of coal and coke traffic alone, as they did from the whole of the passenger business. Overall, freight and parcels traffic together were responsible for an enormous 70% of total revenues.

It must be stressed that this is what was happening nationally, but the general direction is clear. It was to be another four years before the publication of Dr Beeching's controversial 'Reshaping' plan. Even so, in 1959 the British Transport Commission was warning about the financial problems of the intensive suburban services around London.

The replacement of steam traction by electric and diesel trains in the London area, except on much of the Southern Region, was then still largely in the future.

There was also a general expectation by both politicians and the public that the railways should be financially self-sufficient, at least in terms of operating costs and revenues. Grants from public funds for capital schemes, where justified, were however becoming more acceptable. That the competition from (in particular) road transport was at an altogether different level than the situation in 1939, had yet to sink in.

Eastern Region trains

New electric trains were needed in quantity in London for the Modernisation Plan works, notably for the Eastern Region London area. Broadly in order of appearance, these were as follows. The TOPS classification is included, but that was not carried until the 1970s.

The first type, what later became the Class 306, for the Shenfield DC services, was the precursor of what much later became the sliding door standard for suburban operations. They were followed by the Class 307s for the extensions to Southend Victoria and Chelmsford. When wide-scale electrification of much of the rest of the Great Eastern and the London, Tilbury & Southend lines was authorised, those units and the infrastructure had to be converted to the new AC system. This was done in 1960.

From the 1966 electrification, outer suburban services from Euston were in the hands of AM10 EMUs, later known as Class 310. Here unit No 079 arrives at Leighton Buzzard on 30 May 1967. The BG (Brake Gangwayed vehicle) being loaded in the bay is a reminder of the past importance of parcels traffic. *John Glover*

All remaining units working on these sections had to be built to cope with a voltage changeover 25kV AC to 6.25kV AC to suit safety clearances at physically restrictive locations in the inner areas. This dual-system approach was eventually deemed unnecessary and the 6.25kV AC arrangement had been abandoned by the 1980s.

The units are listed in Table 3.2.

Table 3.2. Great Eastern/LT&S electric units, 1949–1980

Class	Description	Introduced	Units	Formation
306	Shenfield 001-092	1949	92	3-car
307	GE Outer Suburban 101-132	1956	32	4-car
302	LT&S 201-312	1959	112	4-car
305/1	Enfield/Chingford 401-452	1960	52	3-car
308/3	Enfield/Chingford 453-455	1961	3	3-car
305/2	GE Outer Suburban 501-519	1960	19	4-car
308/1	GE Outer Suburban 133-165	1961	33	4-car
308/4	LT&S 313-316 (parcels units)	1961	4	4-car
308/2	LT&S 317-321 (luggage units)	1961	5	4-car
309/1	Clacton 601-608 2-car	1962	8	2-car
309/2	Clacton 611-618 4-car buffet	1962	8	4-car
309/3	Clacton 621-627 4-car	1962	7	4-car
312/1	GE Outer suburban	1976	19	4-car
315	GE inner suburban	1980	61	4-car

The fleets of Modernisation Plan electric multiple-units (EMUs) did not impress. With box-like bodies painted dark green all over, perhaps with some minimal yellow lining, they were later adorned in BR corporate blue with yellow ends. As a statement advertising the modern railway, they failed completely. Matters were not helped by serious traction problems, resulting in persistently high failure rates until the faults were diagnosed and corrected.

Internally, gangways between vehicles were a rarity, though in some cases they were added later. Similarly, tungsten bulbs were replaced with fluorescent strip lights. Compartment stock would be rebuilt as open saloons. Second class seating was either 3+2 each side of a central gangway, or six across. Basic, inside and out, would be a fair description of the fleet as a whole.

Maybe that was the best that could be afforded, but there was an exception, and that was the Class 309 Clacton units in lined maroon livery. These were built to the highest standards that could be achieved with Mark 1 vehicles, with no fewer than eight of the four-car sets including a Griddle Car. These would be teamed up with one ordinary four-car set and a two-car set, 10 cars in all. After leaving Liverpool Street the two-car set would be detached at Colchester to form a stopping service to Clacton, the non-Griddle set at Thorpe-le-Soken to proceed to Walton-on-the-Naze, and the Griddle Car set to Clacton.

Other than the Class 306's, the whole of the fleet for the next 30 years was built with drop windows and slam doors. That included the Class 312/1 units, which did not appear until 1976. It was only with the Class 315s which replaced the Class 306s on inner-suburban services from 1980 that sliding doors finally became the accepted way to proceed.

London Midland

On the London Midland Region, matters progressed in a similar manner, but without flagship trains like those used on the Clacton services. Thus the LMR had a fleet of EMUs for the North London line services; these were completely replaced by a new build of three-car units in 1957 (later Class 501). Notably, the centre Trailer Seconds of these vehicles, 57ft long so there were only nine compartments, seated a whopping 108 passengers. They were however decidedly uncomfortable if you had to stand, especially for those not tall enough to reach the luggage racks to steady themselves.

Longer distance services made use of the AM4 units, later Class 304 and similar to the Eastern Region outer-suburban stock. These were replaced from 1965 by the Class 310s with a much more modern look to them, but still slam door stock.

Southern Region trains

Of interest is the huge volume of rolling stock needed to operate the Southern's electric services, which were formed almost exclusively of multiple-unit stock. Covering the post-war period from 1951 to 1974, when the last of the Southern slam door trains were produced, the overall picture was as follows.

Express stock for the Southern's main line operations, were built using the Mk1 Standard coach components, very much in the style of the locomotive-hauled main line fleet. All had gangways both within and between vehicles, with (normally) three slam doors for passenger use on each body side.

The Modernisation Plan saw a 24-strong fleet of what became Class 71 Bo-Bo electric locomotives for the Southern Region. They were built 1958–60 and intended for freight work. In 1967-68, 10 were converted to electro-diesels. On the left is E6106 at Stewarts Lane MPD on 18 July 1968. At the higher level is 4-CEP No 7196 in Southern Region green. *John Glover*

Beneath the front of Brighton station may be found this delightful mural depicting Pullman Car *Doris* as part of the famed 'Brighton Belle' service. It shows a view through the arches of the station. It is seen here on 27 January 2017. *Carol Glover*

The earliest fleet was that for the newly electrified Kent Coast services in 1959 (4-CEP/4-BEP). These were followed by similar units for the Brighton line in 1964 (4-CIG/4-BIG), with further deliveries for the Portsmouth services in 1972.

The 4 represented the number of vehicles in the unit, the letters could be rather obscure. Thus EP stood for Electro-Pneumatic (brake). CIG referred to C for Corridor, with IG as Intermediate Guard. (IG was also the one time telegraphic code for Brighton). The inclusion of a catering vehicle was denoted by B for buffet or R for restaurant car.

Last of the main line sets was the build for the 1967 Bournemouth electrification. This consisted of high-powered tractor units (4-REP sets), which were used to work push-and-pull with one or two unpowered control trailer units (4-TC). This enabled the trailer units to work similarly with diesel power (Class 33/1) over the (then) non-electrified line beyond Bournemouth to Weymouth. Other than the two Driving Motors of the tractor units, all the other vehicles were conversions from locomotive-hauled

A typical 4-EPB formation headed by No 5038 passes through Denmark Hill on 1 November 1969. These slam door trains formed the backbone of the Southern Region's extensive suburban network for many years, later displaced on the Kent lines by the Class 465/466 builds. *John Glover*

stock. In many respects it was electrification on the cheap, but it did get the job done!

As many as 65 of the 348 four-car units in this group would include either a buffet or restaurant car. These catering sets would run in conjunction with one or two ordinary units; they were most unlikely to run on their own.

For working independently on quayside lines at Dover or Folkestone, 10 Driving Motor Luggage Vans (MLV) were built. These relied on traction batteries when working away from the third rail. Their purpose was the carriage of parcels and passengers' luggage and formed part of boat trains of Kent Coast stock.

Were double-deck suburban trains a good or a bad idea? This plaque outside Dartford station showed a Motor Brake Second of the 1949 4-DD train for the Southern. These end vehicles had 55 seats lower deck and another 55 upper deck, with 10 tip-up seats. The equivalent for the intermediate trailers was 78 lower deck, with 66 upper deck and 12 tip-ups. But they were airless inside and took an age to load and unload. *John Glover*

The original units for semi-fast or secondary services were constructed for use on the South Western Division from 1967 (4-VEP), but further builds found them in use all over Southern territory. The 195 units were gangwayed throughout, making them very versatile; they had (mostly) separate doors for each seating bay.

Rather less grand were the units built from 1954 for outer suburban and semi-fast services (2-HAP). One of the two cars was divided into three traditional first class compartments and a second class saloon. Both sets of passengers had access to their own separate lavatories in the centre of the vehicle.

The remaining group was primarily for London suburban services. They were non-gangwayed and usually with a high-density configuration. These were built from 1951 onwards (4-EPB, 2-EPB). A typical 10-compartment trailer might have five straight-through compartments and an open saloon with a further five sets of doors. The compartments seated 60 passengers, the saloons only 52, but the ability to move around did give passengers a better chance of finding any empty seats.

The overall picture showed the building of 1,402 vehicles of Express stock, 1,198 vehicles for outer suburban or other secondary services, and 1,390 vehicles to be used primarily on the inner-suburban routes.

The use of Southern 2-EPB units on the North Woolwich services was short lived, but it served its purpose at the time. Here Class 416/3 no 6316 stands at the desolate terminus in August 1988. These trains had to have the drop windows fitted with bars due to the restricted clearances in Hampstead Heath tunnel. To the left and in the station building behind was the North Woolwich Old Station Museum, with railway displays. Opened in 1984, it closed in 2008. *John Glover*

The lines of the preserved 4-VEP Class 423 unit no 3417 *Gordon Pettitt* are nothing like as sleek as that of South West Trains' 444019 alongside, and the Rail Blue livery would be even more drab were it not for the window surrounds being picked out. The place is Clapham Yard and the date 24 March 2014. ***John Glover***

Thus in the space of a little over 20 years, the Southern built very nearly 4,000 vehicles or over three a week for its electric services. That is not the whole story, either, as many trains built in earlier periods were kept running.

They included the popular all-Pullman car train, the 'Brighton Belle' (5-BEL), dating from the Brighton line electrification of 1933. This continued until its demise in 1972. 'No more breakfast kippers!' as the renowned actor Baron (Sir Laurence) Olivier wailed. Remarkably, 45 years later, Michael Portillo was still lamenting the loss of kippers on trains that serve breakfast, in his 'Great British Railway Journeys' series for the BBC[9].

New build trains with sliding doors started to arrive from the late 1970s onwards. There were of course also the hauled services and the diesel units.

It was the decision to eliminate slam door stock that saw all such trains withdrawn from main line Southern service, which was completed in 2005.

Long before Gatwick Express was thought of, in 1978 the Southern Region converted 12 sets of 4-VEP Class 423 stock to 4-VEG Class 427 stock. This enabled them to launch the Rapid City Link service between Gatwick Airport and London Victoria; this is a commemorative beer mat. The conversion consisted of the removal of 24 seats in the second class accommodation and their replacement with luggage racks. The result was that the number of seats reduced from 232 to 208. First class seating remained the same at 48; do they not have so much luggage? ***John Glover***

Rapid City Link
LONDON VICTORIA - GATWICK AIRPORT

A light sprinkling of snow in February 2003 is not impeding the progress of a Class 442 unit on the up fast line at Surbiton. This adaptation of the Mk3 coach body with power doors in an EMU was provided for the extension of the Bournemouth electrification to Weymouth. Surbiton station is perhaps one of the best of the Southern Railway's inter-war offerings, with its two island platforms and station entrances on both sides of the line. *John Glover*

Diesel traction

Elsewhere, many varieties of the original diesel multiple-units abounded. The Western Region fleet was based at Reading, mostly three-car units of 1959 vintage built by Pressed Steel, latterly Class 117. Other builds were used for services from Marylebone and St Pancras.

Their later replacements are being largely eliminated from Paddington with the completion of Crossrail 1 in 2019 and other GW electrification, while the Bedford-St Pancras (Bed–Pan) electrification meant their withdrawal from Midland line London services in 1982. Of all the London termini, Marylebone alone remains entirely diesel unit operated, again not with the original vehicles.

On the main lines the East Coast began to improve markedly with the delivery of the 3,300hp Class 55 'Deltic' diesel locomotives from 1961 and the West Coast Main Line electrification from Euston with its (eventual) fleet of 236 locomotives in 1966. Coaching stock progressed to the Mk2 version, the later builds of which were air-conditioned, and then to the 23m-long Mk3s.

Further real improvements came with the 125mph High Speed Passenger Train (HST), 200 of which entered service progressively from 1976 on the Great Western, East Coast and Midland main lines.

4 Slow Progress

The Minister asked whether the £55 million the Victoria line would cost would pay a better dividend were it spent on off-street parking or some other project. London Transport in 1959, Annual Review.

It is time to recap on progress with the post-war Underground system. On the Central line, it was finally decided to electrify that problem child inherited from British Railways, the remote Epping–Ongar branch, in 1956. The work was completed in the following year. It was hardly a success story and eventually services were withdrawn in 1994.

It has since been revived as a heritage line between North Weald and Ongar.

Metropolitan line

On the Metropolitan, the electrification north of Rickmansworth to Amersham and to Chesham was a barely started part of the 1935/40 New Works Programme. The work included the four-tracking of the railway north of Harrow-on-the-Hill to the divergence of the Watford branch. A re-start was authorised in 1956. A new build of rolling stock for all Metropolitan services was placed in service from 1961.

This was the well-liked A stock, constructed in two batches by Cravens of Sheffield. These 116 four-car units, usually operated in pairs, were an ingenious attempt to combine sliding doors (three sets per car side or two double and one single door if there was a driving cab) with plentiful transverse seating on a 3+2 arrangement. This gave a not quite central gangway. With cars a modest 55ft long, that worked out at 54 seats in each of the two intermediate Trailers, 58 in each Driving Motor.

Amersham, Watford and Uxbridge to central London were among the longest journeys that most passengers would make on the Underground. The car design and internal layout was aimed at making such journeys as agreeable as possible, given that they replaced six-a-side compartment stock with slam doors.

Most of the A stock trains survived in service until the coming of the S stock from 2010; they were certainly the last Underground stock to feature overhead racks for the briefcase and the brolly!

Circle line

The equivalent trains for the Hammersmith & City line, the Circle line and the District's Edgware Road services were the C stock, the first appearing in 1970. Trains were made up of three sets of pairs of Driving Motor and Trailer, running as six-car sets. Here the slightly shorter (49ft) Trailers had four sets of double doors, but only 32 seats. These were arranged in facing pairs, later changed to a

Some of the A stock saw out its final years as four-car sets on the East London line before that became part of the Overground. Here a southbound train from Shoreditch to New Cross is seen at Whitechapel in May 1987. The subterranean nature of this station will be noted. The line north from here was to be rerouted to a new station at Shoreditch High Street and then onto the former Broad Street line formation, the former Shoreditch station was closed permanently. ***John Glover***

longitudinal arrangement but seating the same numbers. The Driving Motors had the same saloon arrangement and length; the driving cabs were 3ft 7in add-on.

The A stock, the C stock as well as the rather later D stock for the District line, built from 1980, were all ousted in that order by the S stock between 2012 and 2017.

The A and C stock examples are given to illustrate how the number of doors influence the seating capacity that can be provided, but offset by the number of standing passengers that could also be accommodated.

How many standees is it reasonable to expect to carry? The Railway Plan for London of 1965 gives the one-hour loading standards of that period. These were:

- Underground (except Metropolitan main line), Waterloo & City line and British Railways sliding door stock: 100 standing per 100 seats.
- Metropolitan main line, and inner-suburban services of British Railways: 50 standing per 100 seats.
- British Railways outer-suburban services ('corridor' stock): 25 standing per 100 seats.

These standards related to the inner trunk sections on which traffic builds up to its maximum, not over the entire length of the lines. In such ways was the capacity of individual lines determined.

Victoria line

What was to become the Victoria line of London Underground was given high priority in the 1940s plans as already discussed, and in 1953 this was agreed by the Minister. Parliamentary powers to build it were granted in 1955, but it was not until 1962 that ministerial approval for the building of the original section from Walthamstow Central to Victoria was received. The extension to Brixton was approved later.

Why did it take so long? Though the official reason for its eventual implementation was the relief of street congestion and the improvement of travelling conditions on the Underground, political reality meant that the government's anxiety to relieve unemployment may have been a major factor. The Select Committee of 1965 on London Transport[10] were scathing, specifically exonerating London Transport from being the cause of delay.

On 24 April 1997, a train of 1967 Victoria line stock is seen in Northumberland Park depot, the only above ground point on that line. This stock was retired after a 40-year life, to be replaced by a slightly larger fleet of 2009 stock. ***John Glover***

They were however sold on the principle of social benefit analysis. This was then a new technique which suggested (with supporting calculations) that while it was right for the LT Board to be responsible for the operational costs and revenues in running the railway, the capital cost of building the new line should be shared with other beneficiaries. Prime amongst these were road users, from the relief of traffic congestion.

This, the Select Committee hoped, was the right approach to future capital schemes put forward by the Board for which social benefit could be calculated. The methodology as it was developed has since been widely used, and was a distinctly different approach from that set out in the 1961 paper[11] on the obligations of nationalised industries to 'pay their way'.

But scepticism among the public was still widespread in that many thought there was no need for the Victoria line anyway. Opinions did change very quickly following its opening, in sections, between 1968 and 1971.

All the Victoria line's 16 stations except Pimlico have interchange with other lines on the Underground, the main line network, or both. Some links as at Brixton or Seven Sisters are a little tenuous, but great efforts were put into making the Victoria line a useful addition to the existing system. That it was done so well is a lasting tribute to the professionalism of those concerned.

Tube Rolling Stock

The early post-war years saw further deliveries of rolling stock to designs dating from pre-World War 2, both sub-surface and tube. This included what was in its time a revelation in what could be achieved in a tube environment, notably the 1938 stock, already discussed. Originally, this was for the Northern and Bakerloo lines, with some operating on the Piccadilly.

Subsequently, very similar builds but with rubber-suspension, light alloy construction, fluorescent lighting, plastic interior finish, much improved control gear and better conditions for drivers were provided for the Piccadilly line (1959 stock, seven cars) and the Central line (1962 stock, eight cars).

Two sets of double doors and two sets of single doors (at the car ends) were provided. Seats were longitudinal at the end sections, transverse in a 2+2 arrangement in the centre section.

This general saloon design was perpetuated in the Victoria line (1967 stock, eight cars), though the trains themselves were fitted for Automatic Train Operation

Finchley Central was once part of the Great Northern Railway; it is now part of the Northern line of London Underground. A 1959 stock train is approaching from the High Barnet direction, seen here from the station footbridge on 24 April 1997. The line straight ahead led to Edgware, part of the never achieved Underground extension beyond the present terminus of Mill Hill East. ***John Glover***

One of the small batch of 1960 stock which might have formed the Central line replacement fleet is seen at Woodford, just having arrived with the shuttle from Hainault on 21 April 1990. Only 12 Driving Motor cars were built; the centre car was purloined from the 1938 stock, suitably repainted. ***John Glover***

(ATO). Similar trains but for crew operation were built for the Northern line as the 1972 Mk1 stock and for the Jubilee line 1972 Mk2 stock, both seven cars).

The 1972 Mk2 trains remain in service, where they operate the Bakerloo. The 1973 stock trains of six cars were delivered new for the Piccadilly extension to Heathrow Terminals 1, 2, 3 in 1977, with allowances made for accommodating passenger luggage. They too remain in service.

Other stocks in present tube use are 1992 (Central, Waterloo & City), 1995 (Northern), 1996 (Jubilee) and 2009 (Victoria).

BEECHING RESHAPING

On the national railway, The Reshaping of British Railways was published in March 1963. Much of this report was the work of the Chairman of the British Railways Board, Dr Richard Beeching. It was best known for the extensive list of line closures in the years which followed, and for which he was long remembered.

The peak problem was explained in terms of the huge variations in demand across the day. 'The peak load, measured over half an hour is about ten times the average level over the hours from 06:00 to 24:00'. This resulted in what amounted to appalling utilisation of trains, track and train crew, and in spite of that practically the whole of the peak traffic was carried at reduced fares. This was a reference to season tickets, which offered a considerable reduction when compared with paying daily rates.

Beeching also drew attention to the ability of railways to carry people over longer distances on commuting journeys of up to 100 miles and that it was in their commercial interests so to do. Each fare paid would be that much more than for short distance journeys; it was the congestion caused by the latter where the real problems arose.

But these were problems outside the railway's ambit and were in effect left for another day. The London lines were relatively unscathed in the scheme for service withdrawals. The list shows the passenger services which were identified as likely to be withdrawn, and their subsequent fate. Closure dates given are those for passenger traffic; freight may have continued for some time afterwards.

- Camden Road–Richmond (service now provided by London Overground)
- Clapham Junction–Kensington Olympia (service extended to Willesden Junction 1994, subsequently electrified, now provided by London Overground)
- Harrow & Wealdstone–Belmont (closed 1964)
- Hatfield–Luton–Dunstable (closed 1965, part now a busway in the Luton area)

The Clapham Junction–Kensington Olympia shuttle, then consisting of a Class 33 and three Mk1 coaches, had to run round at the end of each journey. The locomotive is in the process of being coupled at Clapham Junction's Platform 2 in this March 1983 shot. This was very much a hands-on at ground level job. *John Glover*

- Kentish Town–Barking (services diverted to start from Gospel Oak 1981, electrified 2018, services now provided by London Overground)
- Romford–Upminster (electrified 1986, services now provided by London Overground)
- Seven Sisters–Palace Gates (closed 1963)
- Watford High Street–Croxley Green (closed 1996, most of track bed could be used for Metropolitan line extension to Watford Junction)
- Watford Junction–St Albans Abbey (electrified 1988, services now provided by London Northwestern)
- West Drayton & Yiewsley–Uxbridge Vine Street (closed 1962)
- West Drayton & Yiewsley–Staines West (closed 1965, part of track bed may yet be used for southern rail access to Heathrow)

Below: This pre-electrification shot of 23 May 1995 shows 117701 of the first generation of DMUs at Clapham Junction's Platform 2 with the 10:03 to Willesden Junction. All that has to be done now to reverse a train is for the driver to change ends before returning. *John Glover*

The Euston/Broad Street–Watford Junction group was to have the stopping services modified in an unspecified way. In the event, the services from Euston remained intact and are now part of London Overground. Services shown as such are operated as a concession by contractors. This has been the case since 2007, following the acquisition of the franchise from the previous operator, Silverlink.

Broad Street services ceased on the closure of the line south of Dalston in 1986. A few peak services were rerouted via the purposely constructed Graham Road curve to Liverpool Street, but these were discontinued in 1992. Interchanging at Highbury & Islington to the Great Northern suburban services to Moorgate proved to be a more popular (and considerably quicker) alternative.

Most of the line from Dalston Junction towards Broad Street was to be used later for London Overground services.

It can be seen that in reality the closure programme had little long-term effect in London, but it did provide a timely warning on the unsatisfactory financial position of many suburban railways.

RAILWAY PLAN FOR LONDON

A further report on London services, A Railway Plan for London[12], was produced in March 1965 on behalf of the Passenger Transport Planning Committee of the British Railways Board and London Transport.

The result was to be a plan for matching railway capacity in the London area to the likely requirements over the ensuing 20 years. Project evaluation would need to take account of financial viability and social benefits, as well as the planning of future population and employment distribution.

This report focussed extensively on the changing locations of homes for those commuting to work.

Typically, the primary role of British Railways was seen as bringing in commuters from the outer suburbs and dormitory areas to termini at the edge of the central area of the capital, while London Transport provided a distribution network for those passengers within that area. London Transport also catered for the whole journey to work for most of those living in the inner suburbs and in the central area.

The North London line with a Class 501 DC set crosses over the Midland line with a Class 127 DMU on 25 August 1976. The location is just to the east of West Hampstead and West Hampstead Thameslink stations respectively. There is no physical connection between the two, nor indeed with the nearby West Hampstead Underground station, where the Jubilee line today runs side by side but on different tracks to the Metropolitan and the Chiltern line from Marylebone. There are no platforms for either of the latter. ***John Glover***

Commuters await no 465155 with their homebound train at Elephant & Castle in August 2004. The entrances to the Underground station of the same name are nearby, but their location is far from obvious. ***John Glover***

At that time, the heaviest commuter flows by British Railways were to the south and east of the capital, with London Underground dominating to the north and west. British Railways services in those areas were relatively underused. Looking 20 years ahead to 1985, the expectation was something like a 45% increase in British Railways commuter traffic (much of which would then result in a busier central area Underground), but a modest increase in Underground-only passenger volumes.

The study assessed urban Underground lines as able to provide an optimistic 40 trains per hour (tph). On British Railways, with high speed outer-suburban services and longer trains, 24tph was more realistic. Catering for the two traffic types on double-track lines would seriously reduce the potential.

'This is why', said the Plan sternly, 'growth in long distance commuter traffic can make it imperative to reduce the number of stopping trains ...' In some cases it might be necessary to eliminate certain stations on the approaches to the main termini.

On the other hand, this was nothing new. One of the objectives of the New Works Programme 1935/40 was to rid parts of what became the British Railways network of shorter distance service, so that the lines concerned could concentrate on providing for the longer distance passengers.

In brief, the proposals made by the Working Party were:

- Building the Fleet line using the Stanmore branch of the Bakerloo, thence new construction from Baker Street via Charing Cross and Ludgate Circus to Fenchurch Street and New Cross, with the option of continuing to Hayes on the Mid-Kent line, or via the Bexleyheath line to Barnehurst. The Fleet line proposal is discussed more fully later; there was at this stage no interest in going to or via Docklands.
- Extending the Victoria line to Brixton to relieve the Northern line. This was completed 1971, though the possibility of taking it further to Crystal Palace, in part over British Railways tracks, was never pursued.
- The Holborn-Aldwych shuttle to be extended to Waterloo to cater for growing commuter traffic. In view of the short journey time, it was suggested that it would be acceptable for people to cram themselves in tighter than normal, to maximise the capacity at minimum cost. (The line was closed in 1994 due to falling patronage and the cost of lift replacement at Aldwych).

Waterloo is the most used London terminus, seen here beginning to get busy for the evening peak on 29 June 2008. The very large clock is suspended over what was once the cab road, long since gone. 'Meeting under the clock' was never a real option here. *John Glover*

- Platform and train lengthening on the Metropolitan, Hammersmith & City and Circle lines, to increase capacity. Modifications would also need to be made to depot accommodation. The disparity in platform lengths is still seen today with S8 (eight-car) trains on the Metropolitan and S7 (seven cars) on the other subsurface lines.

Other anticipated needs due to overloading were relief of the Northern line north of London Bridge, similarly for the Central line west of Liverpool Street. There was however thought to be no justification on traffic grounds for the extension of the Bakerloo line from Elephant & Castle to Camberwell.

On British Railways, the main considerations were the rationalisation of services and terminal facilities north of the river, where capacity much exceeded demand and seemed likely to continue to do so. South of the river, the need was to separate inner-suburban stopping trains from the faster outer-suburban services which were much in need of improvements to their capacity and quality.

A line by line summary follows.

Fenchurch Street. The anticipated growth of one third in commuter traffic could be met by increasing train lengths to 12 cars, with platform lengthening on the Tilbury line, since achieved.

Liverpool Street. The Enfield and Chingford services are not pulling their weight and some trains should be transferred to the Bishops Stortford line, where commuter traffic is expected to double. This would be much helped by electrification of the Lea Valley (completed 1969). Outer suburban services on the Colchester main line, already very heavily loaded, were expected to see considerable increases, to be met by train lengthening,

King's Cross, Moorgate, Broad Street. The Great Northern electrification scheme was very much in the mind, but this was still more than a decade away. 'The prospects … would be enhanced if additional population could be settled in Great Northern territory, thus absorbing the latent capacity of the system.' Use of the Widened Lines to access Southern destinations via Blackfriars had too many physical limitations, and was not favoured.

St Pancras. The expected doubling of the peak hour load can be met by more trains and resignalling. Meanwhile, the Moorgate service via the Widened Lines was financially unjustified and its withdrawal was planned.

Euston and Broad Street to Watford Junction. Depending on the changes brought about by the

The Euston–Watford DC lines are separate from the West Coast Main Line for much of their length. A train for Euston formed of 313120 approaches the Primrose Hill tunnels, seen here from the South Hampstead platforms on 26 March 2010. First, though, it needs to pass beneath the Chiltern main line, which crosses its path at right angles. ***John Glover***

West Coast Main Line electrification (to be inaugurated the following year), it was likely that while Euston–Watford Junction DC lines service would be maintained, the Bakerloo service could be cut back to Queen's Park and the Broad Street link withdrawn. Alternative arrangements would need to be made for the lightly loaded Richmond–Broad Street service.

Marylebone to Aylesbury. Even with a doubling of peak hour traffic due to anticipated population growth, trains on the line via High Wycombe could be diverted to Paddington. Aylesbury services could be diverted via the Underground to Baker Street, given fourth-rail electrification north of Amersham. But the Metropolitan line on its own would not have quite enough capacity, so an alternative approach would be to see if additional population might be settled on that line to make the Aylesbury service from Marylebone viable. Either way, the line and the lightly used stations between Northolt Park and Wembley Hill (now Wembley Stadium) would be closed.

Paddington. Short distance suburban services to Hayes were causing operational problems; traffic was small and not rising. The most effective means of increasing line capacity for the longer distance commuter traffics would be the elimination of the uneconomic inner-suburban service and the closure of Acton (now Acton Main Line), West Ealing, Hanwell and Southall stations. It was thought that an express bus from Hayes to Ealing Broadway might meet passenger needs.

Southern Region South Western Division. Comparatively light traffics with limited growth on inner suburban services were countered by buoyant longer distance traffic. Suggestions were re-timetabling, elimination of the Hounslow loop stopping services, a flying junction at Woking for the line to Guildford and Portsmouth and an extra track on the approaches to Waterloo.

Southern Region Central Division. As with South

The cramped Willesden Junction Low Level station sees no 313134 leaving with a train from Euston to Watford Junction on 12 September 2009. The footbridge and ticket office building are of recent construction, associated also with much improved access to the High Level station out of sight in the background. ***John Glover***

Western, there was a problem of outer-suburban growth and inner-suburban stagnation. Resignalling would help, but the conflicting movements at Windmill Bridge Junction north of East Croydon and the lack of sufficient running lines through the station itself were major difficulties. The extension of London Underground lines over existing rail routes, or below ground level, needed to be examined.

Southern Region South Eastern Division. To paraphrase, 'unless you can sort out the London Bridge area, you won't get anywhere'. And so it has since proved with major works, discussed later, being undertaken in very recent times. Interestingly, the possibilities of projecting services from the south via Blackfriars to Farringdon (as a terminus? – not stated) was more or less dismissed as impractical. 'In the longer term, the most effective single measure of providing major relief will be the proposed transfer of either the Bexleyheath or Mid-Kent lines to the Underground's Fleet line'.

This left the Waterloo & City line, which remained part of British Rail until 1994. Here, an increase in train frequency was seen as likely to be sufficient, but if it wasn't the complete removal of internal seats on trains should do the trick. The possibility of line extension from Bank to Liverpool Street had been examined, but was found to be physically impracticable.

Such infrastructure works would be costly, at around £4.5 million a year for the next two decades (at 1965 prices). Plaintively, the report notes that this might be compared with the £20 million a year that the Greater London Council planned to spend on roads, *and this was exclusive of the cost of urban Motorways.*

The Plan remained a limited circulation item as the then Minister felt that 'it was not ready for publication', according to the Permanent Secretary of the Ministry of Transport[13]. Such matters were very sensitive in the wake of the Beeching 'Reshaping' report.

GRANT AID

There was still the nagging fear of many that the closure programme post-Beeching would at some stage be resumed. To counter this, the then Transport Minister Barbara Castle and the Chairman of the Railways Board Stanley Raymond published jointly a map in March 1967. This was entitled British Railways Network for Development. The purpose of this map was to show the stabilised rail network planned to meet social as well as economic and commercial needs. This specified the large majority of the then network which would survive for passenger and freight, or freight only, and gave an assurance that those lines would have a long-term future.

That has proved to be the case and, with a few exceptions, the lines specified in that document as well as some others are still in operation today.

In November of that year, the Government paper 'Railway Policy'[14] was published. This provided the outline of how in future 'socially necessary services' (those which were unable to be self-supporting) should be specified by Ministers and then grant aided by the Exchequer. The procedure became law under the Transport Act 1968.

Review

That, though, was not the end of the story. The Transport Act 1968 assumed that most of the railway could be made commercially viable and break even without the need for grant. The 'unremunerative' services of the rest of the railway would require subsidy for 'social or economic reasons'. These were identified, assessed, and grant aided. It may be noted that the Southern Region's commuter services were grant aided as a single group.

Unfortunately, the unsubsidised railway (freight and non-aided commercial railway) was unable to achieve its commercial remit, so six years later in 1974 a Rail Policy Review (unpublished) was conducted by the Department and the Board. Apparently, the main conclusions[15] were:

- The railway existed primarily for the purposes of the passenger system.
- The standards and therefore the costs of track and signalling were determined primarily by the requirements of the passenger system.
- On that basis, where freight shared passenger facilities, it should pay only its avoidable costs.
- That should enable the freight business to achieve financial break-even without the need for grant.
- The passenger system as a whole, at anything like its then size, was incapable of breaking even.
- The cost of the passenger system could not be reduced without service closure on a scale disproportionate to the expected savings.
- Grant should therefore be paid to the passenger system and not on a service by service basis.

These changes were accepted by the Government and such provision was made in the Railways Act 1974. This became the Public Service Obligation (PSO) under EEC Regulation 1191/69. The Direction imposing it provided that 'The British Railways Board shall, from 1 January 1975, operate their railway system so as to provide a public service which is generally comparable with that provided at present'.

These however were loose words, to be much criticised by the Monopolies and Mergers Commission in 1980; could they be read as preventing the Board from making any changes at all to the services then provided? This general situation survived until the mid-1980s, when the passenger business was divided into InterCity, Network SouthEast and Other Provincial Services (later Regional Railways), each with its own remit.

The 'avoidable costs' principle for freight track access charges is still extant.

FARES

The fares charged by bodies such as British Rail and London Transport were still subject to much external control. The result tended to be fares at a uniform rate per mile for all lines of each railway undertaking in London, but these were not necessarily calculated on a common basis.

For how long might this last? In May 1968 the National Board for Prices and Incomes reported[16] on an increase for which British Rail had applied. It was clear that new ideas were around.

The Prices and Incomes Board was not happy with perpetuating the status quo, while accepting it for the application before them. In the longer term, they concluded, 'British Rail in conjunction with the Ministry of Transport and the Greater London Council should proceed on the basis of charging different fares where this is justified on the ground of different costs, different qualities of service provided and different social consequences'.

Rightly or wrongly, such views were completely at odds with what many years later resulted in the staged introduction of that best-selling product, the London Travelcard.

That same report also commended the introduction of greater differentiation in the pricing of fares for longer distance rail services by route and by class, known at the time as selective pricing. Developments of this approach have become entrenched in present day railway commercial practices. It is fair to say that the results meet with far from universal approval among passengers or, indeed, at least some politicians.

GREATER LONDON DEVELOPMENT PLAN, REPORT OF STUDIES, 1969

Over the years, the major main line networks south of the Thames had guarded their territory (and their revenues) from interlopers as best they could, with the aim of keeping the tube railways out. In this they were largely successful; in this period the Morden branch of the Northern line was the main one that breached this wall. Others were the District to Wimbledon and Richmond, the Bakerloo to Elephant & Castle and the East London line to New Cross/New Cross Gate, but with all of these the incursion was only modest.

There were then 566 railway stations in Greater London. British Rail served 347 and London Underground 248, with some stations being served by both operators. There were gaps in provision, the Greater London Development Plan (GLDP) citing the northern part of the London Borough of Havering, Biggin Hill, New Addington (which now has London Tramlink) and Hillingdon.

Even so, 94% of London's population lived within a mile of either a British Rail or a London Underground station. In the central area London Underground stations average 0.45 miles apart, or 0.8 miles elsewhere. Table 4.1 shows the areas in which London's railways are located and the heavy reliance on tunnelling in the central area but much less so in inner London. Freight railways in terms of those where there was no passenger service accounted for only 41 route miles and this was diminishing.

Table 4.1: Distribution of railways in Greater London, 1967

Area	Route miles, passenger	Total route miles	of which on surface	of which in tunnel	% in tunnel
Central area	51	51	9	42	82
Inner London	166	193	155	38	20
Outer London	384	398	387	11	3
Greater London	601	642	551	91	14

Source: GLDP

London Underground was generally more successful than British Rail in attracting off-peak passengers; they had the advantage of frequent services which offered direct transit, or with usually no more than a single change, to 55 stations within the central area. But longer journeys on the Underground were usually rather slow.

British Rail services were less frequent, but were often able to offer higher average speeds. For journeys to central London, there was also the problem of onward travel from the main line terminus and how best to proceed. Travel by British Rail was strongest over longer distances; 3.5 million people living outside the Greater London area were within 60 minutes travelling time of central London by rail, and a further 3 million within 90 minutes journey time.

In policy terms, maximising the use of the existing facilities had some obvious benefits. There were three scenarios:

- Intensify the service on British Rail routes into London where there was spare capacity, particularly in the arc from Paddington round to St Pancras. This could open up more sources of labour, providing residential areas were located suitably.
- Reshaping bus services to radiate from main railway stations (in central London as well as in the suburbs) to provide a service more closely aligned with the public need.
- A change in emphasis in British Rail services, with efforts concentrated on longer distance routes to increase labour catchment areas for employment in central London, but also with the maintenance (and preferably development) of the standard of service on the shorter routes.

New legislation

All the above was in preparation for new legislation, which was embodied in the Transport (London) Act 1969.

Under this, the GLDP said:

- The Greater London Council (GLC) will become the statutory planning authority for London, with wide responsibility and powers for public passenger transport services.
- The Council will appoint the members of a newly constituted London Transport Executive and will have power over policies, finance and the broad lines of operations, without becoming involved in day-to-day management.
- The Government will set the London Transport undertaking on a sound financial basis before the transfer.
- British Rail commuter services will not come directly under Council control, but the Council will be enabled to bring rail services into a common plan and will be consulted over fares.

There would also be new Council powers over roads, not included in this list.

The Greater London Council acquired the London Transport undertaking from the Government on 1 January 1970, but minus its Country Bus division which became part of the National Bus Company. Thus London Transport, which was nationalised in 1948, became municipally controlled.

The lack of control over services on the national rail network was to be a continuing sore of the GLC and successor bodies. The problem was that most services on the national rail network in London cross the boundary into Essex, Hertfordshire, Buckinghamshire, Berkshire, Surrey or Kent. Few were contained wholly within Greater London.

There is thus a potential conflict of interest, with those living outside the boundary reluctant to see their rail services placed under the control of an elected body which has different interests and over whose actions they have no say.

A similar situation arises on London Underground, though to a much lesser extent, with the Metropolitan line services beyond Northwood and the Central line north of Woodford plus the stations to Grange Hill. Here, for a time, much higher fares were to be imposed than those for journeys wholly within Greater London.

GREATER LONDON COUNCIL

How then did the Greater London Council rate its new acquisition? A booklet[17] published in October 1970 included a summary of the then less than encouraging situation, of which the following is an abridged version.

When London Transport was formed in 1933, the possibility of losses were not anticipated. The market was buoyant and there was little competition. It therefore seemed reasonable to give London Transport two equal statutory obligations: to provide an adequate service and to pay its way (including interest charges).

For a long time, these twin aims were capable of achievement, but there was a very marked change in the 1950s and 1960s. Economic conditions had improved considerably, but social and technological changes had made the market more difficult. Increasing car ownership had made inroads into the off peak and leisure markets. Even the decline of cinema-going and the almost universal ownership of television had contributed to passenger loss.

For a labour-intensive industry, a combination of manpower shortage and rises in rates of pay inevitably meant difficulties in manning and relatively high costs to the user. Unreliable services and higher charges taken together positively urge customers to use cars instead if they can.

But there were opportunities to be grasped, particularly in North London.

HEATHROW AIRPORT

Access to Heathrow from central London has always been problematic and in 1969 a study team was commissioned jointly by the then Minister, Fred Mulley, and the President of the Board of Trade. At that time, the only direct public transport service available was that by express coach from the West London Air Terminal, near Gloucester Road Underground station.

Their Report[18] was published in 1970. There were four schemes to be considered, three from British Rail and one from London Transport. These were:

- BR 1 An exclusive British Rail link between Victoria and Heathrow, with check-in at Victoria and with the then coach service withdrawn.
- BR 2 Similar to BR 1 but with coach link continuing.
- BR 3 Again similar to BR 1, but without check-in at Victoria and coach link continuing.
- LT Extension of the Piccadilly line to Heathrow, with coach link continuing.

The British Rail link would involve the building of a spur into the airport from the existing line near Feltham. Non-stop electric rail services would operate every 10 minutes during the day and every 15 minutes at night. The estimated journey time was 23 minutes.

With check-in at Victoria, passengers would also hand in their luggage there. This would be sorted by flight and placed in containers. These would be carried on the train to the Airport, where the containers would go to the appropriate terminal. Passengers would not need to handle their luggage between Victoria and their flight destination. The Report however admitted that no satisfactory baggage system had yet been devised, but the advice from the airline representatives and British Rail was that 'given enough time and money, this could be done'.

The London Transport scheme would see the Piccadilly line extended from Hounslow West to the Central Terminal Area at Heathrow, with an intermediate station in the maintenance area (later to emerge as Hatton Cross). Trains would run at 4-minute intervals at the peak and at up to a 7½-minute intervals at other times, but not overnight. The existing (1959) rolling stock could be used, with four seats removed in each car to provide luggage space. Two additional trains would be needed.

The journey would take around 35 minutes by the Underground, half as long again as British Rail, but fares at five shillings (25p) would be rather less. British Rail had suggested ten shillings (50p) with a check in at Victoria or eight shillings (40p) without.

Given various assumptions about air traffic growth levels and passenger preferences, it was found under all conditions that the London Transport option offered the highest level of social benefits in relation to costs. It would also be far more useful for airport workers. But what it could not offer under any circumstances was the in-town check in. This would be at the airport, while the transport of baggage would be left entirely to the passenger.

In the British Rail case, the Victoria check-in etc was optional. Travel by British Rail was also likely to be more comfortable 'and could offer every passenger a seat at all times'. But passengers on the Piccadilly looking for greater service could still opt to travel by the express coach on the basis that it was likely to be retained.

The conclusion was that the Piccadilly line option should be chosen and would make a worthwhile investment.

In the event, the Piccadilly line was opened to Hatton Cross in 1975 and to Heathrow Central (now Terminals 2, 3) in 1977. Trains of new 1973 stock were provided, designed to meet the baggage requirement. The looped extension of the Piccadilly via Terminal 4 opened with that terminal in 1986, followed by the new route to Terminal 5 in 2008.

The idea of a heavy rail link from Victoria was abandoned, though this might yet be revived with Waterloo as the in-town terminal.

5

Future Needs Defined

In 1971, journeys to work formed 62% of all journeys by Underground and 77% of all journeys on the London Commuter Network. Barran Report, 1974

On 1 January 1969 the nationalised London Transport Board, shorn of its Country Bus interests, had become an Executive responsible to the Greater London Council (GLC)[19]. The GLC took on the responsibility for transport planning in London and for the overall policy and financial control of London Transport.

The London Rail Study of 1974, the Barran report (named after its Chairman Sir David Barran), looked at what should or shouldn't be done in developing the network. This was a joint study team involving the GLC, the Department of the Environment (which then included transport), the British Railways Board and the London Transport Executive.

This was in respect of railways wholly or mainly in Greater London. It too came up with a number of investment schemes which tended to cross London from one side to the other, notably what became the Fleet (later renamed Jubilee) line of London Underground, but where should the eastern terminus be? It also included early ideas on orbital routes, which were later to form the basis of those run today by London Overground.

Freight transport was not within Barran's terms of reference.

Changing numbers

The post-war era had not been a happy one for the railway industry in the vicinity of London. Since 1948, passenger carryings on London Underground had been remarkably stable; post war recovery saw a high spot of 702 million journeys being made in 1951. This was then to fall back slightly and reached the lowest level in the ensuing 20-year period of 657 million in 1965. In 1969, on the eve of the GLC takeover, 676 million passenger journeys were recorded. To anticipate matters a little, a further drop in numbers to 559 million was recorded for 1980 and it would soon go lower still.

It may be noted that this was with a system which showed little change in its size or coverage over the period, and that the opening of the Victoria line between 1968 and 1971 had little discernible effect on the total passenger carryings. Maybe passenger numbers would have been that much less without it.

Table 5.1 gives the details of what was happening in the morning peak period over the years from 1961 to 1971 and, subsequent to the London Rail Study, in 1976.

Table 5.1: Passenger Traffic into Central London 07:00-10:00

	Thousands, daily			
Year	**1961**	**1966**	**1971**	**1976**
British Rail	446	450	460	400
London Underground	547	539	503	424
Total rail passengers#	**883**	**878**	**843**	**725**
Road services	209	175	145	151
Total public transport	**1,092**	**1,053**	**990**	**876**
Private transport	138	133	175	195
Total, all modes	**1,231**	**1,186**	**1,165**	**1,071**

'#Excludes double counting of rail passengers who use both British Rail and London Underground services.
Source: London Rail Study, London Transport Report & Accounts

Thus carryings were declining on British Rail as well, and for bus travel too. To some extent the slack was taken up by private transport, but the overall reduction in demand is noticeable.

Reporting in 1974, Barran noted that from 1962 onwards employment in central London had been in slow decline, with the population of inner London falling fairly rapidly. This had been offset by slight population increases in some outer London boroughs, but with an overall loss in the GLC area as a whole. At the same time there was a growth in commuting from the surrounding counties.

Overall, said Barran, there had been a decrease in total commuting to central London, but the proportion of that related to British Rail had not changed significantly. Passengers travelling only by the Underground had reduced, but this was offset by the numbers arriving at British Rail termini and transferring to the Underground to complete their journeys.

Table 5.1 confirms that these trends were continuing.

Definitions

The Barran Report made a useful distinction between London Underground and British Rail services. It remains relevant today and complements the views of the earlier 1949 BTC Working Party. It is quoted here in full:

> 'London Transport's rail operations are confined solely to running London passenger services. Nearly all their lines run through central London. This means that train frequency outside central London is usually determined by the frequency of trains needed in central London, and rolling stock design generally reflects the need for heavy passenger carrying and speedy loading and unloading in central London.
>
> 'British Rail faces the different situation of running several operations, inter-city and freight as well as the London Commuter Network, using the same track and signalling. So priorities have to be established. On the radial routes, freight movements are restricted to times where there is no serious shortage of capacity, and where passenger overcrowding is a problem, virtually no non-commuter trains are run within the London Commuter Network boundary during the peak. (The London Commuter Network's outer boundaries were defined as Bournemouth, Bletchley and Clacton.)
>
> 'On non-radial routes, the impact of other services, especially freight, is very much greater. British Rail also has passengers travelling into London from widely differing distances, and provides slow, semi-fast and fast trains to cater for this. But where, as so often, these different trains operate over the same tracks, there can be problems in preventing the fast trains being held up by the slow ones, and yet still providing sufficient train paths[20]'.

In some ways these were statements of the obvious, but messages of this nature need to be spelt out. In more recent times, bodies such as Transport for London sometimes seem to take little heed of the constraints inherent in running a national railway network. It cannot be all things to all men at all times. As Barran rightly said, 'priorities have to be established'.

Characteristics of London's Railways

According to Barran, most of London Underground's passengers board their trains in inner London, but British Rail services in the area north of the Thames are not used very much for short distance journeys. In some cases, even though it takes longer to go all the way by bus, passengers prefer to make a through journey this way.

Overcrowding (in 1974) was said to be almost entirely a peak hour problem, but each operator measured it differently.

On the Underground, the planning standard stated the maximum number of passengers to be carried in the peak hour. This was designed to ensure that in any one train the number carried was not more than the total number of seats plus 60% of crush standing capacity (the maximum number of standing passengers that could physically be crammed into a train).

On British Rail, the number of passengers at the point of maximum load was averaged over the peak hour for each service. This should not exceed 110% of the seats available for inner suburban services, 100% for outer suburban services and 90% for long distance services.

The maximum load point on British Rail was usually the in-town terminus, but not necessarily so. Account needed to be taken of the level of interchange to and from the Underground at places such as Finsbury Park and Stratford, or between British Rail trains on different routes at Clapham Junction.

There were and are substantial flows of people to and from non-central London locations such as East Croydon, Hammersmith or Harrow and, further afield, Watford, Reading and Southend. Peak travel is not just about movements to and from central London.

Where were the problems?

One of Barran's biggest difficulties was in assessing future needs. Was the then decline in passenger numbers going to continue indefinitely, or was an upsurge in rail usage either probable or likely? If so, how could it be quantified?

The critical factor in the future demand for London rail travel was the peak demand for travel, the key factors of which are population and employment in the South East. It may be noted that the then trends were a low Greater London population, a predominately centralised employment pattern and a declining level of public transport use.

Investigations took into account matters such as would there be high or low population growth, would employment be decentralised, and would there be severe, or less severe, restraints on the use of the private car?

For example, on employment, new office development could be concentrated at or in the vicinity of British Rail or London Underground stations in the suburbs, at strategic interchange points, or close to the British Rail London termini. All could be designed in such a way as to have the effect of spreading the peak hour, forever the problem with commuter travel.

Service standards then were clearly less than ideal; Barran records that in 1972/73, staff shortages were resulting in the cancellation of substantial numbers of trains, leading to scheduled cancellations. This led to a recommendation that operators should move as fast as they could in installing capital equipment which would result in staff savings.

One important way in which this could be achieved was the one-man (later driver-only) operation of trains. Forty years or so later, progress on this matter still has a long way to go on the National Rail system, though it became universal on London Underground passenger operations in the year 2000.

Another identified means of reducing the requirement for staff was more area signalling schemes, replacing individually manned signal boxes.

New schemes

What were the investment priorities? Perhaps not surprisingly and wholly reasonably, the first requirement was seen as maintaining the existing system and services. This was followed by improving their quality and then extending the system by new construction.

Electrification

The following electrification schemes were recommended, in order of priority (present status in brackets):

- Moorgate/St Pancras–Bedford (completed, but Farringdon–Moorgate subsequently closed to allow the later Thameslink scheme to proceed)
- South Croydon–East Grinstead/Uckfield (completed to East Grinstead, but Uckfield remains diesel unit operated)
- Bishop's Stortford–Cambridge (completed)
- Tonbridge–Hastings (completed)
- Paddington–Oxford/Newbury (part of present Great Western electrification scheme, some of which is presently in doubt.
- Marylebone–Aylesbury (not currently proposed)
- Salisbury-Basingstoke (not currently proposed).

Interchange

Proposals for interchange improvements produced some schemes of long standing from the wish lists, such as Euston (main line) to Euston Square, Fenchurch Street to Tower Hill, and the Hammersmith station on the District & Piccadilly lines to the Hammersmith & City/Circle lines station. Also considered were the three close by but non adjacent stations of West Hampstead (Jubilee line) on one

Predictions that the whole of 'the Southern' would be electrified were not fulfilled in the case of services to Salisbury and Exeter. Basingstoke, was reached from Worting Junction, in 1967 with the Bournemouth electrification, but beyond that the field is open for 159013 and other members of the class. This is a down train passing Raynes Park in November 1997. ***John Glover***

side of a busy road, with West Hampstead (North London line) on the other, and West Hampstead Thameslink still on the other side but rather further away. Could platforms also be added to the Chiltern lines at this point?

Suggestions for major extensions to existing rail services were examined.

Ringrail

The Ringrail scheme envisaged a frequent orbital service connecting the North, West and South London lines. On the east side, use would be made of the Stratford-North Woolwich branch of British Rail as far as Canning Town, thence by new cross-river underground tunnelled construction to link in with the South London line at Lewisham.

This was in many ways an early suggestion of what would be seen as the core of the much later London Overground scheme, opened in sections 2010-12. The main difference was on the eastern side; the Overground scheme used a combination of the Dalston Junction–Broad Street formation, new construction in Shoreditch to join with the East London line on the approach to Whitechapel, then using a restored alignment beyond Surrey Quays to reach the South London network between South Bermondsey and Queen's Road (Peckham) stations.

That would all have to wait. The Barran report was not enthusiastic: 'On the face of it, Ringrail is an attractive proposition ... but there are other schemes that would provide better value in relation to their cost.' Estimates of likely usage were very modest and the study team clearly was not convinced.

British Rail also had schemes for improving the services on the North London line and related branches, with or without complete electrification. A novel proposal was the extension of a service from Willesden Junction over existing trackage to Acton Main Line and Ealing Broadway, thence by the branch from West Ealing to Greenford. This was not progressed.

However, it did result, in increments, in through trains between Richmond and North Woolwich, with new stations at Hackney Central, Homerton and Hackney Wick, electrification throughout and the closure of the North London City terminus at Broad Street. This work was completed in 1986. The present services on this line, too, are operated by London Overground.

Thameslink

The Report was much in favour of joining the Midland route from Bedford via Farringdon and Blackfriars to the Southern Region (destinations at both ends unspecified), but with some reservations. At this early stage the route suggested was not via London Bridge, preferring that via Elephant & Castle. It did not involve the Great Northern lines.

The problem seen was that as soon as trains from a previously self-contained system start working onto another system, there was the risk that any operating delays on one would be transmitted to the other. Was that an over-cautious approach by operators? If so, was the risk worth taking, or was it a real problem area? Certainly, the complexity of the Southern system could give plenty of opportunities for problems of this nature to arise.

The recommendation was that a scheme should be evaluated, but for reasons of that nature it should be given second order priority.

It will be interesting to see how the actual and much more extensive Thameslink scheme which has been adopted can avoid such difficulties.

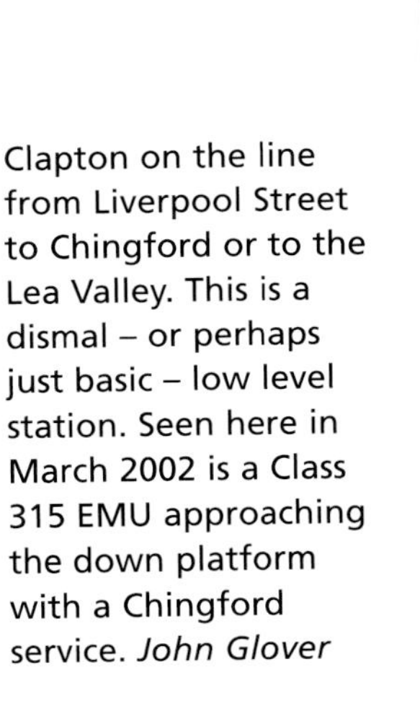

Clapton on the line from Liverpool Street to Chingford or to the Lea Valley. This is a dismal – or perhaps just basic – low level station. Seen here in March 2002 is a Class 315 EMU approaching the down platform with a Chingford service. *John Glover*

The Hastings DEMUs were built to a narrow loading gauge because of the limited tunnel widths on the route. Any rolling stock, diesel or electric. would need to be built specially. Here, Class 20s Hastings unit built on the longer underframe, No 1014, hurries through Crowhurst en route for the Sussex resort. The space occupied by the diesel electric engine and thus not usable for passengers, is all too clear. *John Glover*

London Underground Fleet line

Stage 1 construction of the Fleet line, later renamed the Jubilee line, was intended to relieve the Bakerloo between Baker Street and Charing Cross. Starting from the 1932 terminus of Stanmore, it was to take over the Bakerloo thence to Baker Street, with new construction thereafter. Following the grant of powers to build Stage 1 in 1969, construction began in 1971. On the new section there were intermediate stations at Bond Street and Green Park, and new terminal platforms at a reconstructed Charing Cross (interchange with the Northern and Bakerloo). The Stage 1 section was opened to this point on 1 May 1979.

This required substantial rebuilding work at all four stations. At Baker Street the separation from the Bakerloo required a new Northbound platform well away from and on the 'wrong' side of the Southbound, but it all seems to work well enough.

The key question then was 'what happens next?' The Stage 2 proposal was for the line to continue eastwards to Aldwych (the tunnels and safety over-run being constructed nearly to this point), thence underneath Fleet Street to stations at Ludgate Circus, Cannon Street and Fenchurch Street. Amongst other uses, this would provide a useful distribution service for people arriving at the latter two stations.

Stage 3 would carry the Fleet line on from Fenchurch Street to Lewisham, with a branch from Surrey Docks (later Surrey Quays) to New Cross Gate. Stage 4 would extend from Lewisham, running over the existing British Rail lines from Ladywell to Hayes and the branch to Addiscombe (closed 1997).

'Withdrawal of British Rail services on these lines', the report said excitedly, 'would enable additional trains to run to Charing Cross and Cannon Street, while users of the Fleet line would enjoy a more frequent service.'

The conclusion though was not encouraging. Taking the Fleet line east of Fenchurch Street 'could be justified if there proved to be considerably more funds available for rail investment than at present, but as a low priority.'

River line

That, though was not all. What this all missed out was Docklands, but redevelopment here was still a decade away. However, the concept of the River line was now introduced. Leaving the Fleet line at Fenchurch Street, there were two options.

River line North would run through Stepney East (now Limehouse) and Poplar on disused rail alignments, before crossing the River Lea to connect with what was then the British Rail line at Custom House and then leaving it again to continue to Beckton. Up to this point it would use surface alignments, but it would then go into a new tunnel beneath the Thames to terminate at Thamesmead.

River line South (which the Barran Study Team preferred) would still go to Thamesmead but cross beneath the Thames several times on an alignment that could include Surrey Quays, the Isle of Dogs, North Greenwich, Custom House, and Woolwich Arsenal, connecting at the latter with the BR North Kent line. This route would be wholly underground.

Together, these schemes offered the potential for three eastern termini, at Addiscombe, Hayes and Thamesmead.

'There is, on the face of it, a strong case on general planning grounds for linking the proposed development area of the Docklands to central London and at the same time give the growing new community of Thamesmead a direct link to central London.' The caveat here is 'planning grounds'; Transport investment is crucial for moving people to, from and around an area, but until that development is undertaken incrementally, there is negligible traffic for a new railway.

In the event, only Stage 1 was constructed, and even then the section from Green Park to Charing Cross was abandoned for passenger purposes after only 20 years of use. In 1999 what is today known as the Jubilee line was opened, in stages, from Green Park to Stratford, via Westminster and under the Thames to Waterloo, Southwark, London Bridge, Bermondsey and Canada Water. Another pass under the Thames took the Jubilee line to Canary Wharf. The third pass under the Thames took it to North Greenwich, and for the fourth time to Canning Town, a surface station. The Jubilee line then paralleled the North London line tracks (now part of the Docklands Light Railway) with stations at West Ham and Stratford, incorporating in its route some of the alignments anticipated for the River line.

Much of what was proposed for River line North was to resurface as parts of the Docklands Light Railway.

Thamesmead remains unserved by railway, although 2016 saw two new proposals for rail service provision.

Chelsea–Hackney

This London Transport scheme was for many years the predecessor of what in recent times was to be proposed as Crossrail 2 between New Southgate/Broxbourne in the north and various South Western destinations west of Wimbledon in the south.

The 1974 proposal by Barran was to separate out the Hainault branch of the Central line, with new construction via Central London on a route that took in Hackney, Old Street, Farringdon, Aldwych (interchange with the Fleet Line), Waterloo, Lambeth, Victoria, Sloane Square and Chelsea, before joining the District at Fulham Broadway, terminating at Wimbledon.

The relief of overcrowding was a principal reason for this new line.

There were clearly some worries about overlapping schemes reducing potential benefits. Not for the last time, Chelsea–Hackney was relegated to a lower priority in the investment programme. The Barran report did however feel that the alignment should be protected.

British Rail Crossrail original, 1974

The Crossrail of that era was quite different from later proposals with the same name. The suggestion was that two, separate, deep-level lines of full-sized structure gauge should be built to provide links across London.

A northern tunnel would join the British Rail Western Region lines west of Paddington to the British Rail Eastern Region main line east of Bethnal Green, with intermediate tunnelled stations at Paddington, Marble Arch, Bond Street/Oxford Circus, Leicester Square/Covent Garden, Holborn/Ludgate and Liverpool Street/Moorgate.

London Rail Study, 1974, Crossrail proposed routes.

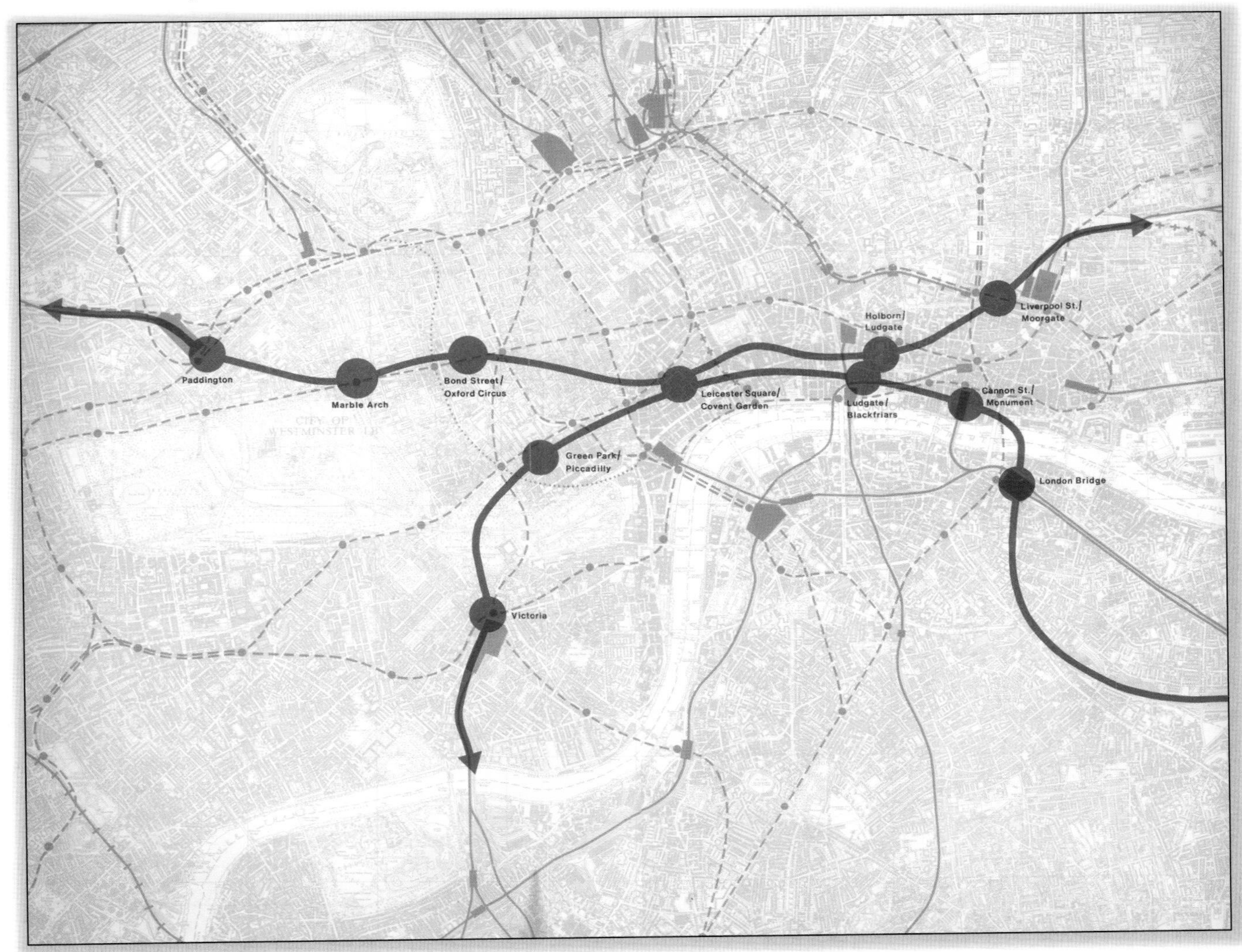

The PEP trains consisted of two four-car units and one two-car unit; the latter was painted silver. A mixed formation with no 4001 leading arrives at Clapham Junction on the South Western up slow line on 9 October 1976. The derivatives of these trains eventually produced Classes 313, 507, 314, 508 and 315, none of them much loved. *John Glover*

A second southern tunnel would connect services of British Rail Southern Region's Central Division which terminated at Victoria with an unspecified group of British Rail services east of London Bridge. There would be intermediate stations at Victoria, Green Park/Piccadilly, Leicester Square/Covent Garden (where there would be interchange with the northern tunnel services), Ludgate/Blackfriars, Cannon Street/Monument and London Bridge.

The double naming of many stations, albeit for illustration purposes only, reflects on the length of the trains concerned and their platform requirements. This is a similar situation to that of the present day Crossrail.

Barran deemed this project 'imaginative and exciting', noting the potential for substantial relief of overcrowding on the Underground at peak. The Steering Group were particularly taken with the potential for interchange at Leicester Square and the easing of cross-London travel for passengers making longer journeys. The freeing up of some main line terminal capacity would, it was thought, result in more reliable service provision.

Notably, British Rail were keen on the usage potential of the northern tunnel for diverted cross-London freight, which would ease the introduction of enhanced passenger services on some non-radial lines such as Ringrail (qv).

But the great disadvantage would be cost, so the Barran Report played safe and suggested a feasibility study. The Report never quite seemed to decide on the market at which it was aimed. For the Northern tunnel, was it the penny numbers travelling from Plymouth to Norwich, a modest requirement between Reading and Shenfield, or the mass market of Ealing Broadway to Leicester Square?

Bakerloo and Victoria lines

The extension of the Bakerloo line to Camberwell and Peckham, and the extension of the Victoria line to Streatham or even beyond to Croydon were both given the thumbs down. 'We believe it is unlikely that the passenger flows ... would be sufficient to justify their construction and that only a weak case can be made for either of them in planning or transport terms'.

In the north, four Bakerloo trains were extended from Queen's Park to Watford Junction in the 1974 peak hour, in addition to the seven British Rail trains from London Euston. Off-peak, there were four British Rail trains an hour only. The Committee's comments, paraphrased, were that there should be a proper all-day Bakerloo service as far as Harrow & Wealdstone, with the rest left to British Rail.

This has been the situation since 1984, though the preceding couple of years saw no Bakerloo service north of Stonebridge Park. This was the site of the newly created Bakerloo line depot, following the split with the Jubilee line.

Sub-surface lines

The Metropolitan line extension from Croxley to Watford Junction was alive and kicking as long ago as 1974, Yes, it was a scheme worthy of examination, but it was seen very much a local matter for the operators and Hertfordshire County Council. This remained the situation for the ensuing 40 years, though progress has again stalled for financial reasons.

Between King's Cross St Pancras and Farringdon a new station at Mount Pleasant was suggested, with no result, and a new platform at West Ham British Rail North Woolwich line for interchange with the Hammersmith & City/District lines. This was opened in 1979 and is now served by the Docklands Light Railway line to Stratford International.

West Ham is now also an interchange with the c2c Tilbury line and the Jubilee line; platforms for both opened in 1999.

The railway in London

Overall, the Report affirmed that rail comes into its own as a fast and efficient means of transporting large numbers of people. It is essentially a mass carrier, but even after the legal powers have been obtained, a new railway line takes a long time to install. It is also expensive to provide and is inflexible once built. In other words, to justify the provision of a new rail facility, there must be a heavy demand, a continuing and not a short-term demand, and a reasonable return on investment. This need not necessarily be in financial terms, but in terms of the overall benefits to passengers and to the community as a whole.

Fares

The study team looked at various fares schemes against the following criteria:

- Operational feasibility
- Passenger convenience and acceptability
- Social factors
- Financial and economic implications and
- Compatibility with planning aims.

The results were inconclusive. Zonal fares were seen as attractive, but beset with problems of practicability and public acceptance. Perhaps these could be overcome? This was in the early days of Automatic Fare Collection.

Priorities

In the difficult financial situation of those inflationary times, Barran's investment priorities were three-fold. The most important job was to maintain the existing system and services, following which the aim should be to improve the quality of that system and the service offered. Only then should effort go into extending the system by new construction.

The preferred investment packages for extensions, most important first:

1. Improvement in the British Rail non-radial services in North London
2. Early start to Fleet/River line extensions from Charing Cross to Fenchurch Street and the south route to Thamesmead
3. The Thameslink scheme
4. Chelsea–Hackney scheme
5. Fleet line to Hayes and Addiscombe, if thought justified.

313001, now on the North London line, is forming a train from North Woolwich to Richmond as it arrives at Willesden Junction high level platforms on 7 February 1994. This commands a good view of the West Coast main line, so there is never a dull moment. ***John Glover***

Other reports were to follow, notably the Central London Rail Study of 1989. To what extent was there a political commitment or public wish to make large public sector investments in improving the rail transport options? As noted at the beginning of this Chapter, the then recent history showing 15 years of continuous decline in usage was hardly encouraging.

GREAT NORTHERN ELECTRICS

So far, this book has concentrated on the really major investment schemes, usually carried out as part of one big programme. But what of the rest? The Great Northern suburban improvements and eventual electrification is one such scheme, which took the best part of 30 years to achieve. It might be noted that those such as the West Coast Main Line electrification which only involved the London area incidentally do not concern us here, nor do national events such as the long drawn out replacement of vacuum brakes with air brakes.

The Great Northern's local London services did not do well in the post-war period. The Northern line extensions of 1940/41 which took in the High Barnet and Edgware branches were partly aborted, with the result that local services on Alexandra Palace branch expired finally in 1954. However, the conundrum of how to serve adequately the three London terminals of King's Cross, Moorgate (Widened Lines) and Broad Street remained unresolved.

What did happen though was that the two-track section between Greenwood (south of Hadley Wood) and Potters Bar, about three miles, was converted to four tracks. This required the boring of three new double-track tunnels, totalling over a mile in length, as well as the reconstruction of Hadley Wood and Potters Bar stations. Completed in 1959 after four years work, these works much reduced the conflicts between suburban and longer distance trains, to say nothing of freight.

Like most of the system north of the Thames, this was at the time a wholly steam operated railway. Local services were provided mainly by Gresley 'N2' 0-6-2 tanks dating from the 1920s, most of which were fitted with condensing apparatus for working on the Metropolitan Widened Lines. They hauled the venerable Quad-Arts. These were the pairs of four-car slam-door articulated coaching stock, of very 'sit-up and beg' type seating, but with a huge seating capacity.

Some more modern coaching stock was the British Ralways-built Mk1 57ft vehicles, all un-gangwayed and with six-a-side seating. What was originally a standard third class coach could thus seat 108 people in nine compartments. Their length was determined by the limited clearances when working to Moorgate.

Outer-suburban passengers did slightly better, with similar coaches. The non-Brake versions had internal gangways, with a pair of lavatories in the centre of the vehicle. The first/second class composite vehicles also had two lavatories, but partitions ensured that passengers could use only the one appropriate to their class of travel. Haulage for these trains was mostly in the hands of Thompson 'L1' 2-6-2 tanks, introduced in 1945.

Dieselisation

The 1955 Modernisation Plan[21] seemed to promise change. The Great Northern lines were included in the list of suburban electrification schemes to be undertaken, but there was a caveat – *unless any unforeseen difficulties should emerge …* The services concerned were described as King's Cross and Moorgate to Hitchin and Letchworth, including the Hertford loop. (The route to be used between Moorgate and Finsbury Park had not been finalised at that stage.)

Alone of the five groups of lines in this list, the Great Northern had in practice to make do with a half-hearted dieselisation programme.

For the inner-suburban operations, basically those to Welwyn Garden City on the main line and Hertford North on the branch, the diesel multiple-unit was the preferred choice. For the Great Northern, these consisted of a batch of 50 Cravens two-car diesel multiple-units (DMUs), intended originally for the Midland & Great Northern. This line which meandered across the open spaces of Cambridgeshire and Norfolk to reach Great Yarmouth was closed, virtually in its entirety, early in 1959. The Great Northern suburban became the reluctant recipients of these vehicles, which had only two slam doors per coach side, hardly ideal for a busy suburban operation. Each two-car set offered 115 seats, 12 of which were declassified First Class.

More damning, though, was their lack of power. With only two 150bhp B.U.T. engines per two-car set, they had a tendency to stall as they tried to depart as four-car (or six-car) sets from the steeply graded Platform 16 at King's Cross (the hotel curve) with a full peak load. The result was that they had to be banned from peak usage on trains originating at Moorgate, which thus became another job for the locomotive-hauled sets of stock. This prolonged the use of the Gresley Quad-Arts, which did not disappear finally until 1966.

For main line work, modest numbers of three different types of Type 2 diesel locomotives were allocated to the newly built maintenance depot at Finsbury Park. (Type 2s were defined as line service locomotives of between 1,100hp and 1,499hp.)

The 40-strong fleet consisted of 20 Birmingham Railway Carriage & Wagon (BRC&W) D5300s (later Class 26), 10 North British Loco D6100s (later Class 29) and 10 English Electric D5900s (later Class 23). The latter two types turned out to be very poor performers and so bad did the situation become in operational terms that strong action was needed.

As a temporary measure a further six of the best types, the BRC&Ws (Nos D5330–5), were diverted away from Scotland and sent new to Finsbury Park. Only the arrival of batches of Brush Type 2s from the D5500 series (later Class 31) and the acquisition of 25 BR/Sulzer D5000s (later Class 24) from the London Midland Region was to ease the power situation. All the original locomotives were drafted away, the Class 26s to Scotland and the others to storage or for possible rebuilding.

These locomotives were intended for the outer-suburban services to Cambridge or intermediately; the coaching stock remained unchanged from steam days. Trains might start from the King's Cross suburban platforms, then Nos 11 to 15, Moorgate Widened Lines via Farringdon (No 16) or Broad Street (via Dalston Junction). All these services came together at Finsbury Park.

In the summer 1964 timetable, the down Mondays to Fridays evening peak service indicates the complexity of what was then offered. From 16:00 to 19:00 there were 14 trains starting from King's Cross main line platforms, 11 from Moorgate and 14 from Broad Street. There were also four services starting at Finsbury Park. Neither Moorgate nor Broad Street were served during the off peak, when a basic five trains per hour from King's Cross sufficed, plus a Finsbury Park starter.

Five years later in 1969, some rather more suitable diesel units were found. These had been displaced from the Great Eastern's Lea Valley services, when that line was electrified.

Meanwhile, the electrification of the East Coast Main Line, which in the Modernisation Plan was envisaged as far as Doncaster, Leeds and (possibly) York, was only lightly endorsed. The case for electrification was not then as accepted as it later became and, perhaps unsurprisingly, there was no progress. Nevertheless, in a dose of reality, the Plan included a sentence that 'the use of atomic power in relation to railways seems likely to be indirect, namely through the use of nuclear energy at power stations rather than through the development of atomic-powered locomotives'[22].

Suburban electrification

This was a situation which could not endure indefinitely, and in August 1971 suburban electrification was at last sanctioned by the Government. The construction of the Victoria line of London Underground offered the opportunity for British Railways to acquire the Finsbury Park to Moorgate tunnels of the Northern City Line for their own use. The use of this 3½-mile self-contained branch by main line services had been thought likely ever since its construction in 1904, and in anticipation it was built to main line structure gauge.

The result was the making of new permanent connections from Drayton Park (as it happened the only open-air part of the line) to the main line platforms at Finsbury Park. Its below ground Finsbury Park platforms were reshuffled between the new Victoria line and the Piccadilly, and a pair of new platforms was created at Highbury & Islington. These enabled passengers to make cross-platform interchange between the Victoria line and the Great Northern Electrics.

This was an essential part of the plan, since the new Great Northern Electrics were to run between Welwyn Garden City or Hertford North and Moorgate, but not to serve King's Cross. Such a service would be fine for City commuters, but of much less value for those wishing to reach the West End. That function would be provided by the Highbury & Islington connection, taking users to the heart of the West End at Oxford Circus.

A particular problem with this approach was the electric traction system to be adopted. By now, the use of 25kV AC was standard on all main lines, but could not be used in the tunnels for clearance reasons. Consequently, dual-voltage trains were required; while stopped for passenger purposes at Drayton Park, the changeover between AC overhead and 750v DC third rail takes place.

This resulted in the construction of a fleet of 64 three-car trains with two sets of sliding door pairs on each vehicle side, the Class 313s. They were built at BR York in 1976–77 and were the first production examples of what was heralded at the new standard inner-suburban electric multiple-unit. As built, the 232 seats were second class and open plan, facing or back to direction of travel.

A site at Hornsey on the up (eastern) side of the line was used for the construction of a maintenance depot and sidings for all suburban electric traction. This remains in use today, as subsequently much extended. There was also a facility for overhead line maintenance and both were operational by 1975.

Stage 1 of the electrification extended from Moorgate to Welwyn Garden City/Hertford North and full services on this section were inaugurated on 8 November 1976. All Eastern Region services to Broad Street were withdrawn.

Great Northern Electrics, schematic route diagram as originally authorised. *BR/Author's collection*

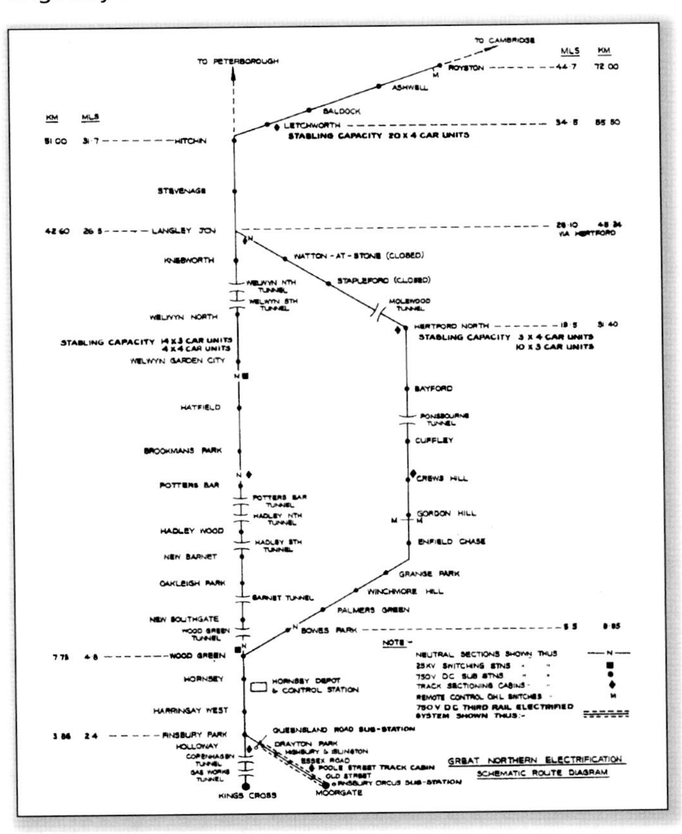

The Gresley 'N2' 0-6-2T tanks were the mainstay of Great Northern suburban services. This undated photograph shows No 69543, complete with condensing gear, heading a train made up of two Quad-Arts (Quadruple Articulated sets) up Holloway Bank on the down fast line. The destination board says Welwyn Garden City but it is upside down, which usually meant that it was going somewhere else this time! *P. Wilson*

Stage 2 included King's Cross and (initially) Royston on the Cambridge branch; these services began on 6 February 1978. For this, 26 four-car Class 312/0 EMUs with 90mph capability were built, again by BR York, in 1977. They had 25 First and 297 Second Class seats.

Collectively, these 49 Class 312 units proved to be the last slam-door stock to be constructed for use in Britain. They were of traditional open plan, with 3+2 seating in the second class. But slam doors made them completely unsuitable for Driver Only Operation. Those on the Great Northern were transferred to the Great Eastern in 1985, to be replaced by 24 broadly equivalent new Class 317/2 units. These were equipped with sliding doors and had a 100mph capability.

The extension of electric suburban operations to King's Cross in Stage 2 made the rebuilding of that terminal highly desirable. The connections to the Widened Lines to Moorgate were no longer required and were thus removed, though little did those planners imagine that a link between Farringdon and Finsbury Park would be restored 40 years later.

The flyover at Holloway, then used to route trains to the Freight Terminal, was rebuilt on an adjacent site. This was used to change the order of tracks as part of the complete revision of King's Cross station layout and its approaches. The result was much better terminal working; the only real shortcoming was the reduction of the suburban platforms to only two (today's 9 and 10); a third (No 11) was later reinstated.

This and much more was associated also with the East Coast Main Line electrification, which would extend to Leeds, Edinburgh and Glasgow Central. Also included was comprehensive resignalling, with the whole route as far as Biggleswade on the main line and Royston on the Cambridge branch placed under control of the new King's Cross Power Signal Box (PSB). This became operational in 1971.

The story does not of course end there, but it does perhaps illustrate some of the huge number of tasks which need to be addressed in (sometimes) very trying circumstances. But what were the results, from the point of view of users?

Electrification results

The GN suburban area is in Hertfordshire from Potters Bar (Cuffley on the Hertford loop) to Baldock and then Royston, and the County Council carried out a study of electrification and suburban development in 1980[23]. The Greater London area which lies to the south was excluded.

The above is divided into three sections for analysis. These are the three Hertford branch stations, the four stations from Potters Bar to Welwyn Garden City (main

Table 5.2: Peak period departures from Hertfordshire GN stations

Section	1951	1961	1971	1979
Hertford loop	23	30	35	45
Main line, inner	37	53	58	96
Main line, outer	53	66	67	88
Totals	**113**	**149**	**160**	**229**

Source: BR public timetables

line inners) and the seven stations from Welwyn North to Royston (main line outers). The resited Stevenage station which became important in InterCity terms had already opened, in 1973. Watton-at-Stone did not open until 1982, with Welham Green in 1986.

First, the service patterns, for the important commuter traffic. It is noticeable from Table 5.2 that improvements had been continuous from the early post-war period, doubling overall from 1951 to 1979. This was most noticeable after 1971, though the least significant rise in train service provision was on the Main line outers.

More trains suggests more passengers to be carried, and indeed this was what happened. In essence, the further away that people lived, the more significant were the growth rates. Stevenage had the additional benefit of New Town status and was expanding, but so too were the other more distant communities. Nearer the Greater London borders, the change was more marginal; the negative result at the remote Bayford station was in respect of relatively few passengers in total.

Summarised by section, the patronage on the Main line inners increased by 14%, that on the Hertford loop by 16%, but the Main line outers by 89%.

Table 5.3: Peak period traffic flows, passengers boarding 1969–1979

Major increase (by 101% or more)	
Royston	+181%
Letchworth	+121%
Hitchin	+104%
Stevenage	+102%
Large increase (by 51% to 100%)	
Hatfield	+76%
Ashwell & Morden	+75%
Hertford North	+66%
Increase (by 11% to 50%)	
Baldock	+33%
Welwyn Garden City	+17%
No change (-10% to +10%)	
Knebworth	+3%
Welwyn North	no change
Brookmans Park	no change
Potters Bar	-2%
Cuffley	-7%
Significant decline	
Bayford	-33%

Source: BR traffic data.

These were better results than they may appear, since over the nine-year period 1969–1978 British Rail commuting to central London (total, all lines) decreased from 454,000 per day to 409,000, and by London Transport Underground from 405,000 to 325,000.

Of interest are the destinations of those using the stations in each group (in 1978). Most are probably commuters, but the proportions refer to all rail passengers. Travel to and from London comprised 56% of those using the stations on both the Main line and Hertford inner areas; this dropped to 37% for the stations further north, where the same number again travelled to/from other stations in Hertfordshire.

The travellers within Hertfordshire went down to 20% of those on the Main line inners. The remaining group, those who were travelling to/from stations outside the GN Electrics area, ranged between 20% and 35% of the overall station totals.

The split for significant traffic flows on the Great Northern line in Hertfordshire taken all together came to 49% to/from London, 26% within the county, and 25% to/from other areas.

Post-electrification time savings were significant; using Hatfield to King's Cross as an example, journey times went down by a quarter to 25 minutes, and to Moorgate by a third to 34 minutes. But the savings were little better than marginal in the generalised cost terms used by planners.

Over the previous half century, there had been a massive growth in the population living in Hertfordshire, coupled with more people living in towns and in reach of the railway. Those areas nearer London were thus developed from the 1930s onwards; it was the towns further away that electrification really benefitted. At Letchworth and Royston, growth had been continual over the years, but electrification seemed to have been followed by a jump of about one fifth in traffic. Stevenage too had seen heavy growth.

Thus on the inner suburban sections settlements had matured, with little more residential growth expected. Many if not most of the potential users were already railway travellers. The very substantial increase in service frequency and quality brought in some extra traffic from those who could reach more than one line.

In the outer sections which were still developing, relatively modest proportions of those living there commuted to London. This is where the real growth was taking place, fuelled by the generally improved but, crucially, much faster services. Because of the longer

Brush Type 2 No D5648 (later a Class 31) heads a down evening outer suburban service through Hadley Wood on the fast line on 30 May 1968. The use of corridor Mk1s suggests that this is a King's Cross to Cambridge working. *John Glover*

This afternoon shot shows an unidentified Finsbury Park Class 31 with an empty stock of BR Suburban Mk1s approaching Farringdon on the Widened Lines. The date is 5 August 1976. It would subsequently form an evening peak service to a Great Northern destination from Moorgate. *John Glover*

distances involved (Royston is 45 miles from King's Cross, Stevenage 27½ miles), higher speeds provide a rather greater benefit in terms of the reduced time spent travelling. These were also the areas in which substantial new housing was appearing.

The report concluded that while the immediately measurable growth generated by electrification was not great, it had diverted some car users to rail and overall had enabled rail to at least keep up with private transport. Individual improvements had been small, but the total effect was substantial. The real benefits would come from the use of the results in future land use planning policies, especially of residential location, and on transport management.

Electrification comes at a cost in terms of service disruption for the users. A six-week period in pre-electrification days in late 1975 recorded Great Northern services as achieving 65% right time arrivals at final destination, with 20% of trains between one and five minutes late, and 15% later still. These would have been on schedules which had already been extended to allow for the necessary work to take place, but during the timetable period the situation changes in terms of precisely what is being done at the time, where that work is taking place, and the impact of similar works under way elsewhere.

In this context it is perhaps of interest that (according to Hertfordshire County Council) British Railways actually reduced the fares to Moorgate on the inauguration of the Great Northern electric services.

Performance

Sadly, the electrified services were to prove troublesome in performance terms. During the first half of 1980, the Monopolies & Mergers Commission (MMC) found that fewer than half of the GN Inner Suburban services arrived on time during the peak periods and only 70%–80% arrived within five minutes of scheduled time[24].

The Great Northern station at Oakleigh Park retains some of its original features, seen here on 26 April 2012. The station building at footbridge level is just that and not a signal box, despite some similarities in appearance. ***John Glover***

The Class 312s for the Outer services were a little better, with just over 50% arriving on time and over 80% within five minutes of time.

The Class 313s were achieving a dismal 7,600 miles between failures, the most significant faults relating to the sliding door mechanisms, the tripcock gear (for working underground to Moorgate) and wheelslip control. By contrast, the next worse were the 1949-built Class 306s for the Shenfield services, at a still poor 19,940 miles between failures.

As the MMC commented, rather acidly, the PEP stock prototypes from which the Class 313s were derived underwent extensive trials, but a number of major components were changed in these, the first production models[25].

What were the expectations of unit reliability in those days? Working straight out of the box doesn't seem to have been one of them.

Revisited 1987

The MMC revisited the Great Northern electrics in 1987, but it was difficult to find much enthusiasm in their report[i26]. Electric services had been extended from Hitchin to Peterborough from May 1987, but the punctuality and cancellation levels of all services were less than ideal. It was noted that Driver Only Operation (DOO) had been introduced on the inner-suburban services in November 1985 'after a period of disruption'. The outer-suburban services were then in the process of conversion to DOO. Staff shortfalls were a problem for the King's Cross area generally.

Disappointingly, what was now the Network SouthEast (NSE) part of British Rail reported that they had had to take vigorous action to match capacity more closely to demand. Consequently, night services too had been reduced. The original fleet of Class 313s for the GN Inner-Suburban totalled 64 units; by March 1987 they were down to 47 units. (The 17 spare units were transferred to Euston and North London services.)

In 2017 the number of units allocated to Hornsey to provide much the same set of services was 44.

AFTER THE LONDON RAIL STUDY

The 1976 Transport Policy consultation document[27] of the Labour Government elected that year made soothing noises about the importance of the London & South East rail network. But it all cost too much, and British Rail should aim at the Outer Suburban services meeting their full costs by 1981. For the Inner Suburban services, which had no prospect of viability, as far as could be seen, the aim should be to contain and if possible reduce the need for Government support.

The Northern City Line platforms always seemed rather oversized and gloomy, as seen here, reflecting the use of tube tunnelling for full-sized trains. This is the Highbury & Islington station platform for services to Moorgate on 4 June 2013, when it still carried some Network SouthEast branding. *John Glover*

The proposed method was more effective integration between bus, Underground and surface rail operators in Greater London, through a new London Rail Advisory Committee (set up in 1976) in which the Government, the Greater London Council and the transport operators would be represented.

Its aims would be to keep the commuter services under review, and advise on the coordination of fares policy and investment programmes. But other questions arose, one of which was the use that the GLC might be expected to make of their powers to support British Rail services? Could British Rail and London Transport services be coordinated more effectively?

But other things were changing too, and the Transport Policy document of 1968 foreshadowed the transfer of the London Transport undertaking to the Greater London Council (GLC). The enabling Act[28] gave the GLC a general duty 'to develop policies ... which will promote the

Harringay is the first station on the Great Northern beyond Finsbury Park. On 4 July 1987, No 317859 on the up slow line is passed by a rapidly approaching HST set. It would be a few years yet before electrification extended north of the Border, though HSTs were still to be used for another 30 years of so to provide services to Inverness and Aberdeen. *John Glover*

provision of integrated, efficient and economic transport facilities and services for Greater London'. It also gave the Council the powers to make grants for transport purposes to the London Transport Executive and also to the Railways Board for passenger facilities they provided to meet the needs of Greater London.

But while the Railways Board were enjoined to cooperate with the GLC, the railway itself and the services on it would remain their responsibility, for which they were given the objective of achieving viability by the end of 1982. They would also determine the fares to be charged.

The London Rail Advisory Committee was disbanded in 1980, its functions absorbed elsewhere.

NORTH LONDON UPGRADES

The North London line electric services ran from Richmond via Willesden Junction, Camden Road and Highbury & Islington to (pre-1986) London Broad Street. At Willesden Junction it crossed over the DC electrified lines from London Euston to Watford Junction. It was also associated with services on the West London line from Clapham Junction to Kensington Olympia and thence to Willesden Junction, though there was no local passenger service north of Kensington Olympia.

At this time, another non-electrified line was that from Gospel Oak to Barking, while the East London line, part of London Underground, ran from Shoreditch via Whitechapel to Surrey Docks, where the line bifurcated to the two termini of New Cross and New Cross Gate.

The North London was an important freight route with additional running lines eastwards from Camden Road to the former Dalston Western Junction. The line continued east as a freight only route (since 1944) to join the Great Eastern line at Stratford.

Thanks to the funding of the Greater London Council, in 1979, passenger services were restored on the eastern section as part of a diesel-unit operated service from Camden Road to Stratford and then over the former Great Eastern branch to North Woolwich. The line was later electrified on the third-rail DC and services were operated throughout from Richmond by 2-EPB units from the Southern Region.

The four-track section Camden Road to Dalston Western Junction was later largely reduced to three tracks when electrification at 25kV AC was undertaken for the benefit of freight traffic. This provided an electrified freight route from the London & North Western lines through to the Great Eastern. New stations were opened over the years at Dalston Kingsland (1983), Hackney Central (1980), Homerton (1985) and Hackney Wick (1980).

The creation of London Overground is discussed later.

Somehow, 313001 sporting a blind reading Watford Junction in Platform 1 at the yet to be rebuilt Liverpool Street doesn't quite look right, but right it was following the closure of Broad Street. The train was to form the 16:12 departure in May 1987. *John Glover*

6

Cross-London Alternatives

London Transport starts from the premise that public transport in urban conditions is a good thing and, within the financial limitations, the more of it the better.
Memorandum to the House of Commons Transport Committee, 1981

In October 1980, the Monopolies and Mergers Commission (MMC) reported on the London & South East Commuter Services[29] of the British Railways Board (BRB).

About two thirds of the traffic was carried by the three Divisions of the Southern Region. The other major carrier was the Liverpool Street Division of Eastern Region, with around 20% of the traffic. By comparison, the other (London Midland and Western) Regions and the King's Cross Division of the Eastern Region did not have any major traffic flows.

The MMC was decidedly critical about the way that standards[30] were set for the Board. Thus: 'Although BRB are set several specific financial targets, there are no specific formal targets or constraints on the quality of service expected of them'. The only external guidance was the very general 1974 direction by the Secretary of State, discussed earlier.

As the MMC pointed out, what constituted a public service was not defined, there was no guidance on how priorities for track access (the modern term) should be determined where there were competing claims for service, nor any mention of such financial constraints that there might be. Markets change over time; how much discretion did the Board have in varying the service it offered the public?

This resulted in a firm conclusion[31]: that 'the problem of the inter-relation of service, costs and charges cannot be tackled satisfactorily unless the business is being conducted with a clear objective. The 1974 direction, however useful it may have been in the past, is no longer adequate for this purpose.' The Government needs to set out what it expects the Board to achieve in operating the social railway in London and the South East.

HEAVY RAIL OPPORTUNITIES

The means of crossing London by heavy rail services has exercised many minds from time to time, history having provided mostly peripheral routes such as the West London line from Willesden to Clapham Junction. The only one to traverse central London was that from the Metropolitan Widened Lines (King's Cross/St Pancras), via Farringdon to Blackfriars, to be discussed later.

It will be apparent that the schemes for cross-London rail operation discussed so far have concentrated on the shorter distance journeys. That was perhaps to be expected, especially when local authorities have been involved. But what potential might there be for linking up journeys which are essentially of a length associated with InterCity operations?

The BRB decided to find out and in 1980 published a discussion paper. This began with the education of its readers, telling them that there are two basic alternatives for linking routes north and south of London – via central London, or around central London.

The idea was to link the main rail routes south of London with those to the north and west. It explored issues relevant to the long-term future of transport in suburban London and accessibility of the area south of London – including air and sea ports – to the rest of the country. The link across London would be provided by through trains, cutting out inconvenient interchanges between train and Underground or taxi, thus saving valuable time for the passengers. It would help commuters from the outer suburbs and InterCity travellers alike. Those using the main lines south of London would also benefit from an extension of the quality of InterCity travel.

Going back nearly 40 years, it needs to be remembered that the East Coast main line electrification was still a decade away from completion, the Midland Suburban Electrification was unfinished and the then Southern Region of British Rail was very largely operated with slam door and often high-density rolling stock.

The Channel Tunnel, too, was still only an idea; not until 1986 was the Franco-British Treaty of Canterbury signed, paving the way to award a concession for the construction and operation of the Channel Tunnel fixed link to private companies. Regrettably, what was to become High Speed 1, the rail link from the Eurotunnel boundary to London St Pancras International, was not to be considered until much later.

Existing alternatives

The West London line between Willesden Junction and Clapham Junction had never really been intended for passenger purposes and it was used mainly as a busy freight route bypassing the central area of the capital. It saw spasmodic passenger use; a minimal and largely unadvertised passenger service was operated between Clapham Junction and Kensington Olympia for Post Office Savings Bank workers. The latter station came into its own for a while as an alternative London terminus for the Great Western Main Line during the Paddington resignalling.

It was also to be used for enhanced Cross-Country services, though the West London line's less than ideal physical construction in terms of curvature, junctions and network connections meant generally that it never really succeeded. In those days, the only interface with London Underground was at Kensington Olympia station and it was perhaps wishful thinking to consider this as being in central London. Kensington Olympia provided direct (and nowadays very limited) Underground services to Earl's Court and High Street Kensington, only.

West Brompton became another interchange station between the West London line and the District line of the Underground in 1999.

The third cross-London railway was that of the East London line, latterly part of London Underground and now part of the London Overground network.

What, then, might have been on offer?

Cross-London Rail Link

The scheme that was pursued was the construction of a new line to run between low level stations (ie beneath the present terminals) at Victoria and Euston. Each of these would have four platforms. Fed by junctions on the existing lines in the area of Battersea, beyond Euston there would be branches to each of the West Coast Main Line (surfacing at Primrose Hill), the Midland Line (coming to the surface in the Kentish Town area) and to the East Coast route (exiting from tunnel at Holloway).

It was considered that a link to the (then) Western Region lines out of Paddington could be provided by upgrading the existing connections between Willesden Junction and Acton.

There would be no intermediate stations at all in central London and a Travelator connection was shown as linking Euston with St Pancras and King's Cross.

Selected existing services, north and south of London, would be linked to form through trains. On the assumption that all the lines concerned would be electrified by the time this link might be operational, the changeover between DC and AC traction would take place while trains were stationary at Victoria. This would be a similar situation to that already in use at Drayton Park on the Great Northern suburban services.

Routeing via central London was much superior to a round London strategy. In principle, two existing trains, one north of London and one south of London, could be combined to make a single through train. The example given was Birmingham–Euston and Victoria–Brighton. In this way, the needs of existing passengers who found the traditional terminal convenient would be safeguarded, others would have a greater choice of stations in London at which to join trains, and those crossing London on this corridor would have a through train available.

Even passengers whose journey was perhaps from Birmingham to Eastbourne would have only one change of train to make, with no need for the use of the Underground or a taxi.

This, it was averred, could all be achieved with no significant increase in train mileage and without producing capacity problems on the rest of the network. Given that turnround of trains at central London stations would also be eliminated, it was estimated that this manner of operation would mean that almost 200 fewer rolling stock vehicles would be needed.

Intriguingly, no estimates were given of the capacity of the proposed link in terms of trains per hour. What little information that there is suggests that around 15tph might have been the target for the basic service pattern. It was stated that additional trains for peak requirements would continue to use the existing termini. Two key destinations south of the Thames were said to be Gatwick Airport and Dover, both for their importance in international traffic.

Today, Office of Rail and Road statistics show that Gatwick Airport is the busiest station in the Government Region for the South East (ie excluding London), handling 19 million passengers a year, and Birmingham New Street is the correspondingly busiest station in the West Midlands at 42 million passengers a year (estimates for 2016/17).

Evaluation

Both financial and economic evaluations were made of this scheme using a number of different criteria, and these were sufficiently encouraging to suggest that further work should be undertaken. A major barrier which put people off travelling by rail for cross-London journeys would be very much reduced. More specifically, it was concluded that:

- A deep level cross-London link between Victoria and Euston was technically feasible;
- Its planning, the obtaining of Parliamentary powers, followed by construction was estimated to take nine years;
- The real rates of return to British Rail made it commercially attractive, and the benefits to the community as a whole would be even greater;

- The scheme would benefit commuters, business, leisure and international travellers alike;
- It would help decongest London Underground services and the Victoria line in particular; also the roads where taxis were used for transfer between the main line termini.

The idea was not pursued, though it might be considered that there are certain similarities in the objectives of the Thameslink scheme as it was later developed, to be discussed later. To that extent, work on Cross-London Rail Links would have been a useful preparation.

Discussion of the practical problems that were anticipated in the post-war conclusions of the London Plan Working Party was absent, though at least nominal provision was made for the handling of parcels at the proposed Euston Low Level station. Notably, the markets and train services which the BRB had in mind were the medium to longer distance InterCity type. Did the scheme have potential?

How the future might look as seen in 1980; an Advanced Passenger Train stands on the third-rail at East Croydon station. ***British Railways Board***

FARES FAIR

As already recorded, rail traffic over the years had hardly been buoyant, and for the Underground the low of 498 million passenger journeys being made in a year was to be reached in 1982. That was very largely a result of the events associated with the Law Lords' ruling on the Labour-controlled Greater London Council's 'Fares Fair' policy.

In this, fares on London Transport services were reduced by 32% in October 1981. Its legality was challenged by the London Borough of Bromley, objecting to their residents having to pay extra taxes to fund the Underground, given that rail services in Bromley were provided solely by British Rail.

This went to court and on appeal in December 1981 the Law Lords ruled that the policy was illegal. This resulted in fares being doubled in March 1982, with results as described above.

In a further change in May 1983, the legality of which was tested beforehand, fares were again reduced by 23%. This put Underground fares in real terms at around 20% below the pre-October 1981 levels.

What did come out of this, though, was the introduction of the popular Travelcard. This would evolve to offer fares for unrestricted travel by bus, Underground or rail within up to six concentric zones, for one day or any period from one month to one year.

The merits or otherwise of 'Fares Fair' are not discussed here[32], only to note that policy variations of this magnitude put an enormous strain on the service operators. This episode was to be instrumental in the government's decision to take back control of the London Transport Executive in the form of London Regional Transport. This became effective from 29 June 1984, a year in which Underground carryings were back to 672 million.

This was followed in 1986 by the abolition of the GLC itself.

A Metropolitan line train of the stalwart A stock hurries through Neasden with a train for Aldgate, running non-stop from Wembley Park to Finchley Road. Unusually, the slow lines for the trains of the Jubilee line are in between the fast lines on this section. ***John Glover***

The 1972 Mk2 stock was to spend some time on the Northern line until its transfer to the Bakerloo, where it still operates. A train of this stock, noted at the time for the unusual red-painted doors, is approaching Finchley Central on the single track branch from Mill Hill East in August 1976. *John Glover*

The situation is very different today. Underground carryings in 2016/17 were approaching three times the numbers carried in 1984. The system is now larger, yes, but the growth in demand has been phenomenal. Many of the causes such as changes in the rates of economic growth, population, employment and its location, housing and so on, are external to the transport providers. They have to meet with the requirements for service expansion, wherever possible, as best they can.

Adapting to growth rather than continuing slow decline needs a completely different mind-set. But, again, how permanent is that growth and what happens if, or more likely when, circumstances change?

The Underground's D stock was built around 1978 and was retired by early 2017. Here a Wimbledon-bound train departs from Parsons Green on 28 April 1997. The effect of the body overhang when negotiating curves can be seen in the chunk purposely taken out of the nearside platform because of the crossover between the tracks. *John Glover*

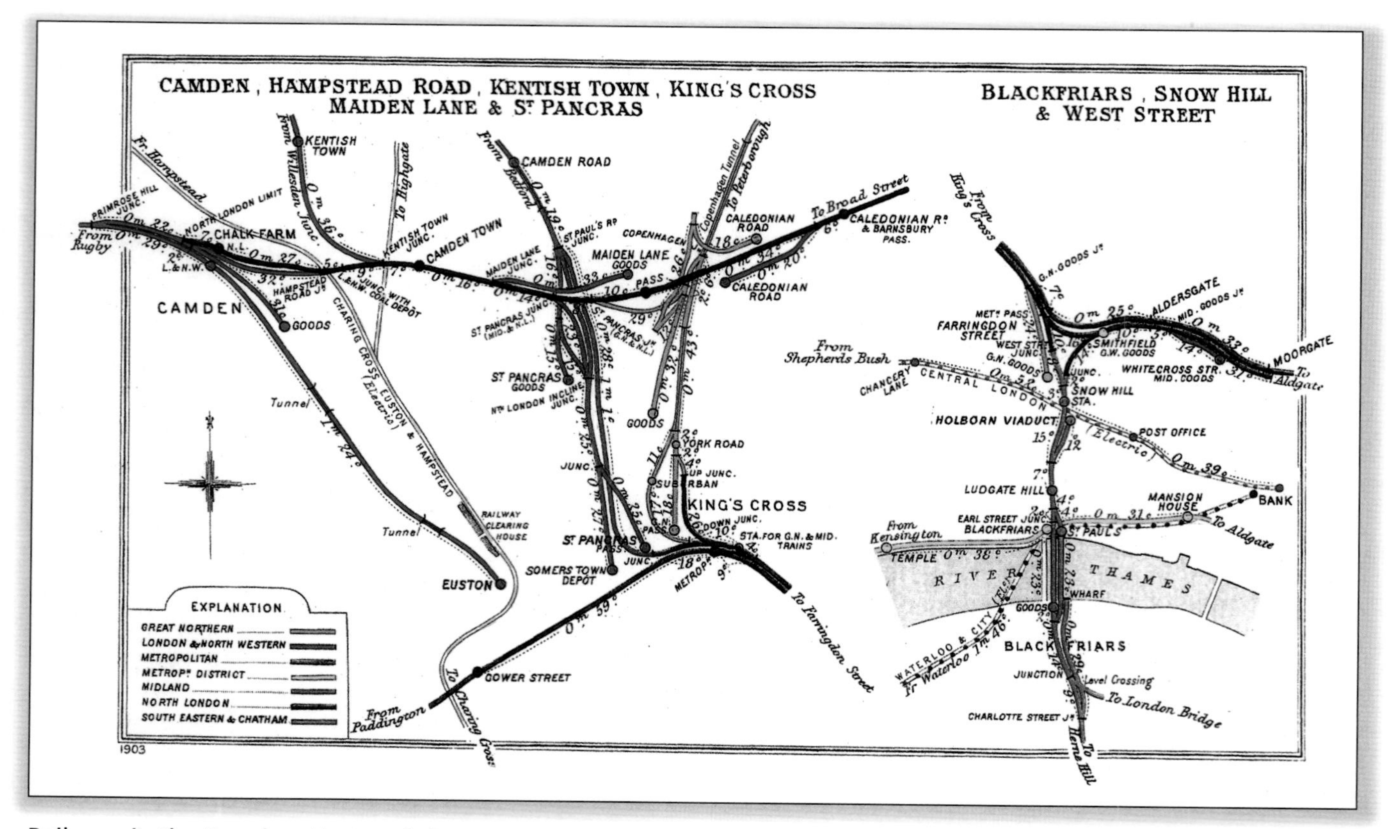

Railways in the Camden, Euston, St Pancras, King's Cross and Blackfriars areas. *Railway Clearing House, 1903*

WIDENED LINES NEW ROLE

The Metropolitan Railway's original section of double track line between Paddington and Farringdon Street was opened in 1863; it was soon to go further. The Metropolitan's location was ideal for rail access to the City for passenger traffic, but also the wholesale food markets for goods.

This new facility was quickly oversubscribed by other railways. What amounted to four-tracking between King's Cross, Farringdon and Moorgate was started as early as 1867. The result became known as the City Widened Lines, built by the Metropolitan to relieve their own system of excess traffic. The result was to see the appearance of trains from the Great Western, the Great Northern and the Midland railways. A number of goods depots were to appear. The Railway Clearing House Junction diagrams of the area show the situation in 1903.

Established long-term passenger operators were the Great Northern via the curves at King's Cross (from York Road, and back via Platform 16), and the Midland via the present Thameslink route. Also attracted was the London, Chatham & Dover Railway, which built a link from their terminal at Blackfriars to a junction just east of Farringdon station. From here their trains could proceed west towards King's Cross, or east to Moorgate over a now long-vanished south to east curve just short of Farringdon.

This involved the use of locomotives from those companies. Ownership of the infrastructure remained with the companies concerned, and those Metropolitan, and other companies paid dues for its use.

Passenger trains over the Farringdon-Blackfriars link did not prosper. With the establishment of the electrified Underground, this link was used for freight only from 1916. It fell into total disuse with the post-war decline of wagon load traffic. The track here was lifted in 1971, though importantly the formation remained intact.

The situation that then existed saw the Widened Lines being used by passenger services to Moorgate from both the Midland and Great Northern railways. The Great Northern services were to be withdrawn and diverted via a new connection to the Northern City line north of Drayton Park and to Moorgate via that route, as already discussed.

This left only the Midland services, operated latterly by Class 24 diesels and BR non-gangwayed suburban stock, and that at peak times Mondays to Fridays only.

Pointwork connections to and from the Underground had been removed, so that all that remained was a wholly British Rail operation.

Midland Diesels

The St Pancras/Moorgate–Bedford outer-suburban services were dieselised in 1959 using a Derby Works build of 30 four-car slam door units, later Class 127. These were of the DMBS-TS-TS(L)-DMBS configuration, Second Class only and seating 348. Unusually, they had hydraulic transmission, and were thus unable to couple with mechanical units. There were no end gangways between vehicles; those who thought they might want to use a

An up service formed of a Class 127 DMU is seen at Radlett, a station still with its Midland style buildings, on the up fast line. Like so many of the original examples of the DMU fleet, these trains were kept in service well beyond the time when prudence would have retired them. ***John Glover***

lavatory during the 50-mile journey from Bedford had to choose their vehicle carefully.

The poor quality and low reliability of the diesel service had led to a steady reduction in passenger journeys, despite population growth in the north of the area. By the autumn of 1981, morning peak travellers numbered less than 7,000.

Midland Suburban Electrics

The Midland Suburban Electrics (MSE) scheme was designed to replace the ageing diesel units and make some real improvements to the operation. The Bedford – St Pancras scheme (or Bed-Pan, as the then Chairman of the British Railways Board Sir Peter Parker referred to it), was inaugurated on 18 April 1983. This followed a year-long industrial dispute with the Unions over what was to be the first application of Driver Only Operation on British Rail.

The Class 317 AC electric replacement stock was of four cars as were its diesel predecessors, with as many as 45 units being provided. These were sliding door trains, seating 273 second class passengers plus 21 first class and two lavatories. They were gangwayed throughout and ran to Moorgate in an eight-car formation.

The 25kV AC electrification extended via the Kentish Town junction to Moorgate. The MSE involved complete resignalling and the Widened Lines were closed, the last diesel trains to the Midland running on 14 May 1979. As the Widened Lines were now of no relevance to London Underground operations, the whole of the infrastructure apart from the stations themselves became the property of the British Railways Board.

Consequently, the new signalling for the whole of the Midland Suburban electrified area was controlled from the new West Hampstead power box, with electrical control from Hornsey.

Once the industrial relations disputes and certain technical failings of the rolling stock were resolved, the newly electrified service began to attract passengers back. The original service offered was 2tph all stations between Bedford and St Albans, then fast to St Pancras, plus 2tph all stations Luton to Moorgate. There were some limited stop trains between Bedford and St Pancras in the peak. Decline was reversed, and the autumn passenger count of 1986 showed nearly double the numbers of 1981. In short, the service went from strength to strength.

But was the best use being made of the infrastructure? The Greater London Council certainly thought that it was not and was keen to see services restored over the Farringdon–Blackfriars section, today's Thameslink.

One of the original AC only units for the St Pancras–Bedford electrification, 317302, stands at Flitwick in British Rail blue and grey livery. This is a down train on 18 May 1983, shortly after the electric services had been introduced. *John Glover*

RAILWAYS INTO ROADS?

As was noted earlier, Dr Beeching in his 'Reshaping' report of 1963 let the London area off relatively lightly, with nearly all lines scheduled for retention. But others had different ideas, the Railway Conversion League being one of them. Their proposition was that all railway routes could better serve the community as a whole if they were converted into roads. At its extreme, 'it would allow the creation of a duplicate motorway network'.

Unsurprisingly, the British Railways Board (BRB) took a different view, in that such a case was supported neither by facts nor by valid argument. It also argued that such ideas in general were physically impractical and would be uneconomic to carry out.

Furthermore, railways had a continuing and key role in the nation's economic and social development. 'Can it really make sense to replace one man driving 1,000 tons of coal or 800 commuters with 50 lorries or 20 buses, each individually driven?' was the view expressed by BRB Chairman Sir Peter Parker, in 1982.

Such allegations however do not go away and might there be places where conversion into roads could be advantageous? The outcome was the setting up in 1984 of a Steering Committee consisting of Sir Alfred Sherman, a known advocate of railway conversion, Michael Posner, a member of the BRB who was known to be sceptical about the idea, and Professor Christopher Foster, an independent expert.

The approach was to have a study carried out by consultants, who would then report back to the Committee.

A sample consisting of a number of less heavily used rail route sections was identified. It was selected to include both radial and orbital railway routes, with a range of rail volumes and traffic types, and which might make useful contributions to the road network.

The following routes were identified for examination and the findings for each are given.

Great Central line Marylebone–Northolt Junction, 16.1km

Options were seen as cars only or bus only. There is a prima facie case for conversion on the assumptions that profitable tolls could be negotiated and that acceptable road standards could be achieved. All substantial flows of rail traffic could be diverted elsewhere (presumably to Paddington).

In the further sections of the Great Central railway, namely Northolt Junction–Princes Risborough (42.2km), Princes Risborough–Aylesbury (11.7km), and Aylesbury–Claydon Junction (17.4km), there was insufficient road demand to warrant conversion.

Platform width at Farringdon is not over-generous, as can be seen here in this view of 319455 bound for the Midland line in April 1998. Constrained sites like this are always potential problems, as there is so little room to manoeuvre. *John Glover*

West London Line Willesden Junction–Latchmere Junction(s), 8.0km, also Cricklewood–Acton Central–Kew Bridge, 10.3km.

Only one of these two schemes would be selected, as both would serve largely the same ends for road traffic. However, the volume of rail traffic makes it profitable to retain both as railways, so there is no case for conversion.

If a choice had to be made, the West London line would be preferred for conversion if, and only if, an alternative route could be found for InterCity services and that road tolling was acceptable. This would be an all-purpose road, 5.5km long.

Kew Bridge–Barnes, 4.1km

Potentially of some interest, but all rail traffic would have to be diverted to the (double-track) route via Richmond. This contains four level crossings, some or all of which would need to be replaced and a substantial number of commuting journeys would be affected. These disbenefits make a conversion scheme no better than marginal.

North London line, Willesden Junction–Hampstead Heath–Hackney Wick, 16.4km

The North London line in total is a key linking railway route with many junctions. Formation width, gradients and track curvature, and bridge/tunnel clearances are often limiting factors. A 4.5km section though is to four-track width. The line was then used by 180 passenger and 90-100 freight trains a day.

It was considered that the physical constraints ruled out conversion west of Camden Road, and that the loss of (mostly) freight revenues east of that point made the whole route unprofitable for conversion.

Clapham Junction–Peckham Rye, 5.5km

This line, which was primarily on viaduct or embankment and in a densely developed area, was used by 33 trains in each direction every day. Given also its physical limitations and its likely use for local road traffic only, there was no case for conversion.

Fenchurch Street–Shoeburyness, via Laindon or Tilbury, 63.6km

For the first 4.6km the line is on continuous viaduct with a sharp curve at Steney East (now Limehouse) station. And from Bromley-by-Bow to Upminster it runs adjacent to the fourth-rail electrified District line. A total of 125 passenger trains operate in each direction out of Fenchurch Street, and there is heavy freight operation on the route via Tilbury. Overall, there was inadequate width for conversion to a road, and bus substitution for rail commuter flows would be uneconomic.

It may be noted that it was later found possible to reduce the formation used by British Rail trains between Fenchurch Street and Limehouse from four tracks to two, to provide for the construction of an initial section of the Docklands Light Railway. This was opened in 1987.

The conclusions were that a generalised case for rail conversion into roads did not exist, other perhaps than in a very few localised cases. Given the huge explosion in rail volumes that has taken place since this report was published in 1984, the case now must be that much weaker. Of the remaining examples, no case could be made for conversion of the railway into a road of any description.

PUBLIC TRANSPORT IN LONDON, THE NEXT 10 YEARS[33]

This Greater London Council 1985 document looking a decade ahead is of particular interest in terms of its suggestions as to how the South Central rail network might be developed.

It started from the premise that parts of British Rail's network were complex and difficult for the occasional passenger to understand. This applied particularly to the Central Division of the Southern Region. There was a good case for running a less complicated system, at least off-peak. Each line could be given a separate identity, with more emphasis on the opportunities for interchange at key points; Sutton, Tulse Hill and Norwood Junction were mentioned specifically in this context.

At the same time, the frequency of each of the simplified services should be not less than every 15 minutes. It was recognised that many sections of the network did have a combined service frequency of 15 minutes or better, but typically this was made up of two (or more) low frequency routes to different destinations. Overall, this appeared to the user to be a less frequent and less attractive service than it might.

It was also suggested that the low marginal cost of increasing off peak frequencies from (say) every 30 minutes to every 15 minutes, if adequately advertised, should be self-supporting,

The matter of service frequencies was to be pursued in much of what became Network SouthEast, though that of simplified service patterns tended to be put in the 'too difficult' box. The problem with the South Central services was the impossibility of trying to serve both the West End (at Victoria) and the City (at London Bridge, but also sometimes Charing Cross or [then] Holborn Viaduct) with one service. To do otherwise meant enforced interchange for some; while this might be acceptable on the Underground, it was likely to be strongly resisted on the main line network.

The same sort of problem affected the Northern line's High Barnet and Edgware branches. If they were to be separated, with services from one branch running via Bank and the other via Charing Cross, there would be a lot more interchanging between services at Camden Town. That station would need a major rebuild, and depot accommodation for the trains rethought out. Passengers with seats might well lose them in the process of changing trains, although in theory others would gain in equal numbers.

As one senior Underground manager put it to the author, 'you spend a lot of money separating the two lines, to make life more difficult for a large number of people'.

Such conundrums take on a different aspect when viewed in the light of growing passenger numbers, line capacity and service frequency. 'Every second counts' is far from a meaningless slogan. If the operational objective is to maximise the number of trains provided on any service or group of services, the lines concerned need to have as simple a layout as possible, a repetitive timetable and the least sharing of operational resources.

That is easier said than done. Thus Underground lines serving busy National Rail stations will sometimes find their platforms crowded, sometimes with very few passengers waiting. This can reflect the gaps between successive main line trains arriving at the platforms above, and particularly long-distance services.

Yet it will be essential to get the utmost value out of the railways that already exist, before turning to new construction. In very recent times, the prospect of 'Metroisation' – making service provision more like that of an urban metro - is discussed further in Chapter 11.

The ritual of suggesting new stations, in this case no less than 50, met with little success. Fewer than 20% of those put forward have been constructed, with most of these being associated with line openings such as Imperial Wharf and Shepherd's Bush on the West London line. Evaluation appeared to be seen only in terms of capital costs; potential passenger usage and hence fares revenue. Staffing and maintenance costs were ignored. But new stations on existing tracks also bring a cost in terms of overall extended journey times, discouraging passengers travelling over most or all of the route. This will also result, at some stage, in the need to commit additional trains and train crew to the service.

This report also contained early ideas on what was to emerge eventually as London Overground, and the basic elements of what was later to become Crossrail 1. The suggestion was 'the extension of British Rail Western Region local services from Reading or Slough onto the Hammersmith & City line to Liverpool Street. This could be linked with an Eastern Region service either via Liverpool Street to Chingford or Enfield, or onto the Southend Central via Tilbury line which starts at Fenchurch Street.

Western Region services [were then] not yet electrified, but a through service could be operated initially using dual traction electric/diesel units'.

The touching faith in the ability of the north side of the Circle line to accommodate such an extra service and the proposed arrangements at Liverpool Street, all operated by dual traction vehicles, suggest that this represented little more than early thoughts. Diesel traction on the sub-surface lines is not an attractive proposition and the associated fire risk would today probably rule it out..

Even so, the linking of railway lines from each side of the capital is increasingly becoming a reality, with both Thameslink and the Elizabeth line fully open in 2019.

LIGHT RAIL OPPORTUNITIES?

If the conversion of railway lines to roads was not a starter, would conversion to light rail fare any better?

By 1986 the first stage of the Docklands Light Railway (DLR) in East London was under construction. This was designed to kick start the reinvigoration of the by now near derelict docklands area, rather than for direct transport reasons. The scheme was given government approval by the then Secretary of State for the Environment, Michael Heseltine, in October 1982. Among the conditions attached were that the scheme must not cost more than £77 million in total and that the project had to be completed by 1987.

After some toying with street running at least in part, the initial stage of the Docklands Light Railway (Tower Gateway to Island Gardens, with a branch to Stratford) was an unconventional railway. Crucially, it was to be on a reserved track with no pedestrian (or road vehicle) conflicts. Maximum use was made of a number of existing but disused railway alignments, plus as mentioned two tracks between Limehouse and Tower Gateway and, very importantly, enough space for a single line from Bow Road to Stratford).

The DLR performance specification in 1987 was that of a single two-section articulated car train running every eight minutes. This was on a 13km railway with 15 stations. It was built on time and to budget. The DLR used 80lb/yd flat-bottomed steel rails on slab track, and basic concrete structures. By contrast, swing-nose crossings installed to give continuous wheel support through pointwork were both complex and expensive.

Much of the original DLR was at viaduct level, which did not make passenger access easy; the simple stations were all unstaffed. Trains were controlled initially by a fixed block system; there was (and is) always a staff member on board. Current collection was by underside third rail at 750v DC. A fleet of 11 trains was all that was needed for the initial system.

About two thirds of the route from Tower Gateway and Stratford to Island Gardens was built on the trackbed of former heavy rail lines.

This first section was opened by Her Majesty the Queen on 30 July 1987. Public opening came a month later.

The building of the initial DLR system was planned and managed by eight people.

What other opportunities might there be?

Next move

In 1986, a group from British Rail and London Regional Transport undertook a general review of the prospects for light rail[34]. Did the concept have a place more generally in meeting passenger needs for movement in London?

The Docklands Light Railway was test running in 1987 and this picture is of the embryonic Canary Wharf station with two of the original DLR cars passing. As there was clearly little prospect of traffic from what was no more than a building site, the station was never opened. Good times came along later. This view was from Heron Quays. *John Glover*

First, the team's Report gave a general definition of its role:

> 'Light rail is the application of appropriate rail technology and operating practices to an intermediate level of passenger demand (say from 3,000 to 15,000 passengers per peak hour per direction), to provide a more cost effective and efficient service in this range than is possible with conventional bus or rail operations.'

Light rail was defined broadly as any system of:

- driver only, manual operation, standard gauge, steel wheeled vehicles on steel rail
- operation on wholly or partially segregated rights of way, or completely unsegregated from road traffic
- simple, low cost, closely spaced stops
- minimal signalling
- lighter vehicles built to less onerous end loading and other design criteria, capable of negotiating sharper bends and curves and steeper gradients than conventional vehicles
- generally but not exclusively electrically powered, with simple overhead collection where street running is required
- potentially lower vehicle, operating and engineering costs of route alignment, structures and track.

Less easy to define were the benefits of a high-quality image, a permanent infrastructure and service reliability (when compared with a bus route).

A train of 1992 Central line stock calls at Chigwell on the line towards Hainault in March 2007. The unusual height of the Great Eastern canopies above the platform level may be noted, accentuated by the diminutive tube train. This section of the Underground was one of those seen as a potential light rail conversion. *John Glover*

It will be seen that this suggests a wide possible field of application, in which the group listed 32 possible schemes for the London area. They did not however include the Euston–Aldwych–Waterloo Cross-River scheme, which later received attention for a time. Of those listed, the vast majority were aimed at getting better value out of the existing infrastructure and the rights of way associated with it.

Was it a good idea, and if so could it work? Five schemes were selected for further consideration, listed here together with the present writer's comments:

- Convert and extend the East London line from Shoreditch to Liverpool Street, to maximise the potential of the cross-river link.

Author: The lack of physical capacity of Liverpool Street main line station and its approaches, even after the 1990s rebuilding, made this a difficult starter. The East London line later became part of the extended London Overground operation where the capacity of a heavy rail service has been amply justified.

- A comprehensive study of the possible role of light rail in the Croydon area, defining the traffic potential, technical and operational feasibility, likely capital costs, operating costs and revenues, effects on existing passengers, overall benefits and disbenefits, and the methodology and implementation issues.

Author: This seems to have been the Group's favourite, even if the eventual scheme adopted was rather less ambitious than that which they outlined. Thus it was unlikely that light rail construction across a chunk of Epsom Downs between Tattenham Corner and Epsom Downs stations would have been well received.

This 87.5km network would have made much more extensive use of railway lines which remain open for passenger traffic today than the scheme finally adopted.

- Hainault–Woodford–Epping–Ongar, and/or Greenford–West Ruislip. In an era when rolling stock and signalling would shortly be replaced, would a conversion to light rail technology, perhaps with extra stops, be worth pursuing?

Author: The Study itself commented on the complications which would ensue in reaching Hainault depot and the need to find alternatives. If schemes for the replacement of British Rail lines were included, perhaps something radical for the Underground was also necessary? In the event, Epping–Ongar closed in 1994, and it seems unlikely that conversion to light rail would have made much difference to such an outcome.

- Rickmansworth–Croxley–Watford High Street–Watford Junction. Linking the lightly used British Rail service to Watford High Street and Watford Junction (and in those days Croxley Green) to Rickmansworth, closing the unsatisfactory

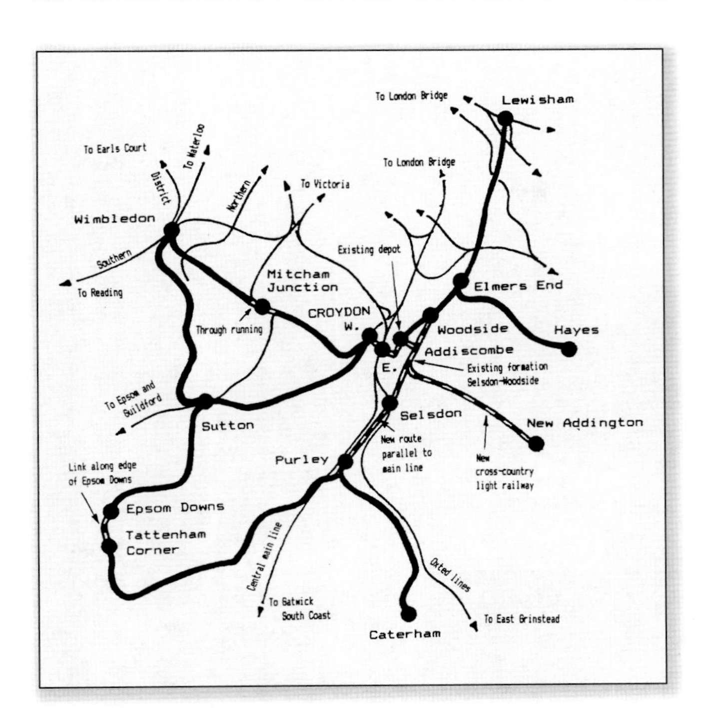

Original 1986 proposal for Croydon area, Light Rail. *BR/LRT liaison group*

The Wimbledon–West Croydon branch always seemed to be struggling; here two-car Class 416/1 set No 5665 arrives at Morden Road with a service to Croydon. Now part of London Tramlink, the track here has been doubled and there are two platforms. All buildings have been demolished. *John Glover*

London Underground terminus of Watford (Metropolitan), and examining the effect on local bus services.

Author: Many years later, the proposed rerouting of the Metropolitan line in this area would have achieved very similar results, but this is at best in abeyance for reasons of cost.

The Croydon scheme

The key to the Croydon scheme as built was an on-street single light rail line providing a clockwise circumnavigation of central Croydon. From this, lines diverge to serve Wimbledon in the west, to East Croydon station and Sandilands in the east and then further splitting to New Addington in the south east and to Elmers End in the north. The latter line then divides at Arena, giving a further route to Beckenham Junction.

All routes serve central Croydon, but only those terminating there serve all stops. Most routes travel through Croydon, making different stops according to their direction of travel.

None of this would have been possible without three events. First was the formal closure of the Elmers End–Sanderstead rail shuttle service in 1983. The others, in 1997, were the closure of British Rail's closely related branch from Elmers End to Woodside and Addiscombe, and their Wimbledon–West Croydon shuttle service. This ran at the uncomfortable headway of every 45 minutes, which was the best that could be achieved using only one train.

The use of these former heavy rail routes provided a major part of the infrastructure. Outside central Croydon, which includes Sandilands, only the sections of line from Arena towards Birkbeck on the Beckenham Junction branch and that from Lloyd Park to New Addington are on newly created infrastructure. The separation of the trams from road and pedestrian traffic is about as complete as it could be.

The system became fully operational in May 2000. It is 28km long and there are 39 stops. Electrification is at 750v DC, fed from 13 substations.

For the initial service 24 trams of three articulated sections were built by Bombardier. Each is 30.1m long and all are fully accessible. They have since been joined by 10 32.4m-long Variobahn trams by Stadler and these have five sections. The only depot is at Therapia Lane.

The assets are owned by Transport for London, but the operator is Tram Operations Ltd, a First Group subsidiary.

Tramlink services now make double use of Platform 10 at Wimbledon by an arrangement which allows two trams to be present at the same time but independently of each other; at Elmers End and Beckenham Junction stations Tramlink uses what amount to redundant bay platforms. At no point are there any running connections with the national network.

The conversion of parts of the Wimbledon branch to double track now enables a 12tph service to be operated and more work may soon be needed. Thus there are plans for a Croydon Westfield centre, while the new Thameslink services from 2018 are likely to bring new passenger demands to and from East Croydon. A further cause of growth is likely to be new housing.

London Tramlink services on the largely single-track line between Wimbledon and Croydon use the passing loop to cross at Mitcham on 27 March 2010. Much of this branch has had a second track installed, together with a second platform being made available at Wimbledon. These trams are both from the original fleet, with No 2549 for Wimbledon on the left and No 2540 for New Addington on the right. *John Glover*

This interior view at the Therapia Lane depot of London Tramlink shows Stadler Variobahn car No 2554 on 29 September 2013. This was the first of an order for 10 vehicles; modern trams too have an open interior layout. *John Glover*

For over 30 years, the four extant bay platforms of Watford Junction (Nos 1-4) to the west of the main lines have had only limited use. They have been host only to the DC services from Euston and (when it ran) the shuttle to Croxley Green. The fourth-rail scheme connecting them to the Metropolitan line at Croxley might one day provide through Underground services from Baker Street. This view of 25 July 2014 shows London Overground No 378229 on a service from London Euston. *John Glover*

New works will need to ensure a reliable and resilient tram network in central Croydon, coupled with an increase in the New Addington service. These are penciled in for 2020. The ensuing five-year period could see further upgrades to the Wimbledon branch, but a possible new on-street route from Wimbledon to central Sutton is unlikely. The present Mayor, Sadiq Khan, has said there is no budget for it.

Route expansion would require more trams and hence a second depot site. A quarter of a century after its opening, London Tramlink carried 29.5 million passengers in the 2016/17 year.

The Report's conclusion that considerable benefits could be derived from the conversion of an existing railway line to light rail operation seems to have been well founded. This would allow the addition of extra low cost stopping places and possible short extensions to better serve a traffic objective. It could also provide a link between existing lines.

However, the severity of the derailment at Sandilands on 9 November 2016, with the consequential injuries and loss of life, has at least the potential to slow the development of London Tramlink and similar systems elsewhere.

Growing the DLR

The subsequent history of the Docklands Light Railway after its original opening in 1987 shows continued system expansion.

Before the Bank extension of 1991, there had been no thought of running underground; the initial fleet had no end access and their use was forbidden. New three-car trains were obtained and the originals disposed of to the German town of Essen. The gradient on the steep exit from Bank, which took the line to viaduct level at Royal Mint Street Junction, was a challenging 1 in 17. Passenger congestion at the deep level DLR platforms at Bank station has always been a difficulty.

The routes newly created since have been as follows:

1994 Poplar–Beckton
1999 Crossharbour–Lewisham
2005 Canning Town–King George V
2009 King George V–Woolwich Arsenal
2011 Canning Town–Stratford International

Further stations have been added to the existing tracks and a certain amount of realignment has taken place. Pudding Mill Lane station, for instance, has had a mixed

Docklands Light Railway B92 car No 76 enters Stratford Market station on 24 March 2014. The Great Eastern origins of the station building may be recognised, but it is no longer in railway use. Passengers approach the platforms by a side walkway. *John Glover*

Passenger Operated Ticket Machines have become a common feature of at least suburban railways and in this case the Docklands Light Railway. This pair of machines is situated on the bridge at the DLR's Royal Victoria station. They were photographed on 18 July 2016. *John Glover*

Docklands Light Railway Car No 152 is of the B07 class built by Bombardier in Germany and seen on 26 July 2014. The location is near West Silvertown station on the Woolwich Arsenal branch and it is pictured from the Emirates Air Line, which links the Greenwich Peninsula with the Royal Docks. Air Line is operated by the DLR. *John Glover*

history. Opened in 1996, it was then closed temporarily for the duration of the London Games 2012, but a couple of years later in 2014 was closed permanently to allow the construction of a ramp to the Crossrail portal. It was subsequently reopened 10 days later as a larger station on a new site.

Pudding Mill Lane is situated on the last single or partially single track section of the DLR between Bow Road and Stratford. This is to become double track throughout.

Other major works have included the rebuilding of Canary Wharf DLR station. Originally constructed with two short side platforms but never opened as such due to the total absence of potential traffic, it was expanded to six full-length platforms with three tracks serving them, plus an overall roof. It was completed in 1991. Tower Gateway station was reconstructed to accommodate three-car operation and the completely revised junction layout in the West India Quay/Poplar/Canary Wharf triangle was designed to reduce the incidence of conflicting movements (both 2009).

Stations located underground started with Bank, later joined by the present Island Gardens, Cutty Sark and Woolwich Arsenal stations. These have always been staffed,

During the 1990s, signalling was transferred to control by Alcatel's SELTRAC Transmission Based Train Control (TBTC) system, which allows frequencies of perhaps 30 trains per hour.

The original single articulated pairs of cars have been replaced by sets of cars working in pairs and in many cases threes. The fleet in 2017 totalled 149 cars. There are two rolling stock depots, the original at Poplar and the main Beckton depot accessed from Gallions Reach.

The DLR system has now expanded to a length of 34km and serves 45 stations. Usage in the first full year of 1988/89 was 8.5 million passenger journeys; this had expanded massively to 122.3 million in 2016/17.

Since February 2014 the system operator has been contractor Keolis/Amey, whose concession lasts to April 2021. This can be extended by a further two years by London Rail (part of TfL).

As might be imagined, there have been and are many ideas of how the DLR might be extended further, but at the time of writing none has any higher status than a proposal. Given the growing volumes of travel on London's railways in recent years, with quite a lot more seemingly to come, the use of light rail vehicles with relatively limited capacity is not necessarily the most attractive policy to pursue.

But did we really need the DLR in the first place? It is interesting to speculate on what (if anything) else might have happened, had the start of Docklands expansion been the building of the Jubilee line extension from Green Park to Stratford.

SECRETARY OF STATE'S VIEWS

After the disbandment of the Greater London Council in 1986, no single body was in charge of transport in London. One result, in 1989, was an explanatory statement with a foreword by the then Secretary of State, Paul Channon[35], on his approach to the operation and development of London's transport systems.

This was also at the beginning of substantial change in London. Thus 'Since 1983, after decades of declining population, London has been growing.' It was up to the Minister to set objectives for British Rail and London (Regional) Transport ... and to ensure cooperation between the two operators in the planning and provision of London's rail services. 'There is not, and never has been, a single authority, responsible for all aspects of transport in London'.

The growth in numbers by rail is illustrated in Table 6.1 below:

Over the same period the numbers travelling by road (bus, car, cycle/motorcycle) went down substantially. Commuter coaches showed an increase, but this was from a very small base. Numbers overall rose by 10%, almost entirely a result of the increased carryings by British Rail and London Underground.

This was also the era in which quality objectives were imposed on British Rail by government, in addition to financial objectives. They were not, as is sometimes supposed, a result of privatisation; this was still a decade in the future. The obsession with measuring everything in sight and setting related targets was well and truly under way.

Thus it was recorded that in 1987 Network SouthEast achieved 92% of trains arriving on time or within 5 minutes of time, 98.8% of services ran (as opposed to being cancelled), 85% of phone calls to enquiry offices were answered within 30 seconds, the maximum queuing time at ticket offices, target (5 minutes at peak, 3 minutes off-peak), was met on 97% of occasions, and carriage cleaning requirements were met 91% of the time.

Load factor requirements were that no more than 35% of passengers should be standing in sliding door trains, 10% in those with slam doors (still in considerable numbers in those days), and no passengers should stand for more than 20 minutes unless they chose so to do.

Table 6.1: Commuting into Central London (07:00–10:00, morning peak)

	1983	1987	change
British Rail	384,000	449,000	+17%
London Underground	323,000	403,000	+25%

Basic stations can still be smartly turned out; the wide platforms here are a result of the four tracks being reduced to two. This is Sudbury Hill & Harrow on 10 April 2005 looking towards High Wycombe, with Chiltern Railways 165.212 on a train for Marylebone arriving. Passengers, though, are not in abundance. *John Glover*

TOTAL ROUTE MODERNISATION, 1988–92

'The experience of the St Pancras/Moorgate to Bedford electrification had shown that improved quality of service can generate a profitable increase in traffic. In that case, a number of conspicuous improvements in quality of service were introduced concurrently, at a high capital cost.' Thus the Monopolies and Mergers Commission in their 1987 report on Network SouthEast.

Could similar results be obtained repeated elsewhere?

Chiltern line

The Great Central Railway lines from London Marylebone had a chequered history. This, the last main line into London (until HS1), was completed in 1899. But it was in effect too late, and all main line services north of Aylesbury (to Nottingham, Sheffield and Manchester) had been withdrawn by 1966 for lack of custom. This left little more than the DMU-worked outer-suburban services.

The Aylesbury service runs over this route, which is largely parallel to the Metropolitan line, with which it merges at Harrow-on-the-Hill (9 miles). The shared line, initially four tracks, but reducing to two at Watford South Junction, continues to Amersham (23½ miles). From this point, the services from Marylebone (only) continue to Aylesbury (37¾ miles), and from 2008 a further 2¾ miles to Aylesbury Vale Parkway.

The lengthy 14½-mile section from Harrow-on-the-Hill to Amersham is owned by London Underground and is thus not part of Network Rail.

The other line operated by Chiltern diverges at Neasden, from which it runs west to join the Great Western's former Birmingham route at Northolt Junction. This line runs parallel with the Central line of London Underground until the latter terminates at West Ruislip (13¼ miles).

The line continues to High Wycombe and Princes Risborough (36 miles). Here the branch to Aylesbury diverges and the main line continues to Bicester North (54¾ miles) and Banbury (68¾ miles). This was latterly the effective terminus of Chiltern services; passengers for Leamington Spa and Birmingham needed to change here.

The local trains on this route from origins such as High Wycombe were diverted from Paddington to Marylebone in 1963 and much of the former Great Western route south of Northolt was singled. For a time a single locomotive-hauled peak service of one train in each direction to Paddington was retained, but there is now a token service only.

In the late 1980s, the whole was in a decidedly run down condition. The fleet of Class 115 high-density diesel units which operated all services dated from 1960 and, regrettably, looked their age. Economies had been carried out; this included the singling of the line between Princes Risborough and Aynho Junction (south of Banbury), with a little used passing loop at Bicester North. This was a considerable constraint on the services that could be operated. The general removal of loops where they had existed at stations such as Denham, Gerrards Cross and Beaconsfield made the running of services in mixed speed bands that much more difficult.

What could or should be done about it all, bearing in mind that the route had not so long previously been the subject of a plan for conversion in part to a road? The decision was taken to use the line from Marylebone to Banbury as the prototype for what was called the Total Route Modernisation programme by the BRB.

Under this, piecemeal improvements were to give way to a Big Bang approach. This would cover all aspects of the railway, thus there would be track renewals with line speeds raised where practicable, semaphore signals would be replaced by colour lights and Automatic Train Protection (ATP) installed. Stations would be rebuilt as necessary to meet modern standards. The whole exercise was to be completed during the years 1988–92.

The Chiltern lines brand had been created by Network SouthEast marketing in 1985. Although originally part of NSE's Thames/Chiltern, it later became the freestanding Chiltern sub-sector.

The Marylebone Integrated Control Centre was installed in a modest sized office at the station, controlling all trains in the Chiltern area. It interfaced with Banbury to the north, while it 'loses' trains to London Underground between Harrow and Amersham.

In 1987, the substantial gap with no station for 18¾ miles between Princes Risborough and Bicester North was plugged by a new station at Haddenham & Thame Parkway. (The earlier Haddenham station, closed in 1963, was about 0.4 miles further south.) Given that this section of line had been singled, it was a reasonably straightforward job to build the platform on the disused track bed. Unfortunately, when double track was restored a decade later in 1998, this meant that a completely new station had to be constructed.

In the 1980s, no Chiltern services ran beyond Banbury, but there was clearly scope for going further, with Birmingham as the most obvious goal. But where could they terminate?

Largely due to the efforts of the West Midlands Passenger Transport Executive (Centro), the long-closed tunnel between Birmingham Moor Street and Birmingham Snow Hill was reopened to a completely recreated Snow Hill station with two island platforms in late 1987. The work included the building of platforms on the through line at Moor Street for the first time. These were replacements for the Moor Street terminal platforms which were then closed, although some of these too would later see a rebirth.

The new trains were known as either Networker Turbos or Chiltern Turbos. These Class 165/0s consisted of 39 units, 28 of which were two-car and 11 three-car, making 89 cars in all. The 75mph Class 165s started arriving from their builders, British Rail Engineering Ltd (BREL) at York, in 1991. Automatic Train Protection could now be implemented. New depot accommodation was constructed to the north of Aylesbury station for the new trains. This was completed in 1990/91.

The same new trains provided the service on the line to Aylesbury, though only stations north of Amersham were those of Chiltern. These, like others elsewhere, underwent substantial uplifts which retained their character, but made them rather fitter for purpose for the late 1990s.

An early success was to see the journey times between Marylebone and Banbury reduced. In that year, an hourly service was provided from Marylebone to High Wycombe, and an hourly semi-fast to Banbury.

Completion of the Class 165 order signalled the end for the Class 115s, all of which had been withdrawn by the end of 1992. By 1993 it was possible to run a Marylebone–Banbury–Birmingham Snow Hill service on a two-hourly headway, which was improved to hourly in 1994.

The next build of the four-car air-conditioned Class 168s introduced a 100mph capability and they were delivered from 1997 in what turned out to be a number of batches. As such, they lie outside the scope of the present discussion on the BR period.

Chiltern Railways became a private sector franchise on 21 July 1996 and the innovations have since continued with a whole series of successive development projects under the Evergreen name. Most recently, a link from south of Bicester North to Bicester Town and the existing railway thence to Oxford Parkway and Oxford has been opened.

What might have happened differently had British Rail continued to exist is pure conjecture.

7

Central London Rail Study, 1989

Of the schemes tested, the least cost-effective appeared to be those which provided new Underground capacity only within the central area. Central London Rail Study, 1989

By the 1980s, much of what had become the Network SouthEast business of British Rail had been electrified, though there were still some noticeable gaps. Many of these were lines omitted from earlier electrification schemes, and may have been at best of marginal benefit.

But there comes a point when the elimination of elderly diesel units and the replacement of their associated depot facilities makes a worthwhile case for electrification. While some more major works such as the routes from Tonbridge to Hastings (1986) and from Bournemouth to Weymouth (1988) were included in their own right, it was also an opportunity to electrify shorter routes such as the complex North London line east of Dalston (third-rail in 1985) and to undertake infill electrification generally.

The classic case of infill work was the Watford–St Albans Abbey branch (1988), though it still had to be served from a depot as far away as Bletchley, later even further at Northampton. Similarly, the line south from East Croydon was electrified between Sanderstead and Oxted in 1986, the section thence to East Grinstead following in 1987. The other rather longer branch south from Oxted (strictly from the junction at Hurst Green) is the truncated route to Lewes. In 1969 it was cut back to terminate at Uckfield, and has remained diesel-unit worked.

A rolling programme of such work brings its own benefits. Staff get used to working with each other; new teams and the necessary equipment do not have to be set up again on each occasion; they just move along from one project to the next. Thus the extension of electrification from Bishops Stortford to Cambridge in 1987 was followed by that from Royston to Cambridge the following year. Both use the same track for the last 2½ miles into Cambridge, and that in itself was a good start for continuing north to Kings Lynn, completed in 1992.

The new three-mile branch to Stansted Airport left the Great Eastern Cambridge main line at Stansted South Junction. This included a single-track tunnelled section; there was also a connection from the branch towards Cambridge. The whole was opened as an electrified railway on 19 March 1991. Other East Anglian branches to be electrified in this period were Wickford–Southminster and Manningtree–Harwich Town, both in 1986.

It wasn't always quite as organised as that, but by the end of the British Rail era in 1995, the only non-electric Network SouthEast services to be found in London termini were those serving Paddington (all), Marylebone (all), Waterloo (for Salisbury and Exeter) and London Bridge (for Uckfield).

Some InterCity services and most freight continued to be worked by diesel traction.

CENTRAL LONDON RAIL STUDY, 1989[36]

In March 1988, the then Secretary of State Paul Channon set up the Central London Rail Study (CLRS). More and more people were coming to work in central London. If that area became too congested, the argument went, nothing else would go right either. What were the demand predictions for the future, and how could they best be met?

The terms of reference included the development of a strategy to meet the anticipated passenger volumes by the turn of the century, making sure that the best use possible was made of the existing assets. What improvements might be financed from fares, and to what extent would an input be needed from external sources?

Peak period traffic had been rising continuously from the early 1980s. In 1983, British Rail was carrying 384,000 peak passengers into London daily, London Underground 323,000. By 1988 that had risen to 468,000 and 415,000

Liverpool Street station has a fine wide and open concourse. Seen here at the end of the morning rush hour on 17 September 2014 at 09:03:42 (precisely), this is the view looking east towards Bishopsgate, with the entrances to the platforms on the left-hand side. ***John Glover***

respectively. Crudely, that represented a 25% rise, but in addition there was another 125,000 passengers in 1983 who transferred from BR to the Underground at or near the London terminals. That 125,000 had become 170,000 by 1987.

That produced decided difficulties for the Underground, but also on Network SouthEast, where growth had been especially prevalent with the longer distance passengers. Continued growth was expected in the future; though in reality it was to ease off for a time due to the recession, only to resume in earnest in the mid-1990s.

Major Upgrading Programme

Congestion is a major problem. Thus if the platform or train are congested, people take longer to board and alight. This results in station stop times for trains becoming longer. That means fewer trains can be run at the very time when they are most needed. Station stop times do vary enormously, from around 15 seconds at a relatively quiet station at off peak to 45 seconds or more at peak at a busy station. Something between one third and one half as much again may be added to the off peak station stop times at peak to aid punctual working, but this will vary according to circumstances.

The CLRS identified five headings under which upgrading proposals might be considered:

- Station capacity – enlarging all passageways, more escalators?
- Service performance – reduce junction conflicts, enforce station stop times?
- More trains – may need resignalling, more depot accommodation?
- Higher capacity trains – new car designs, longer platforms for 12 cars?
- Service restructuring – new service patterns, more trains on each line?

Such a programme, costed at c£1,500 million, was expected to have a significant effect, but on its own it wasn't going to be enough.

On Network SouthEast it wouldn't solve the critical overloads then being experienced between Waterloo and Surbiton or Liverpool Street and Shenfield, while on the Underground Liverpool Street–Chancery Lane (Central), Parsons Green–St James's Park, (District), Clapham Common–Stockwell (Northern), Earl's Court–Knightsbridge (Piccadilly) and Euston–Oxford Circus (Victoria) overcrowding would all remain at more than 20% above the planning standard.

New Lines and Extensions

That then led to the need to construct new lines or extensions to the existing. The Study listed a dozen possibilities, which it then whittled down to a short list. These were:

- The Full Cross scheme consisting of East–West Crossrail plus North–South Crossrail. The latter was described as Euston and/or King's Cross to Victoria with intermediate stations at Tottenham Court Road and Piccadilly Circus There were various possibilities for extension onto the British Rail network at each end.
- East–West Crossrail, plus the Chelsea–Hackney line.

East–West Crossrail as then conceived had one branch only to the east, to Shenfield, but in the west was to proceed via the Metropolitan/Great Central route to (probably) Aylesbury, as well as to Slough and to Heathrow.

Chelsea–Hackney, described later, was then to be a new tube line from Hainault, taking over the Central line branch to Leytonstone, Hackney and one of two alternative routes via King's Cross or Farringdon to Tottenham Court Road, Victoria, Chelsea, Fulham Broadway and the present District line branch to Wimbledon.

The East–South Crossrail proposal (Victoria and Liverpool Street) did not proceed any further.

Of Thameslink Metro (as the study called it), the concept was a railway running from St Albans on the Midland line and Enfield Chase on the Great Northern in the north, then via Elephant & Castle (not via London Bridge) to West Croydon, and to Wimbledon then Sutton (only) in the south.

Despite being the scheme with the best benefit:cost ratio, Thameslink Metro was not selected for inclusion. Not being a new line it had only a limited effect on congestion, but somewhat grudgingly it was acknowledged that it could be considered as a subsidiary option. It will be appreciated that this was a very modest scheme, compared with what eventually emerged.

Interestingly, amongst those routes discarded on the grounds of low benefit:cost ratio was the extension of the Jubilee line (then terminating at Charing Cross) via Ludgate to Liverpool Street and Whitechapel, with an optional extension to Stratford and Ilford. The possibility of a route into or via Docklands was dismissed as not likely to ease central London congestion, while Docklands in those days was still a largely barren landscape.

CENTRAL LONDON RAIL STUDY, PART 2[37]

This was the follow up study of the following year. The preferred lines for construction in the original Central London Rail Study did contain some potential duplication and an early task this time was to narrow the options.

Services between Liverpool Street and Norwich have to share the double-track line from Shenfield to Colchester with other more local services. Driving Van Trailer 9702 is leading as one such service arrives at Chelmsford in October 2005. The signalbox here was in a decidedly unusual position. *John Glover*

A view from the country end of London Bridge sees three trains in this photograph of 25 May 2005. A Class 423 (4-VEP) unit is leaving, while 466018 at the head of a 10-car train is approaching the station. To the right can just be seen a Brighton line train. *John Glover*

First to be discarded was North–South Crossrail, which was found wanting in its ability to attract much in the way of additional passengers and thus hence benefit congestion. Chelsea–Hackney was considerably better in this respect, especially in terms of opening up new markets in the Hackney area and offering shorter routes for some journeys.

How might the Chelsea–Hackney line compare with East–West Crossrail? The impression given was that these two schemes were much of a muchness; neither was outstanding as each had its own good and bad points.

Thus both were rated as feasible. East–West Crossrail would be cheaper; £1,436 million construction cost at mid-1990 prices as against £1,776 million for the Chelsea–Hackney scheme. On the other hand, you got considerably more for your money with Chelsea–Hackney in terms of more tunnelling and more stations.

Benefit:cost ratios (BCRs)* were an unexciting 1.29 for Chelsea–Hackney or 1.32 for East–West Crossrail. Could they be improved? Both schemes scored well in terms of being well loaded in the central area, both did well on relieving congestion in the (different) areas which they would serve.

Or would removing four stations from the planned Chelsea–Hackney scheme improve the result? Only slightly. Adding in a Chingford branch would make it worse, and truncating the line at Victoria put the BCR down to 0.91.

Neither was East–West Crossrail much better. Taking out Bond Street station gave the best result with the BCR up to 1.40; taking out Paddington made no net change, and taking out Tottenham Court Road and Farringdon, replacing them with Holborn, still scored 1.33. Adding in the Chingford branch still gave a low result, but perhaps surprisingly the provision of off-peak services from the LT&S line resulted in a BCR of 1.38.

Such ratios are not everything, though a good result of 2.0 or more provides a rather stronger case for taking a project further. Some matters are not easily quantifiable and these include environmental matters generally, regeneration benefits (mainly inner London with Chelsea–Hackney and regional with East–West Crossrail), or the benefits to London as a whole in modernising its railway system.

In the words of the report, 'there is a reasonably strong argument for East–West Crossrail being the first line to be built and for the Chelsea–Hackney line to be safeguarded for implementation if and when resources permit'.

A Bill for the construction of East–West Crossrail was introduced in 1993, but it was declared 'not proven' in 1994 by the Parliamentary Private Bill Committee set up to consider it. That was the end of Crossrail, for at least the time being.

The Thameslink scheme (no longer Thameslink Metro) did proceed on a rather grander basis, and will be opened in stages from 2018. The present Crossrail scheme's successor, the Elizabeth line, will be opened fully in 2019.

In May 2005, 315803 arrives at Stoke Newington with a Liverpool Street–Enfield Town service. The stations on this line are decidedly close together; Rectory Road (towards Liverpool Street) is less than half a mile away, with Stamford Hill in the other direction about three quarters of a mile and Seven Sisters half a mile beyond that. In an ideal world, at what distance should stations in heavily built up areas be spaced? ***John Glover***

*Benefit Cost Ratios are used by Government as initial Value for Money assessments of proposals to form the economic part of a Transport Business Case. Value for Money is rated as poor if the BCR is less than 1.0, low if between 1.0 and 1.5, medium if 1.5 to 2.0, high between 2.0 and 4.0 and very high if greater than 4.0.

Meanwhile, the Chelsea–Hackney line was safeguarded but progressed no further. It may yet come to pass in a new guise as Crossrail 2. This could also incorporate some aspects of the discarded North–South Crossrail (Victoria–King's Cross) proposals.

All are further described later, but it is now time to consider the East London Rail Study.

EAST LONDON RAIL STUDY[38]

On 23 January 1989 it was announced by the Secretary of State in Parliament that a study was to be carried out 'to examine the best options for improving rail access from central London to Docklands and East Thameside'. This was with a view to depositing a Bill in November 1989.

'Any new line should be paid for by those who benefit, including passengers, property developers and landowners, with government only contributing if such income was insufficient to make the project viable, given benefits to non-users such as road congestion relief.'

The strategic role of extending the Docklands effect required the railway to be rapid (ie relatively few stations located at the major development points or interchanges), to portray a modern image in terms of its technology, comfort and appearance, and to connect effectively with London's suburban and Underground networks. It would also need to be compatible with the new line proposals of the Central London Rail Study.

It might be added that in 1988 developers Olympia & York had progressed to Private Bill stage a proposal for a privately financed and completely underground railway from Waterloo to Canary Wharf. The key issues of the East London Rail Study were seen as:

- Alignment to be followed?
- An independent railway?
- Use of high technology?
- Economic and financial viability?
- Feasibility?

Alternative alignments

The map shows the main alternatives put forward by the consultants. Taking as read the need to connect to the existing Jubilee line, the alternatives were to pursue the more northerly route from Charing Cross via the City to London Bridge, or to build a new southerly route from Green Park to Westminster and Waterloo to the same point. From London Bridge the line would run to Canary Wharf, thence either north or south of the Thames (both with a station) and thence via either alignment towards Canning Town and Stratford, or to Prince Regent and Woolwich. The latter route could, if required, be extended to Thamesmead.

If Waterloo was a major potential generator of traffic, the map shows that the existing Jubilee line, which already extended most of the way to Aldwych in the over-run tunnels, would experience severe curvature in order to call also at Waterloo. That would make serving Westminster even more difficult, and might there not be some benefit in having a station there?

Further east, the alignment to Stratford had major benefits in terms of interchange with the District but also the London, Tilbury & Southend lines at West Ham, and with a large selection of other routes at Stratford (Great Eastern main line and Lea Valley, Elizabeth line, DLR to Poplar and to Stratford International, London Underground Central line and the North London line of London Overground).

It was at this stage possible to choose both the extension to Stratford and that to Woolwich/Thamesmead, with trains on the common section running (say) alternately to both.

The Stratford route was that eventually chosen, with the south Thames alternative providing a station at North Greenwich. Other complementary links from this area towards Woolwich were later to be provided by extensions of the DLR and then the Abbey Wood arm of the Elizabeth line.

East London Rail Study, Alternative Alignments, Jubilee Line Extension.

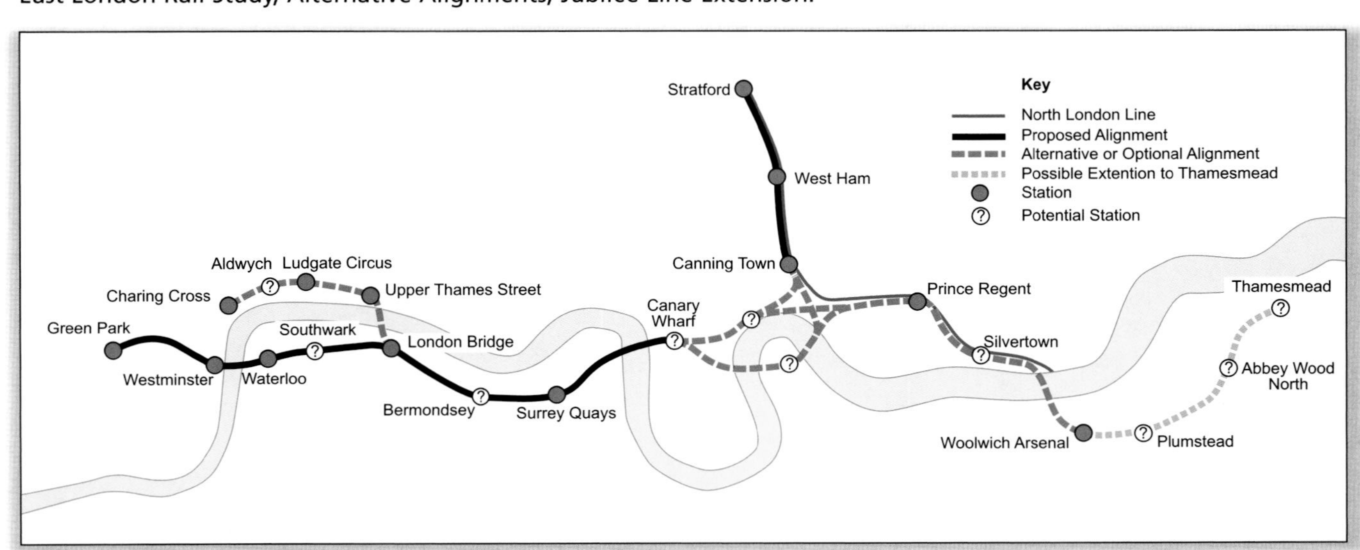

Beyond the southern end of Stratford Jubilee line station, a train from Stanmore is approaching the terminus. To the left is the route to Stratford Market depot, while on the right and behind a very stout fence are the lines used then by the North Woolwich branch of National Rail and now by the DLR Stratford International service from Canning Town. ***John Glover***

Engineering

All options under consideration were feasible in engineering terms. Both of the eastern extensions could by arrangement make some use of the existing surface track beds used then by the Stratford–North Woolwich branch. That to Stratford was at one time four-tracked and the vacant double-track bed could probably be used.

The Woolwich option would require a new under-river tunnel; if proceeded with, the extension thence to Thamesmead would be largely underground.

While it might be possible for the new service to inter-run with the existing BR services, 'it is not clear whether this was either feasible or desirable'.

A comprehensive two-level interchange for all rail services, including also a bus station, could be built at Canning Town.

Operations

The new line could be a continuation of the Jubilee line or a physically independent railway; either was possible.

A depot site would be required and this could be at Stratford (as later constructed), Plumstead or Silvertown. If this were to be an extension of the Jubilee line, use could also be made of the facilities at Neasden.

An early warning was given of the likely demise of the existing Green Park–Charing Cross service if the via Waterloo version was selected.

Independence

Should it be an independent railway, physically separate from other lines but giving operational and management independence, or not?

Independence would allow innovation in design standards and the introduction of larger and more comfortable trains which might be considered attractive, said the report, carefully.

On the other hand:

- an interchange and terminal station would need to be built at additional capital cost at the western end of the line;

A short-lived Underground design was the 1983 stock built for the Jubilee line. Here a six-car train approaches West Hampstead on a southbound working on 28 December 1996; the flyover in the background takes this railway over the North London line. In the centre is a turnback siding for trains proceeding no further north than West Hampstead. *John Glover*

- it would not be possible to use LUL's existing depot facilities;
- passenger benefits would suffer if interchange was essential for many journeys, reducing both patronage and revenues; and
- it would considerably complicate the institutional issues that needed to be resolved, and thus delay the lodging of a Bill to enable construction.

The report thus favoured a running extension of the Jubilee line.

Technology

Wisely, the report firmly recommended that technology should not be pursued for its own sake and that only those technologies which were already proven and in similar revenue service should be considered.

More precisely, the new railway should have the capacity to carry the forecast traffic, with a margin to spare (or at least 25,000 persons per hour, per direction). The trains needed to be compatible in size with the Jubilee line tunnels of 3.85m in diameter, train and platform lengths should also be similar (120m and 140m respectively), and that the signalling should provide for a 105-second headway (34–35 trains per hour). All this would be necessary to provide the speed, service reliability and capacity for the numbers anticipated and to avoid overcrowding.

Larger trains could be provided if greater diameter tunnels were built, resulting in a penalty of 10% additional civil engineering costs, This would have obvious further implications elsewhere, for instance if the line were to be extended from Green Park to Paddington (and thence perhaps to Heathrow?) Nevertheless, it was felt that such options should be further evaluated.

Cost

There was little to choose between the capital costs of around £570 million (1988 prices) of the two options at the western end, but the route to Woolwich at £445 million was significantly more expensive than the

These eight-car 'Juniper' sets were built by Alstom in 1999/2000 for the Gatwick Express service, running non-stop to and from London Victoria. Here unit No 460008 (last two numbers only carried) passes Clapham Junction on a down working on 4 July 2005. ***John Glover***

Stratford option at £350 million. The extension from Woolwich to Thamesmead would cost a further £125 million. Making use of the Stratford–North Woolwich line tracks where possible for either or both routes would be a useful economy.

In June 1988, the Acton Town–South Ealing test track of London Underground was host to the ABB vehicles, which were to be chosen for the 1992 Central line stock replacement programme. A total of three sets of trains (red, green and blue) were produced in 1986 by different manufacturers, for evaluation. This was the design chosen, though unfortunately the production versions currently have the lowest reliability of any London Underground passenger trains. ***John Glover***

Impact on Traffic

The line would have two main sets of beneficiaries. Those travelling to work in Docklands, including the Isle of Dogs, would benefit directly, while it would also afford some congestion relief on the existing lines of the Underground and National Railways. Between central London and Canary Wharf, the result would be consistently high traffic levels in both directions.

The down main platform at Finsbury Park is unusually crowded due to services being severely restricted as a result of a fire near King's Cross Power Signal Box which caused it to be evacuated. Passengers were waiting to be taken to Peterborough to gain their main line trains there. Note how they are standing behind the yellow line on the platform. *John Glover*

Development impact

The clear preference of the development community was for the Waterloo alignment, principally because of the strategic importance of Waterloo as a major commuter terminal, with lesser support for the Stratford option in the east. This though had the advantage of offering a high-capacity link to the Isle of Dogs.

The East London Rail Study provided the necessary impetus for the Jubilee line extension (Green Park to Stratford) to be built, and construction started in 1993. The railway opened in sections during 1999, completed on 22 December. That was just in time for the Prime Minister and others to be conveyed to The Dome at North Greenwich for the millennium celebrations.

The Charing Cross branch closed on 19 November 1999.

Importantly, this new railway was able to demonstrate to everybody the effectiveness of good quality rail connections.

8

Crossrail Gets Close

We were disappointed by the Private Bill Committee's decision not to find the preamble to the Crossrail Bill proved, a sentiment shared on both sides of the House.
Steve Norris, Minister for Transport in London, House of Commons, 20 June 1994

The carrying out of a new major railway infrastructure project used to need the promoters to submit a Private Bill that in due course would become an Act of Parliament. That was the case with the Crossrail project, discussed over many years with various degrees of enthusiasm by all and sundry. By the end of the 1980s, it looked as if this would soon become a reality.

The first use of the Crossrail name (with or without a capital R in the middle) is to be found in the London Rail Study of 1974. Encouraged by the later recommendations of the Central London Rail Study of 1989, the Government gave Network SouthEast and London Underground the go ahead for in 1990. This was a £3 billion project with a five-year construction period, according to the Strategic Rail Authority.

Crossrail route

As a result, the two organisations deposited a joint Bill in 1993 to authorise the construction of a new Crossrail link. The Explanatory Memorandum stated: 'This Bill provides for:

> the construction of a new underground railway commencing west of Paddington Station and terminating east of Liverpool Street Station and connecting, on either side, with existing railways of the Board;
>
> the construction of a new railway on the Thames Valley railway at Old Oak Common to connect the new underground railway with the Metropolitan and Chiltern lines; and

The Crossrail Route, Shenfield, Reading and Aylesbury, 1994.

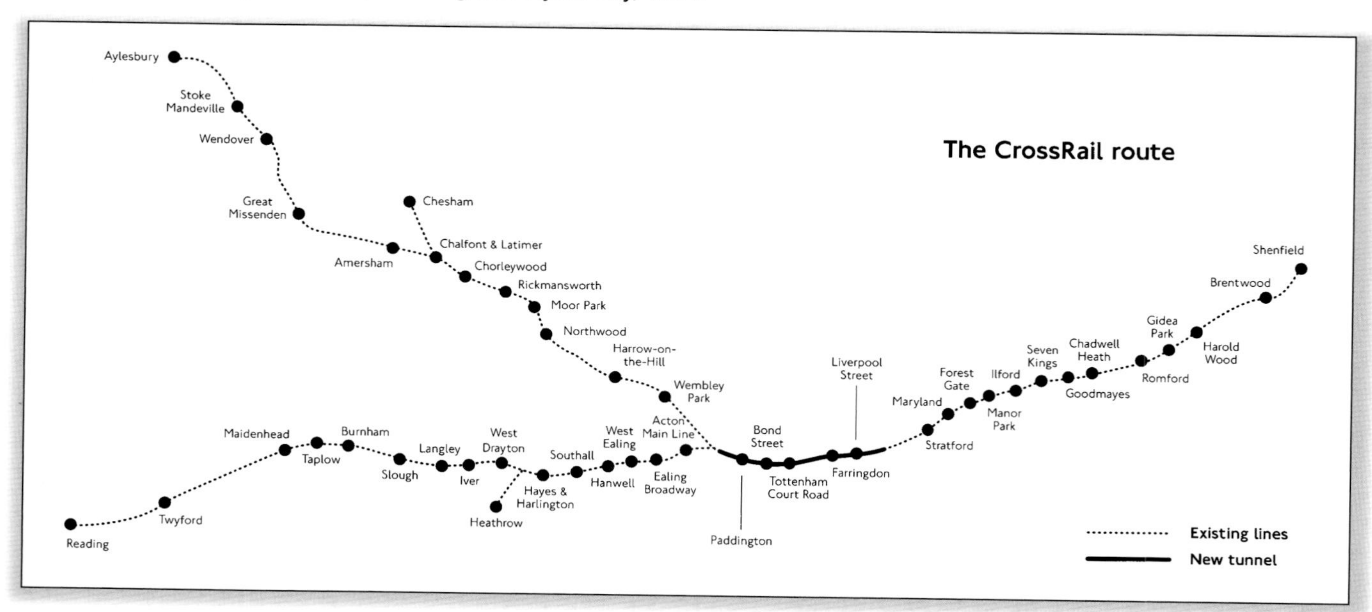

> the construction of a further connection at Hayes on the Thames Valley railway with the proposed rail link to Heathrow Airport authorised by the Heathrow Express Railway Act 1991 for service using the new underground railway.'

To this was added other works on the lines of route.

The aim was to relieve congestion on existing services by linking Reading and Aylesbury in the west with Shenfield in the east. Crossrail would construct a new line on a new alignment through central London. This would require six miles of new tunnelling between Royal Oak and Bethnal Green. At each end, Crossrail would use existing infrastructure wherever possible.

West of Royal Oak, the connection to the lines from Marylebone would be effected by a new link to the freight only Midland Dudding Hill route in the vicinity of Old Oak Common. This would be followed to Neasden Junction, where the link already existed, though the creation of junction arrangements here with the minimum of conflict would have been quite a challenge.

Station sites in the central area were chosen to provide good opportunities for interchange with the Underground and with British Rail. Particularly in the promoters' sights were the very busy sections of the Central line through the City of London and the Shenfield services to Liverpool Street. The locations with new Crossrail platforms and ticket halls were to be Paddington, Bond Street, Tottenham Court Road, Farringdon and Liverpool Street/Moorgate (with exits to both stations).

The central London stations would all need major engineering works. Thus at Liverpool Street/Moorgate large-scale reconstruction of Liverpool Street main line station was under way; a new underground alignment would need to avoid this and certainly London Underground's subsurface and Central lines. The now defunct Post Office Railway might need to be diverted.

In between here and Moorgate was Finsbury Circus, with its listed buildings, and there were other sensitive sites. At Moorgate, the subsurface lines were again an obstruction, plus the City branch of the Northern line and the Great Northern electrics route to Finsbury Park.

Similar constraints were apparent elsewhere.

Services would be operated by new Class 341 trains, a development of the Networkers then in production for South Eastern services as Class 465/466. It was envisaged that Crossrail would operate for 20 hours per day and during the peak at 24tph in each direction. Sample times given were Aylesbury to Paddington reduced from 64 minutes to 51 minutes, West Drayton to Liverpool Street down from 50 minutes to 26 minutes, Manor Park to Tottenham Court Road 32 minutes to 17 minutes and Bond Street to Farringdon 17 minutes to 5 minutes. It was carefully mentioned that not all trains would operate over the entire route.

The Chesham branch and the as yet unbuilt line to Heathrow were shown on the mapping, without commitment.

Crossrail was said to be a vital new rail link for London and the South East.

The route to Aylesbury

This proposed section of the original Crossrail project north of Harrow-on-the-Hill created a lot of problems. For a start, the section of line from Harrow-on-the-Hill to Amersham was owned by London Underground and electrified at fourth-rail DC. It was also to be used by Crossrail.

What electrification system should be adopted? It went without saying that the main part of Crossrail would be at standard 25kV AC overhead, but what about this extension? The following outlines the choices available:

- Extend the 25kV AC over the two fast tracks only from Harrow-on-the-Hill to Watford South

Short two-car trains can look a little lost in platforms of this length. This is Chorleywood on 14 September 2008 with a Chiltern Railways train from Aylesbury to Marylebone arriving. It is in the charge of unit 165006. This is on the section operated by London Underground, as the roundel on the station platform suggests. *John Glover*

Junction (south of Rickmansworth where the four-track section gives way to two tracks and the Watford branch leaves the Metropolitan main line), thence all the way to Aylesbury. The fourth-rail would remain to Amersham (and to Chesham) for Metropolitan line services. This would be costly, with quite a bit of duplication.

- Or the fourth-rail could be removed north of Harrow-on-the-Hill other than on the slow lines to Watford (Metropolitan). That would require some numbers of passengers, eg those from Northwood to Rickmansworth, to change trains, and Crossrail would have to re-electrify and operate the Chesham branch.
- Extend the 25kV AC only as far as Watford South Junction, with Crossrail taking ownership of the two fast line tracks and removing the fourth-rail over this section. Crossrail would use dual voltage units capable of accommodating the fourth-rail DC electrification thence to Amersham. Beyond Amersham the fourth-rail (or even conceivably third-rail) could be extended the 14 miles to Aylesbury, or the 25kV AC system could be installed instead.
- Extend the 25kV AC only as far as Harrow-on-the-Hill, thence using the DC fourth-rail to Amersham, with a choice as to what happened beyond as outlined above.
- Any sections of dual electrification systems would result in questions of responsibility for who owned what, who had what rights of use, and who was responsible for operation and maintenance. As matters stood (and still stand), the section from Harrow-on-the-Hill through to Amersham is owned, operated and signalled by London Underground. Trains from Marylebone are thus 'lost' to the Network Rail signalling system until they reappear miraculously at a location which, it is understood, should be known as Weedonhill Wood. This is a mile or so beyond Amersham.
- This would be coupled with Health & Safety considerations of those whose jobs took them on and about the track and their likely lack of familiarity with both AC and DC systems. It was at least possible that the four tracks from Harrow to Watford South Junction would need to be separated by a fence down the middle. This would mean costly formation widening.

The whole was complicated by the services that would be run, assuming that Crossrail was built. Would there be any future need for the Underground to serve destinations north of Harrow-on-the Hill other than on the slow lines to Watford? Would additional platforms be built on the fast lines for (especially) Pinner or Northwood? (Moor Park station already had them.) But the more stops that might be added, the more that journey times would be extended, to the extent that eventually more trains would be needed to offer a given service frequency. Or should Rickmansworth be the Underground's northern terminus?

- Was there any likelihood of the introduction of direct services from Aylesbury/Amersham to Watford (Metropolitan) (or Watford Junction as might become the branch destination at some time in the future?)
- Rolling stock issues were interlinked. The Underground's A stock Metropolitan trains of the early 1960s were approaching renewal, but the transfer of some services to Crossrail would make a noticeable difference to the quantity needed of what would emerge eventually as London Underground's S stock.
- Much the same question would have to be asked for the quantity of Crossrail trains and whether or not dual voltage versions were required.

It will be evident that there is quite a range of possible answers to the questions posed above concerning what many might think to be a relatively simple piece of railway.

That perhaps only emphasises that operations and maintenance people need to be involved from the start. Standards can change over time, as can legislation. How does one deal with such issues?

Yet, though there are answers, the Private Bill was rejected in 1994 by the House of Commons Committee set up to consider it. Reasons for rejection are not given, but a post-mortem inquiry by the industry did suggest that the railway promoters were not sufficiently single minded in putting their proposals forward. Systems of electrification are important and need to be grasped, but they are not the issues that usually excite Members of Parliament.

Their view, perhaps, was that such technical matters are for the industry to resolve; MPs are more interested in the development potential, user benefits and the financial results of large scale schemes of this sort.

There were perhaps also nagging fears that some relative decline following the strong economic (and passenger) growth of the late 1980s would render Crossrail redundant. Thus, for the Great Eastern corridor to Shenfield: 'Even the basic Crossrail service implies a doubling of patronage. Given the built up nature of the terrain, it is difficult to imagine where such numbers will come from'.

Or should other routes such as the London, Tilbury & Southend line in the east or Northampton in the west be considered for connection to the core Crossrail operation? Was Crossrail really a Metro-type urban operation, or a suburban railway with rather different characteristics?

Such concerns would resurface in relation to Thameslink service provision.

Effectively, this was the end of the proposed Crossrail branch to Aylesbury over the Underground and the lines now used by Chiltern Railways. Crossrail itself was to be revived some years hence, but in a rather different form.

A Eurostar Three Capitals Class 373 set No 3229 brings up the rear of a departure from Waterloo on 4 July 1999. After a decade of virtually no use, these platforms are now being brought back to life for domestic services, International operations having been moved to London St Pancras International (to give it its full name) in 2007. *John Glover*

INTERNATIONAL LINKS

There was also the international dimension. The Channel Tunnel Rail Link, later known as High Speed 1 (HS1), might in its early days have had a terminus in the White City area. Later, it was to have served a low-level station under King's Cross, positioned so that it would be ideally placed to enable the line to be extended later to the west, north and east of Britain.

Under these conditions, the provision of through services between the continent and the regions in Britain would have been reasonably straightforward in operational terms. In reality, there were very considerable problems, given the requirements of HM Customs and that of the Immigration service. These meant that the use of international trains for domestic journeys wholly within

This is Stratford International station from the footbridge looking towards St Pancras in 2011. The platforms consist, from left to right, of No 1 (out of sight) for the up International line, the up CTRL line, the up domestic No 2, the line rising which forms the link to Temple Mills depot, the down domestic No 3, the down CTRL and the down International Platform 4. *John Glover*

Commuter traffic on what was the Southern Region of British Railways was never particularly speedy and a train from Dover Priory to Charing Cross would take, typically, almost 2 hours for the journey. Enter HS1 and services to St Pancras come down to 1hr 5min. Southeastern were thus keen to publicise their six-car dual-voltage Class 395 'Javelin' EMUs with 140mph capability, of which 29 were built from 2006 for use on this route, but also services to Stratford for the 2012 London Games. *John Glover*

Britain could not be permitted. The resulting inability to carry passengers (and collect fares from them) for journeys such as Edinburgh to Newcastle would be a severe setback to the economics of such operations.

The King's Cross low-level station proposal did not happen and trains instead served newly created platforms at Waterloo International. But St Pancras was to be the destination of HS1, so that trains from the Channel Tunnel now terminate in dead end platforms at London St Pancras International, facing south. These platforms (5-10) were opened in 2007, replacing those at Waterloo International.

Also terminating in a separate part of St Pancras (Platforms 11-13) are the domestic HS1 services operated by SouthEastern, which originate from various stations in Kent. (For the sake of completeness, East Midlands Trains use Platforms 1–4 and the Thameslink low level platforms are A and B).

The provision of international services from parts of Britain beyond London was shelved. This was particularly relevant in connection with the decision that High Speed 2 services (from Birmingham and later from Manchester and Leeds) would terminate in an enlarged Euston.

Euston and St Pancras stations are approximately 600 metres apart. Various schemes to make transfer between them easier than walking along the Euston Road have surfaced from time to time; the latest variant is the proposed Crossrail 2 scheme, the double-ended station of which would give access from its underground platforms to both stations.

TRANSPORT STRATEGY FOR LONDON 1996

By mid-1996 rail privatisation was well under way and the Department for Transport felt it was time to issue a large document: A Transport Strategy for London.

Several objectives were identified, starting with the promotion of international transport links. Thus a domestic and (so far unused) international station would be built at Stratford, as part of the Channel Tunnel Rail Link (now HS1). A fast through connection to the West Coast main line would put Birmingham within four hours of Paris (through services later abandoned). Kent commuters would benefit from new services (achieved).

Another objective was enhancing services by rail and Underground. This was mainly an explanation of how the privatised railway worked. On the Underground, while the shape of the investment programme was determined by the management and not the Government, the latter did have a number of roles given the abolition of the GLC a decade earlier:

- monitoring the Underground's safety performance (in the wake of the disastrous King's Cross fire of 1987)
- determining the level of financial support
- setting the investment appraisal criteria, the financial and the quality of service objectives, and
- working with London Underground to identify opportunities for exploiting private finance'.

Also desirable was the promotion of greater use of less polluting forms of transport. Rail and Underground usually scored well, were generally quick, but not always as comfortable or reliable.

Plugging major gaps in the road and rail networks. Helpfully, the London Pride Partnership set out in their Transport First Initiative 1996–2010 the then expected opening dates of what were identified in the Transport Strategy as the three priority rail schemes. A sorry tale it tells.

First was Thameslink 2000, which was assessed as being completed in 2002, though the reality will be the end of 2019. Crossrail 1 was thought likely to be finished in 2005, though the actual will not now be until December 2019. Completion of the Chelsea–Hackney line was then likely to be in 2010, but the continued slippage down the priority list was to result in changes of route, termini and name. It is now Crossrail 2, with completion in the 2030s at the very earliest.

London Pride did describe the timescale as 'ambitious but achievable', so their conclusion was half right.

Regeneration was also an important part of the Government's transport strategy, with four areas identified specifically. These were:

- The Thames Gateway covering both sides of the Thames, broadly from Stratford to Ebbsfleet, both stations on HS1.
- The southern end of the Lea Valley corridor, though Lea Valley rail improvement was not on the then agenda.
- The Wandle Valley (Croydon–Wimbledon corridor), in which due credit was given to the forthcoming Croydon Tramlink.
- West London, particularly the Park Royal area, which was to see developments on the West London line. Much later, the Old Oak Common site would become a major centre of railway activity.

HEATHROW EXPRESS ESTABLISHED

The second airport rail link, when it came, was from Paddington with the (then) British Airports Authority owned Heathrow Express Railway. Leaving the Great Western main line west of Hayes & Harlington, the new privately financed branch from Airport Junction to Heathrow Airport Terminals 1, 2, 3 and then Terminal 4 opened on 25 May 1998. The later branch from Terminals 1, 2, 3 to the T5 station, which is shared with the Underground but on separate tracks, opened for both operators on 27 March 2008.

Other than the main line junction area, all of the rest of this development is in tunnel. Associated with this was the electrification of the main line from Paddington; it was served by Heathrow Express, running non-stop to what is now Terminals 2, 3 at 15-minute headways.

In conjunction with Great Western Railway, a Heathrow Connect service is also operated; this calls intermediately at Ealing Broadway and stations to Hayes & Harlington. The time to Terminals 2, 3 at 32 minutes is roundly twice the Heathrow Express time.

Crossrail will assist rail access to Heathrow, particularly as it is a direct means of reaching many central London destinations to the east of Paddington.

A LONDON HUB?

Twenty years after the British Railways Board put forward their ideas for a London hub, the concept was resurrected in a form less related to long-distance traffic. This was the subject of a 2000 thesis by Dr Peter Gordon; a summary of the findings is included here, with his kind permission[39].

By this time, the original low capacity Thameslink scheme between the Midland and Brighton lines and routed via Blackfriars was operational, though its further development was then at best uncertain.

As discussed, London has a number of railway terminals scattered about the central area, but they are very much around the edge. Charing Cross is perhaps the only one that is truly in the heart of the capital.

London presently has 12 main line passenger termini; in order of their initial opening these are:

London Bridge	1836
Euston	1837
Paddington	1838
Fenchurch Street	1841
Waterloo	1848
King's Cross	1852
Victoria	1860
Cannon Street	1866
St Pancras	1868
Liverpool Street	1874
Blackfriars	1886
Marylebone	1899

There were in addition Broad Street and Holborn Viaduct, closed in 1986 and 1990 respectively. Moorgate (GN&C) was opened in 1904, but did not become a terminus for the National Rail system until 1976.

That much is history, but we have now been living with something approaching the present situation for a century or more. Is it the best we can do, or are there opportunities to do better? What alternatives, if any, might be available? Is the concept of a rail hub for Britain a practical possibility and, if so, could it be made to work?

The Rail Hub benefits

Rail's share of the total transport market in Britain is very low at about 6% of passenger kilometres, even if London Underground is included. This is less than in many other European countries and under half that of Switzerland. However, while rail in Britain is strong in certain corridors, its use in others is almost non-existent.

Research has revealed that while passengers may be unhappy with service quality, the actual reason that they don't travel more is that the service provision on the journey they wish to make is not as convenient as it might

One of the distinctive Heathrow Express units, No 332014 stands at London Paddington station awaiting departure. The fleet consists of 14 trains, all built as 23m four-car units in 1997–98; five of them had an Open Second added in 2002 to make them five-car units. ***John Glover***

be. What amounts to a convenient or inconvenient journey is subjective, but the need to transfer between London termini, usually by Underground, is to many people a major disincentive.

The nearest to a rail hub in Britain at present is Birmingham New Street. This station was once expected to absorb virtually all rail services in the Birmingham area, though against early expectations Birmingham Moor Street was retained. Birmingham Snow Hill, once completely demolished and turned into a large car park, has since been recreated.

Could a means of producing a single rail hub in London to counteract this problem of having to change between termini by Underground or taxi be devised, and if it could, would it stimulate more traffic?

What would this entail and how successful might it be? Under what circumstances might such a large scale project be justified, financially or otherwise?

The above summarises the objectives of Gordon's thesis. This used National Travel Survey data and industry information such as that from CAPRI (Computer Analysis of Passenger Revenue Information) and the Passenger Demand Forecasting Handbook.

On-train surveys were undertaken on the two National Rail services which ran on a north–south trajectory each side of the River Thames. What became known as Thameslink was first established between Bedford, Farringdon, London Bridge and Brighton in 1988, with the Rugby, Kensington Olympia and Gatwick Airport service following in 1997. The latter made use of the West London Line and thus did not really serve central London. Both groups of services have changed substantially in more recent years.

As Gordon puts it, 'making prospective passengers "think rail" is a challenging task with potentially exciting rewards'.

The hub concept

The hub concept is seen in many other forms of transport, especially air. Thus Heathrow is a major hub airport from which flights go in all directions. It is the prime airport for the major traffic generator of London, but as much as 30% of its passenger throughput is changing there from one flight to another. This group of people has no interest in London as such, nor in many cases do they have a need to leave the airport complex. The wide choice of onward flights which need a single change only (albeit not necessarily from the same terminal) can make travel via Heathrow an attractive proposition.

The second flight may require some waiting about, even to the need to spend a night in a hotel, but so much depends on service frequency. The more often the services run, the less that any waiting time becomes a problem. A similar situation can apply to coach travel via Victoria Coach Station.

The 16:33 Heathrow Connect service from Paddington to Heathrow Airport Terminals 2, 3 is formed of 360202, seen here leaving Hayes & Harlington on 12 April 2016. ***John Glover***

On railway networks, Swiss Federal Railways (SBB) have taken the concept one stage further. In Switzerland the Taktfahrplan principle has established a number of hubs throughout the country, between each of which the journey time is similar. Trains are timed to arrive at such hubs at (say) 55–59 minutes to the hour, and depart at 0–5 minutes past the hour. The same thing might then happen again on the half hour and, subject to traffic requirements, at 15 and 45 minutes past the hour as well.

Thus the Zurich Hauptbahnhof terminus can cope with the arrival of 10 trains during a 10-minute time period and their subsequent despatch, but the ability of the infrastructure to accommodate the level of service is clearly an important consideration.

That way the maximum number of rail connections can be made by passengers easily and with a high degree of certainty, and it might be mentioned that this approach extends to connecting bus and ferry services as well. There are however downsides; these are the length of time for which trains may spend stationary in such hubs, which is essentially unproductive time for them and their crews, and the way in which stations can change from being very busy to having a period during which very little happens. It can also be difficult to secure running times between adjacent hub stations that vary little for all the services concerned.

It also puts considerable pressures on operators who wish to change the service pattern. Even inserting an extra stop into one service might destroy a train's ability to reach the next hub point in the time required. That might mean that another stop has to be taken out. Might this have the undesirable effect of making the service operated unresponsive to market needs as they change over time?

Nevertheless, this arrangement makes travel by public transport very straightforward and popular for regular users and visitors alike.

London

Railways are constrained by the tracks that they use. Limited capacity in the London area means that it can be difficult to flight trains, particularly where there are only two running lines. Flighting is the grouping together in the timetable of trains with similar operational characteristics and stopping patterns, to make the best use of the track capacity available. It largely avoids the problem of fast trains catching up slow trains and leaving a widening gap behind them, but it may not suit customer needs.

It might be hoped that long-distance services would depart at least every 30 minutes, with suburban services say every 15 minutes, thus keeping the average waiting times down.

This would represent a fairly small proportion of the journey time and the ambience of the interchange station would be important. Airport-like facilities would decrease the perceived transfer time. Walking time would have to be added and these might be significant, especially for the less able.

A railway hub would be a concentration point for North-South services across London, and perhaps East–West ones as well. Gordon suggests that the most suitable hub location would be King's Cross. This is about the most accessible rail location in London and Gordon postulated the construction of a number of new lines in tunnel which could feed into and out of it. Some of what was suggested is no longer possible given the construction of Thameslink and Crossrail 1, while other uses have been found for the former railway lands north of King's Cross station.

To give an idea of the proposals, these bore a considerable similarity to those outlined in the BRB paper of 1980 discussed above, though differing in that Gordon's target was the Network SouthEast type passenger rather that those using the truly long-distance services. A network with a radius of around 80 miles from central London was seen as the most productive market. Effectively this includes all coastal areas south of the Thames and as far west as Southampton.

It was envisaged that InterCity service to and from places such as Bristol, Birmingham, Manchester, Leeds and Newcastle would continue to run as now into their present terminals. In any event, trains with high seating capacity and minimal numbers of doors are not very suitable for use on tunnelled urban railways operating at high frequencies.

What benefits might such an approach bring in terms of traffic generation? While the rail market share is high for journeys to and from central London at around 65%, it is far lower for journeys beyond London. Thus the proportion of journeys made by rail between Kent and Buckinghamshire was only around 4%.

But does it have to be so? Where there was a through rail service as between Bedford and Brighton, the number of journeys per head of population could be eight times as high as where the only alternative was to make a change between two London termini.

While some of this large increase would reflect the fact that Croydon, Gatwick Airport and Brighton are major traffic attractors in their own right, it seemed to bear out the research that showed that through journeys increased by up to a multiple of six when Thameslink was introduced originally.

How long would the journey take? The comparator is the concept of generalised time, which turns the actual time taken for an activity into a measure of how it is perceived by the person concerned. Thus for a rail passenger who wants to get somewhere, the time spent travelling is counted as the actual time well spent.

However, waiting on platforms for trains, interchanging and walking around stations, and also getting to and from the trip origins/destinations is all counted as unproductive time. The time taken is charged to the total journey at twice its actual level. Thus a four-minute wait on a station platform is counted as eight minutes, whereas a four minute journey on a train is still counted as four minutes. A further penalty of 20 minutes is added with cross-London journeys where a change of location as well as main line train is needed. This reflects the general frustration and effort involved.

The research gives a worked example of a journey between Redhill and High Wycombe, with the following results:

Redhill to High Wycombe

Present total actual time	128.3 mins
Generalised journey time (as perceived)	187.5 mins
Future total actual time with rail hub	115.5 mins
Generalised journey time (as perceived)	144.5 mins

The generalised journey time is thus reduced by 43 minutes, or by 23%. In turn, that might be expected to result in an increase in passenger demand of around 30%.

Given the large and continuing rise in passenger numbers across the rail system in recent years, further increases of this magnitude in addition to the pressures of an expanding London population are quite daunting. On the other hand, if the benefits of the railway system are not being exploited as well as they might be, that itself is a cause of concern.

Times have moved on since Gordon's research was undertaken, with Thameslink and Crossrail 1 fulfilling some types of cross-London operation and on a considerably larger scale than has been experienced in the past. It will be interesting to see how the new opportunities they offer are taken up by the system users.

The distance travelled per head by rail in Switzerland is almost three times that of Britain, though the country lacks a major city such as London which encourages the use of rail. It is clear that quite a bit more can be done to make the rail network attractive. Making prospective passengers 'think rail' is a challenging task with potentially exciting rewards.

EAST–WEST RAIL

In 2000, at the request of the Deputy Prime Minister John Prescott, the Shadow Strategic Rail Authority conducted a review of rail traffic on the East–West axis across London. This was achieved with help from Transport for London, Railtrack and London Underground but not, it would seem, from any Train Operating Company.

Their Report[40] re-trod familiar ground, but it recommended the construction of the deep-level line between Paddington and Liverpool Street as the top priority, together with options for serving Heathrow Airport. Perhaps deliberately, no mention was made of the ultimate termini; enigmatically the map merely showed arrows to Slough, Amersham, Shenfield and Tilbury. Project definition was yet to come.

The Report did however set out the principles that the parties agreed should form the basis of evaluating schemes for new lines in London. These were:

- Rail must be the vital part of a London-wide,

comprehensive and integrated public transport service.

- Individual services should operate on dedicated lines running to similar service patterns to give the highest possible throughput.
- There should be a clear hierarchy that distinguishes between, for example, local, regional and national services. Each level of service should have a unique visual identity.
- Dedicated freight routes are vital if the expected growth in rail freight is to take place.
- Local services should have simplified service patterns that should stop at all stations and offer 'turn up and go' frequencies.
- There should ideally be no more than three branches at each end of individual services, with grade separation at the principal junctions.
- High quality interchange with all relevant public transport modes is required.
- Destinations should be planned to avoid passengers accumulating on tunnel platforms.

'These principles will lead to improved operational efficiency of the system and provide a more attractive and efficient public transport network for passengers' was their rather smug conclusion. Readers may wish to consider the various schemes discussed in this book against these criteria.

WHO RUNS WHAT?

Transport for London (TfL) is a statutory body created under the Greater London Authority (GLA) Act 1999, which gives the Mayor a general duty to promote and encourage safe, integrated, efficient and economic transport facilities and services to, from and within London.

TfL's role is to implement the Mayor's transport strategy and to manage services for which the Mayor is responsible. Currently there are 8.4 million people living in the capital; this is expected to become 10 million in the 2030s.

Transport for London's strategy document of July 2001 set out the plans for a London Metro service. This was to consist of services styled, branded and marketed as an urban Metro, the title of which chosen later was to be London Overground. These services were to have a 'turn up and go' frequency, with a target gap between trains of not more than every 10 minutes.

The services would be integrated with the Underground and buses, as would the fares and ticketing.

These London Metro services would meet agreed standards and improved levels of passenger facilities. That would include the standards of passenger information, and the operation would progressively be made accessible to all with defined security criteria.

The core would be a London orbital network which included the Gospel Oak to Barking line, though not at this stage the Euston to Watford DC lines.

London Underground Ltd. remained a London Regional Transport company for the time being. Following the passage of the Railways & Transport Safety Bill which received Royal Assent on 10 July 2003, London Underground became a subsidiary of TfL. The transfer took place on 15 July 2003.

London Underground is the principal rail operation. In the 2016/17 year the Underground carried 1,379 million people, up 2.2% from the 1,349 million in 2015/16. That is a multiple of 2.7 on the mere 498 million journeys made in 1982. The system is larger, yes, but not that much so; no wonder the availability of capacity has become a major problem.

Over four million passengers a day is likely to become the norm, and demand is likely to continue to grow. It always needs to be remembered that LU's fundamental objective is to provide a safe and reliable service.

Rail for London was set up as a TfL subsidiary in 2003 and deals with the National Rail network in London. The aim is to raise standards by focusing investment in London's railways and developing a more integrated approach to rail governance. The Railways Act 2005 signified the end of the short-lived planning body, the Strategic Rail Authority, giving greater responsibility to TfL and transferred the responsibility for services on the Overground network to them.

Tasks include overseeing major new rail projects related to London Overground, managing the Overground concession and also the operation of the Docklands Light Railway and of London Tramlink. It also supports and develops Crossrail and Thameslink, and supports Network Rail's contribution to an integrated public transport system.

CREATION OF LONDON OVERGROUND

The further development of the North London and associated lines was associated with the creation of London Overground. This is essentially a non-radial operation, excepting the Euston–Watford DC line.

The Overground was not the first to explore the possibilities of a circumnavigation of inner London by rail. The late 19th century saw a number of schemes which tried to do this; what has been termed the Outer Circle ran from Broad Street (next to Liverpool Street and now closed) and via the North London line to Willesden Junction, then to Kensington Olympia via the West London, and to Earl's Court (or beyond) on the District. Such schemes though suffered from low frequency service provision, but even more from bus, tram and then tube competition.

The North London services, as amended, have survived into modern times. From being subject to decidedly mixed traction (DMUs, DC EMUs, AC/DC EMUs), the line was converted to 25kV AC, but only as far west as Acton Central. Third rail was retained from there through South Acton and thence to Gunnersbury, from which point the line to Richmond is shared with fourth-rail London Underground District line services.

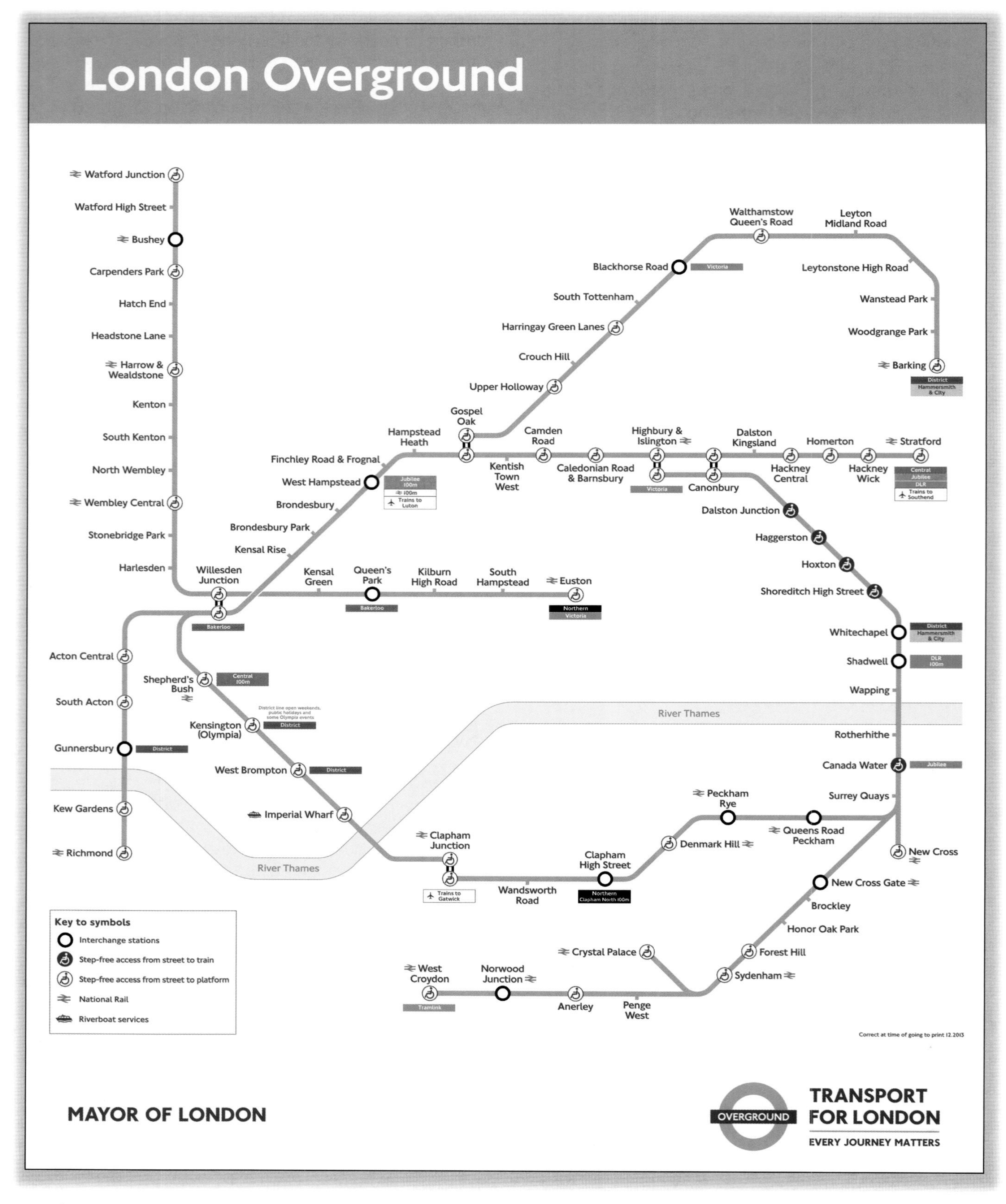

London Overground, initial system, 2012.

Operation was by the dual-voltage Class 313 units. The Stratford–North Woolwich section was closed in 2006 in conjunction with extensions to the Docklands Light Railway and this never saw overhead electrification.

This was associated with the reinstatement of the four-tracked section, with some of it as two separate two-tracked railways, as well as extensive rebuilding. This resulted in the two southernmost tracks east from Highbury & Islington being used exclusively for the operation of services via the East London line. Those from Stratford on the northern side were shared with freight until the four-tracking was resumed immediately to the west of Highbury & Islington.

A major financial contribution to this work was made by the Olympic Delivery Authority as part of the upgrade to public transport in readiness for London 2012.

Elsewhere, third-rail electrification was extended north from Kensington Olympia to just north of the A4 overbridge and thence at 25kV AC to Willesden Junction. This allowed Eurostar trains access from Waterloo to their original North Pole depot. It also enabled electric passenger services to be introduced, both on the LNW lines north to Wembley Central and beyond, and to Willesden Junction High Level with the options of terminating there or continuing east to Stratford.

Meanwhile, London Underground services over the East London line ceased in 2007 when the line was closed for major works in connection with the coming Overground. These included its being taken north of Whitechapel in 2010 over a new formation to a station at Shoreditch High Street, thence onto reclaimed infrastructure to Dalston Junction, with intermediate stations at Hoxton and Haggerston. It was latterly extended to Canonbury and Highbury & Islington.

To the south, the line was extended beyond New Cross Gate via a flying junction onto the Brighton line tracks to both Crystal Palace and West Croydon.

In 2012 a further link was forged over the South London line from Surrey Quays via a long disused formation to Peckham Rye, Denmark Hill, Wandsworth Road and Clapham Junction.

New Class 378 trains of two varieties were procured from Bombardier in Derby, who maintain the fleet. One type is for DC only services, the other for AC/DC operation. Originally intended to be three-car units, the Olympic Delivery Authority funded the construction of additional cars to make them all up to four cars. They have since been extended to five-car length, such has been the success of the new services.

The Class 378s for London Overground were the first stock for National Railways to feature wide open gangways between vehicles and longitudinal seating. This photograph from 28 April 2010 shows how much standing room is available even when the seating is moderately well occupied. What it doesn't suit is those who like to sit in a train and look out of the window. ***John Glover***

The approach to Camden Road Overground station as seen from the road of that name makes it unmissable. Does the rest of the railway advertise its presence sufficiently? It is 14 July 2014. *John Glover*

Caledonian Road & Barnsbury today has a single island platform only, but the Way Out is by the overbridge and a walk along the disused platform on the right. The main use of that track is for freight and the platform edge is protected by railings. London Overground unit 378006 calls with a Richmond-bound train on 4 December 2011. *John Glover*

Freight traffic along the North London line may, as here, be making south west, though Feltham Yard has long since gone. No 66058 is seen here heading west through South Acton station towards Feltham on 4 June 2013. *John Glover*

The Euston–Watford DC lines were built for local electric services. Today, from Harrow & Wealdstone southwards, these are run by both London Overground and London Underground's Bakerloo line. Note that the fourth rail is still needed. No 378229 is arriving at Headstone Lane station on a southbound working to London Euston on 4 June 2013 *John Glover*

The coming of London Overground effectively put paid to the Victoria–London Bridge local service over the Victoria to Wandsworth Road section. Southern's 456024 is seen here on 15 April 2010 departing Battersea Park on the viaduct that stretches eastwards from here. ***John Glover***

The Gospel Oak–Barking service was operated by Class 172/0 two-car diesel units. A prolonged hiatus surrounded the delayed electrification, which was to be completed finally in early 2018. A DMU service was reinstated as a temporary measure, pending the delivery of eight 4-car Class 710 electric trains later in the year.

The Class 710 order extends to 45 units, of which 31 are AC only (Class 710/1) for TfL's Enfield and Chingford services, with the remaining 14 AC/DC (Class 710/2) for Gospel Oak-Barking and other original Overground lines. This will enable a reallocation of the existing Class 378 units to take place. The depots for London Overground operations are at New Cross Gate and Willesden Junction, and Ilford for the Enfield and Chingford services which became part of the Overground network in 2015.

The net result was the introduction of what are now London Overground services, which operate under contract to Transport for London. They include services over the whole network described, including the Euston–Watford Junction DC lines which are largely unaltered.

London Overground was formed in 2007 when the franchise for the North London routes on Network Rail infrastructure was devolved to TfL, having previously been operated by Silverlink Metro.

London Overground Rail Operations Ltd (LOROL) was the original operator, succeeded in 2016 by Arriva Rail (London).

Operation is mostly over Network Rail tracks, for which track access charges are payable as with any other operator. However, the East London line section, broadly that on which operations were previously undertaken by London Underground plus the former Broad Street line north to Dalston Junction and the intervening new construction, are owned and operated by TfL subsidiary Rail for London.

That operating centre is located within the New Cross Gate depot area and this section is known as the East London Line Core Route.

MODERN ROLLING STOCK

The more modern rolling stock on the Underground consists of the 1992 tube stock on the Central and Waterloo & City lines, the 1995 stock on the Jubilee, 1996 on the Northern, 2009 on the Victoria, and the S7/S8 stock on all subsurface lines.

Over the years there has been a general move to less seating (usually longitudinal rather than transverse) and more standing space. The S7 and S8 stocks also feature walk-through vestibules between adjacent cars, which may result in passenger loads being better spread out between (at least) adjacent vehicles.

The end/centre gap on curved platforms is a continuous source of problems in terms of boarding speed and safety; the future possible use of shorter articulated vehicles is a potential way round this. Major orders for stock replacement of the older cars and the need to cope with growing patronage and route additions are anticipated.

On the Hertford East branch, unit 315849 arrives at the terminus in September 2001, with its tail lights already lit for the return journey. It sports the colourless (undercoat?) livery which was at the time common on such services. Signalling was still locally controlled from the Great Eastern box, seen here, with a searchlight-style colour-light starting signal on the right. *John Glover*

A Virgin Class 390 Pendolino with an up West Coast Main Line service approaches Willesden Junction at speed; the fast line platforms were closed to passengers at the end of 1962 and subsequently removed. There are still two 'stations' here; one crosses the main line at high level, the other is for the parallel DC lines services. It is 12 September 2009. *John Glover*

The number of doors per vehicle side is of key importance in terms of fast loading and unloading, very important in urban settings, and the trend is certainly to more doors rather than fewer.

On the main line railways similar conditions apply; the new vehicles for Crossrail and Thameslink are discussed elsewhere. Here too the principle of trains comprising of (typically) four cars which can be combined as necessary up to around 12-cars, is being replaced with longer unit trains that cannot be easily separated. These have no intermediate driving cabs and while that results in capital cost and maintenance savings, the length of the train cannot be adjusted to take account of the traffic currently on offer.

A May 2001 view of unit No 357019 calling at the LT&S line down platform at Upminster. There are 74 of these units, built in two batches from 1999 and from 2001. To these have been added a further six Class 387/3s. Demand pressure has resulted in increased service levels. *John Glover*

The existence of trains with more than one source of traction, ie some combination of AC electric, DC electric, diesel or even battery, seems to be on the increase. This does benefit the choice of where they can be operated, but at the cost of more complexity and hence higher maintenance requirements too. This means that more equipment is going to be carried round, some of which at any one time is likely to be redundant. Tanks of heavy diesel fuel are an obvious example of this, and they will also increase the overall weight.

There is also the question of varying performance levels when working in different modes.

None of this is to argue against the bi-mode, multi-mode, dual-system, or whatever you wish to call its specification; there is always a place for such trains. However, the approach needs to be used with care; in itself, it doesn't seem likely to lead to a reliable, low cost and high performance operation.

Internal layout

Seating is still largely transverse, sometimes 2+2 each side of a central gangway, sometimes 3+2. Longer passenger journeys are usually involved on National Railways than the Underground. This means that the ability to find a seat increases in importance, but 3+2 arrangements can be decidedly tight. The off-peak market too needs to be attracted, and such users tend to look for a little more comfort.

Might that mean, for instance, the provision of toilets? Their availability is very much dependent on individual operators and services. What might be the attitudes to first class? Again, provision is patchy, but it is not normally available on relatively short distance inner-suburban services.

This is the now closed King's Cross Thameslink station with 319453. Perhaps surprisingly, the St Pancras International low-level station which took its place is the best part of half a mile distant. *John Glover*

9

Thameslink, Bedford to Brighton, and ...?

The principal objective of the Thameslink project is to provide for a major expansion of services, having experienced very substantial demand growth since their introduction in 1988. Shadow Strategic Rail Authority, 1999

The Midland Suburban electrification to St Pancras plus the branch to Moorgate was well received, but matters rested there only temporarily. The wishes of the then Greater London Council resulted in a 1984 joint study with British Rail on possible future uses of the abandoned Snow Hill tunnel from Farringdon through to Blackfriars. This had the potential to restore cross-London services by relaying and reopening the line and the introduction of a relatively frequent all day, every day service linking with destinations south of the Thames.

The study showed that for a relatively modest expenditure, 20,000 daily passenger journeys could benefit from reduced journey times, terminal costs would be reduced and turnround time at central London stations would not be needed. That would result in the use of fewer units and fewer train crew working fewer diagrams. Additional passenger revenue would be a bonus.

In the event, the six platforms of St Pancras main line station would then be used only by two Midland line InterCity trains an hour, as use by the Midland Suburban Electrics would cease.

The push for the reinstatement of the route from Farringdon to Blackfriars and beyond had been growing and ministerial approval was received in July 1985. The work included the reinstatement of the Farringdon junction and the track generally, making a new junction with the 'Southern' at Blackfriars.

The Midland Suburban Electric services were operated by the Class 317 fleet, built for the job, but these were for 25kV AC only. There was the little problem of electrical system differences north and south of the river. The means of changing from AC overhead to third-rail DC had been pioneered with the Great Northern changeover at Drayton Park, so the ability so to do was not in question. It did however require the existing trains to be found new work elsewhere, and a series of stock cascades took place. This enabled the elimination of old units with asbestos contamination.

A new build of AC/DC dual voltage rolling stock would be needed, and a fleet of Class 319 four-car units was built by BR at York in 1987–88. Like their predecessors, these units incorporated a single motor car and they too were 100mph vehicles. They were built in two groups, depending on the type of service for which they were intended. The Class 319/0 (60 units) were Second Class only, with a total of 319 seats. The Class 319/1s (26 units) had 16 First Class seats included in one Driving Trailer plus 287 Second Class seats, giving 303 seats in total. Both types of unit included two lavatories which, it might be felt, was a good idea for a run of 103¼ miles from Bedford to Brighton which would take (at that time) about 2½ hours.

The changeover between 25kV AC and 750v DC took place while trains were stationary at Farringdon for services in both directions; this did not apply to the services to Moorgate Widened Lines, which remained at 25kV throughout.

Operations

What sort of service was it practicable to run? While operations north of the river might be considered more or less straight replacements for those already in existence, services south of the river were a different matter altogether. A cursory glance at the network map shows the huge range of destinations to which a train presenting itself facing south at Blackfriars might proceed. Were there markets to support them, and if so were train paths available? What junction conflicts might result and would any services be displaced? These were the sorts of matters that had to be addressed.

How well might it all work? To join two groups of services which until then had been entirely separate does bring risks as well as rewards; Network SouthEast considered it inevitable that when through working via Farringdon was established, there would be a one to two per cent deterioration in punctuality when compared with the self-contained service in the north.

This was however a quite limited proposal compared with the much more extensive one that would follow. Distinct capacity limitations were imposed by the infrastructure and it was also desired to maintain a service to Moorgate (but only at peak times).

The new Thameslink service was opened on 16 May 1988. Shown in Table 9.1 is the basic service pattern operated in the Summer 1989 timetable.

Given that the hourly pattern is represented by six trains only, this still managed to result in six different stopping patterns, three different originating points in the north and four different termini in the south, reached by five different routes. The Widened Lines King's Cross Thameslink station was still open, and City Thameslink station was yet to be built.

Thus the result was a wide-ranging but relatively infrequent service over a substantial range of routes. North of the Thames the Midland line has no branches at all used for passenger purposes south of Bedford; variations here related to where trains started and their stopping patterns.

South of the Thames, was such a variable result in the users' best interests? Should perhaps the longer distance trains crowd out the shorter distance services, or would the reverse be more acceptable? What was in the best interests of the railway business?

Compromises were also possible and in 1993 an experimental hourly service south from City Thameslink (opened 1990 as St Paul's Thameslink) would take the intrepid traveller the 35½ miles to West Croydon, Sutton, Epsom and Guildford, with 14 intermediate station calls, in 1 hour 11 minutes. The average speed was 30mph. These trains originated from Luton, 50 minutes earlier.

By comparison, a fast train from Waterloo to Guildford, 30½ miles, would take 29 minutes. The message here is that 'long distance' is not a synonym for 'fast'.

Such issues would need to be resolved, but in the meantime improvement of the Farringdon–Blackfriars section was taking up everybody's attention.

Farringdon–Blackfriars

There were three main issues here:

- The wish of the post-war planners to see the Ludgate Hill railway underbridge removed on aesthetic grounds, to improve the views of St Paul's cathedral from Fleet Street,
- The wish to close the little used Holborn Viaduct terminus which was a prime City site; it was a short distance north of Blackfriars, but a replacement would be needed, and
- The need to have an intermediate station between Farringdon and Blackfriars on the newly inaugurated Thameslink route.

By good fortune, it was possible to achieve all of these in one large engineering project.

This involved the construction of a steep up direction ramp from the City Thameslink station (two side platforms) on a new 1 in 29 alignment to reach Blackfriars platforms. This would have been impossible in the days of steam without a banking engine, but achievable with electric traction. It compared with the 1 in 31 on the Widened Lines between Farringdon and King's Cross where Thameslink passes beneath the Metropolitan, for which a banker was regularly stabled at Farringdon.

Table 9.1: Thameslink basic service pattern, mid-day Monday-Friday, Summer 1989 timetable

Bedford			xx17			xx47
Luton		xx26	xx39		xx56	x109
Cricklewood	xx41	xx57		x111	x127	
Farringdon	xx55	x114	x119	x125	x144	x139
Blackfriars	x100	x120	x125	x130	x150	x155
London Bridge			x132			x202
Elephant & Castle	x104	x124		x134	x154	
Norwood Junction		x147				
Streatham					x208	
East Croydon		x150	x145		x220	x215
Purley		x158			x228	
Gatwick Airport			x203			x237
Brighton						x315
Bromley South	x131			x201		
Orpington				x212		
Swanley	x143					
Sevenoaks	x200			x227		

St Pancras in February 2002 was a rather sad station. Shorn of the Thameslink services which were now terminating at Moorgate or somewhere south of Blackfriars, the overhead electrification was unused. All that were left were the Midland main line services. 170106 is the only occupant as it stands in Platform 6 with a service to Nottingham. *John Glover*

A substantial lowering of the railway trackbed was needed to pass underground and beneath the road which forms Ludgate Hill.

The effect on the operational railway was minimal, with work taking place from 10 May 1990, the date on which the railway bridge was removed, through to 29 May when services were restored. Holborn Viaduct terminus had closed after the last train on 26 January 1990. The passenger entrance for the new low-level City Thameslink station was very close to that of Holborn Viaduct.

THAMESLINK NEXT STAGE

A more intensive service might be possible, but that would require a much larger programme of works. Thameslink had already improved access to parts of central London and opened up new journey opportunities without the need for interchange.

The general headings for the services adopted by Network SouthEast in 1991 were Thameslink Express and Thameslink Metro.

Thameslink Express with a total of 8tph would serve regional centres, key rail interchanges and would link London's airports. This added Peterborough and King's Lynn to the northern destinations, also (route unspecified) to Bishop's Stortford and Stansted Airport. The proposed route is understood to have been via a reinstated curve at Kentish Town to Upper Holloway, thence to South Tottenham and a new west to north curve to reach the Lea Valley line south of Tottenham Hale.

Heathrow would be accessed by passengers changing to Crossrail at Farringdon.

Specifically, planned service highlights were:

- 1tph Peterborough to King's Cross and Ashford
- 1tph King's Lynn to King's Cross and Ashford
- 2tph Cambridge to London Bridge, West Croydon and Guildford
- 2tph Stansted Airport to London Bridge and Horsham
- 2tph Bedford to London Bridge and Brighton

Thameslink Metro was described as a 10tph service, linking more than 100 stations both north and south of London, 'bringing new life to less developed suburban routes'. Notably, all day operations extended no further south than Sutton, Caterham or Sevenoaks, but in the north to Bedford, Welwyn Garden City and Hertford North.

Tattenham Corner is a substantial terminal station with three platforms that will each take eight-car trains. This may be useful on Derby Day, but not on many other occasions. Southern Electrostar 377706 stands in Platform 2 on 13 June 2016. It does look an unlikely terminus for a half-hourly Thameslink service from Cambridge, which has been suggested. ***John Glover***

It was intended that separate builds of stock would cater for the Express (Class 365) and Metro (Class 319s).

There were warnings also of an urgent need to undertake extensive works to allow all this to happen. Otherwise, despite the success of the initial 1988 Thameslink programme in carrying 10,000 passengers an hour on a limited service, it would be unable to cope with anticipated demand by 1998, and that there would be no rush-hour services through London Bridge station.

By the Winter 1995-96 timetable, the 1989 services set out in Table 9.1 above had altered substantially. In the equivalent hour, a total of 8tph were passing through the central area between Farringdon and Blackfriars, with 5tph from Bedford, 2tph from Luton and 1tph from St Albans. London Bridge saw half of these, 4tph, all of which continued to Brighton as, alternately, fasts and semi-fasts.

The other 4tph via Elephant & Castle continued to Wimbledon via Sutton (2tph) or in the reverse order (2tph) of Sutton and back via Wimbledon. There were now no services towards Kent, illustrating how ephemeral such operations could be.

Thameslink 2000

The principal objective of the Thameslink 2000[41] scheme was to provide the basis for the major expansion of a service which had already seen very substantial demand growth and consequential overcrowding. It would also be of assistance to Channel Tunnel passengers at the (then proposed but not built) low-level international station at King's Cross.

The aim was to offer a more extensive network of frequent high-quality services crossing central London, with the use of longer trains.

Early ideas of further expansion of the route to the south favoured that via Elephant & Castle, but this would require major additional infrastructure works due to the flat junctions at Herne Hill and Tulse Hill. The prime focus was changed to the London Bridge route, which would give a wider range of destinations as well as to London Bridge itself. Mentioned specifically (in 1999) were Guildford, Horsham, Littlehampton, Brighton, Eastbourne, East Grinstead, Ashford, Sevenoaks and Dartford.

In the north, a new connection to the Great Northern line via the unbuilt King's Cross low-level station would have offered a route to Peterborough, Cambridge and King's Lynn. The construction of the Canal Tunnels later substituted for this.

Perhaps ominously, it was also stated that 'alternative destinations could be substituted at the (later disbanded) sSRA's discretion'. It will be clear from the above that though there seems to have been little disagreement about what works were needed in the central area for a successful operation, the choices of routes and service patterns elsewhere on the system commanded far from universal agreement.

An up Southern service with 455823 for London Bridge is leaving Penge West on 12 April 2010 as a Thameslink service approaches on the down fast line. If there are no platforms, arguments as to what should stop where are much reduced. The also give an opportunity to offer faster longer distance services. The bridge in the background carries the line from Sydenham Junction to Crystal Palace, *John Glover*

FINAL SCHEME

In 1999, the Shadow Strategic Rail Authority set out the key aims that the Thameslink project would fulfil:

- to reduce (albeit not eliminate) overcrowding on rail and London Underground services,
- to reduce the need for interchange at congested central London stations, and
- to introduce new services and direct links across South-East England and facilitate the dispersal of passengers from St Pancras International.

The scheme was said to provide excellent value for money with a benefit:cost ratio of 1.6:1, though some would question whether 'excellent' was quite the right word.

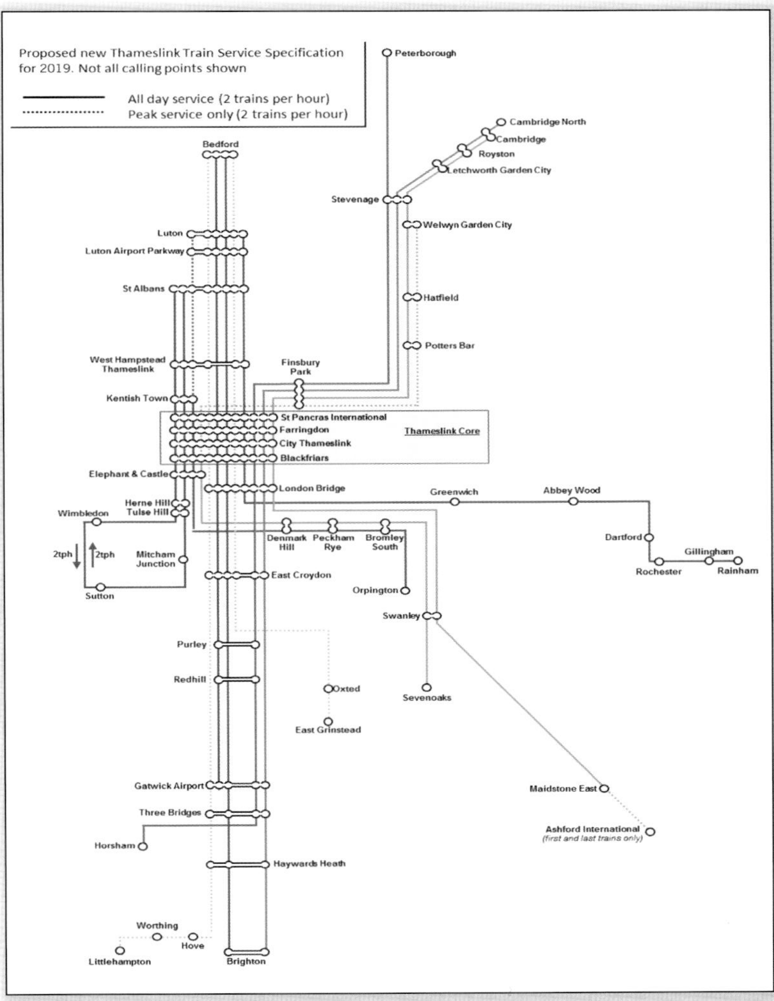

Proposed eventual Thameslink service patterns, to be reached in stages by December 2019

Method

There were to be three separate streams of work:

- Infrastructure investment to allow more services to be operated
- New rolling stock provision (and cascade of existing stock elsewhere), to include depot facilities and maintenance (all specified by DfT)
- To manipulate franchise agreements, later largely achieved with the introduction of the Govia Thameslink Railway franchise, to make one Train Operating Company responsible for the whole operation.

Capital works

Principal works required for what had become the proposed 24tph service were:

- Fitting out the new station at St Pancras (Thameslink) together with the construction of the Canal Tunnels connection to the Great Northern line at a new Belle Isle Junction.
- Reconstruction of Blackfriars station with four platforms (two through, two terminal from the south). This would be extended across the Thames, with a new station entrance on the south side.
- A new viaduct at Borough Market over Borough High Street to provide two new tracks dedicated to the Charing Cross services.
- New tracks and platforms generally as part of a comprehensive total rebuild and reorganisation of the whole of London Bridge station, including the terminal platforms used by Southern services.
- Grade separated junction at Bermondsey and the laying of an additional track at St John's, Lewisham.
- Extended platforms at stations throughout as necessary, to permit the operation of 12-car trains.
- Reinforced power supply and extensive signalling works.

This, it was stated, would enable 24tph of 12-car length to be operated throughout the peak periods of 07:00–10:00 and 16:00–19:00 in both directions between Blackfriars and St Pancras (Thameslink). Crucially, the works in the London Bridge area would provide for the separation of Thameslink, Charing Cross and Cannon Street services, each onto their own dedicated tracks, and also between 'Sussex' and 'Kent' services at Bermondsey.

Work starts

But would all or even any of it ever happen? It was not until 2006 that the Transport & Works Act Order was granted, meaning that work could begin; funding was agreed in the following year, see Table 9.2.

Table 9.2: Thameslink Timeline, 2006-2019

Year	Event
2006	Transport & Works Act Order granted.
2008	Thameslink All-Party Parliamentary Group established. Construction works begin. Luton Airport Parkway platforms are lengthened to 12 cars.
2009	Farringdon to Moorgate Widened Lines section closes. A new footbridge is built at Farringdon between Thameslink and London Underground platforms. Re-railing and track refurbishment, St Pancras to Blackfriars, undertaken. At Blackfriars, a four-year modernisation programme starts; protection arrangements are installed, allowing London Underground services to run between the construction work and the temporary station entrances.
2010	Funding granted by Department for Transport for the full scheme. City Thameslink station platforms usable by 12-car trains.
2011	Platform lengthening at stations north of London, also Farringdon and Blackfriars for 12-car trains. New ticket hall at Farringdon completed. New bridge slid into place across Borough High Street. Signalling works completed Kentish Town–Farringdon (September) and to Blackfriars (November). The London Bridge planning application is submitted. The first 12-car trains on Thameslink enter service. New ticket hall at Farringdon and rebuilt West Hampstead Thameslink station opened.
2012	The first station to span the Thames, the new south bank entrance in Bankside is made available for passenger use and the new northern entrance opened. World's largest bridge solar array completed. London Underground station reopens. Final two platforms opened at Blackfriars and resignalling to Elephant & Castle completed, April. Phase 1 complete. HRH the Prince of Wales and the Duchess of Cornwall reopen Borough Market with its restored Victorian roof. Demolition begins on Brighton side of London Bridge and shed roof removed, part of which is relocated to create a new railway museum in Aberystwyth. Regional signalling control centre completed at Three Bridges. Planning permission for new bus station at London Bridge received and work completed. New viaduct to ease Thameslink bottleneck which benefits the whole network built, though not commissioned. Work begins on Three Bridges and Hornsey depots.
2013	Contract for supply of new trains awarded to Siemens. New track added near St John's station, Lewisham. Start of track renewal on London Bridge approaches. Station redevelopment begins with demolition of the first platforms. Signalling train control testing laboratory complete.
2014	Train stabling south of river now complete, with a new facility at Brighton. Two new platforms built at London Bridge, with canopies, and further platforms demolished. Start move of signalling control for London Bridge to Three Bridges Railway Operating Centre (ROC).

2015 Three Bridges depot connected to system. Train stabling in the north is completed with the facility at Cricklewood. First new Class 700 trains arrive in Britain and are tested. The 650m Canal Tunnels linking St Pancras to the Great Northern are complete, but will not be in passenger use before 2018. In the meantime, they provide a direct route between Three Bridges and Hornsey depots. Vibration reduction measures undertaken. Platforms 10–15 at London Bridge finished and demolition work started elsewhere.

2016 New Class 700 trains on Thameslink enter service and increase route capacity. The depot at Hornsey is connected. Half of the new low-level London Bridge concourse is completed and in use.. The new Borough Viaduct is connected into London Bridge station and Charing Cross trains start to use it.

2017 Bermondsey diveunder completed, segregating Kent and Sussex routes. Thameslink services between London Bridge and East Croydon run at the higher level. By strengthening or replacement work, interconnection of 11 different structures alongside existing viaducts arches, bridges and decks. Trackwork completed.

2018 London Bridge station is longer than The Shard is tall. East meets West and North meets South at Farringdon, which will become a very busy hub providing direct services to Heathrow, Gatwick and Luton airports, as well as facilitating interchange with London Underground. Full operation means 160 trains an hour here on all lines taken together. Completion of major bridge strengthening work on London Bridge approaches. ATO ready, Blackfriars to St Pancras. New signalling installed, with move of London Bridge signalling control to Three Bridges ROC almost complete. ETCS Level 2 ready. Infrastructure needed to provide 24tph now complete. Platforms 1–5 reopen and station work completed. A better station is emerging with the completion of London Bridge with 50% more through platforms. The new concourse has 24 escalators and seven lifts, which means that passengers will have a more comfortable experience at the station.

2019 The Thameslink programme is now complete, all new services operating with 115 new trains in use. Farringdon becomes the place where Thameslink, Crossrail and London Underground meet.

Source: Network Rail

London Bridge station

London Bridge station before the rebuild was not really fit for purpose, despite being the fourth busiest station in Britain. It had a poor reputation, in terms of having no heart and no character. The whole structure was built on arches, with the tracks at such a height as was required to bridge Borough High Street.

Southeastern's Electrostar 376024 enters London Bridge from Cannon Street on 18 July 2016. The capacious canopies were a good point for at least part of the old station. ***John Glover***

The London Bridge Brighton line platforms were the first to be reconstructed and 455801 may be seen, left, in Platform 13, with 455802 to the right in Platform 12. It is 19 June 2016. The end corridor connections from these units, never used for passenger purposes, have been permanently sealed by Southern. ***John Glover***

To say that the station had evolved over the years is probably not far off the truth. The reality is that a decade ago there were three main sections of what is a very large station. Starting on the north (Tooley Street side), they were as listed below. They are shown in pairs of those each side of an island platform. All platforms could accommodate 12-car trains except Nos 8, 14, 15 and 16, all limited to eight cars.

Platform 1	down line, Cannon Street services
Platform 2	reversible line, Cannon Street services
Platform 3	reversible line, Cannon Street services
Platform 4	reversible line, Charing Cross and Blackfriars services
Platform 5	reversible line, Charing Cross and Blackfriars services
Platform 6	up line, Charing Cross and Blackfriars services
No platform (7)	up through line, Charing Cross and Blackfriars services
Platforms 8–16	terminal platforms for Brighton line services.

Despite all this, London Bridge handled an estimated 54 million passengers in the 2015/16 year.

Notable is the shared use of Platforms 4–6 and the through line 7, all for services to and/or from Charing Cross and Blackfriars. This was the major sticking point. All these services shared a very heavily used pair of lines (one up and one down) as far as Metropolitan Junction, west of the station. The junction was not grade separated and thus always a potential source of conflict.

Similarly, east of London Bridge, a series of flat junctions enabled trains to take either the Brighton or the Kent main lines. Both of these have four tracks.

Other than the Brighton terminal Platforms 8-16, which were at a lower level than the rest and reached by a small concourse, passenger access was decidedly difficult. From the street, this was via a low-level tunnel beneath the tracks and then long ramps up to Platforms 1-6. Towards the eastern end of the station, a very long and wide overbridge across the entire station eased the lot of those who were only changing trains. The whole station was decidedly unsatisfactory and parts of it could become acutely congested, despite the concourse, bus station and footbridge having been rebuilt in the 1970s.

This simplified description cannot tell the whole story, omitting for instance the weaves needed for many trains to and from Cannon Street, but the general complexity will be clear.

Reconstruction of London Bridge station meant temporary arrangements for many. This was the informative view which greeted those walking over London Bridge itself on the approach to the station on 29 July 2015. The sign was understood to refer to a kiosk selling Travelcards and similar. *John Glover*

Major rebuilding

The main requirements were to achieve physical separation between as many flows of trains as possible to facilitate the introduction of a much enhanced Thameslink service, making London Bridge a more passenger-friendly station, while catering also for a continuing growth in passenger numbers as time progressed.

The scheme was to divide the platforms into four groups: those dealing with the Brighton line terminating services, the south eastern platforms for Charing Cross trains, those for Thameslink proceeding to or from Blackfriars, and the services to and from Cannon Street. As far as possible in the finished version, such services should be kept separate from each other through new construction. This included the Borough Market viaduct and the grade separation at Bermondsey. By such means, the system capacity could be maximised.

Work started in earnest once London 2012 Games were over and the following major works were undertaken:

- construction of a new double track bridge over Borough High Street, to separate out the Charing Cross trains from those to/from Blackfriars
- reducing the number of terminating platforms for Brighton line trains to six (now Nos 10 to 15), freeing up space for more platforms for Charing Cross trains
- building a Bermondsey diveunder east of London Bridge to remove all conflict between Thameslink Croydon services and those of Southeastern to and from Charing Cross. It also enables the Thameslink Croydon services to be grade separated from Southern trains departing London Bridge in the New Cross Gate direction
- reconstructing the four platforms (now Nos 6 to 9) to be used by Charing Cross trains
- reconstructing the two platforms (now Nos 4 to 5) to be used by Thameslink trains

Railway bridges over roads are not necessarily beautiful, especially in urban areas. This is the bridge carrying the Metropolitan Junction area of the railway over the A3200 Southwark Street, seen on 19 June 2016. *John Glover*

- reconstructing the three platforms (now Nos 1 to 3) to be used by Cannon Street trains
- building a completely new large low-level concourse with a new ticket office and access by a series of escalators to all the platforms above
- major infrastructure works including new tracks, pointwork, signalling and general attention as required.

Such major schemes cannot be carried out without a considerable degree of passenger disruption, and it was decided early on that the favoured approach of closing the station completely while rebuilding took place was not an option. The volume of usage was just too great for this to be feasible and there aren't too many alternatives. Work was therefore divided into a number of separate packages, broadly as outlined above.

This included diverting trains elsewhere wherever practicable, and closing or severely restricting the use of sections of the station progressively. This started with the Brighton services, helped by the effective transfer of the service to Peckham Rye and Victoria to TfL. Charing Cross trains non-stopped London Bridge from January 2015 until August 2016, while Thameslink trains were mostly diverted via Elephant & Castle. The final section was for Cannon Street services, which non-stopped London Bridge from August 2016, continuing until completion in late 2017.

The new railway infrastructure at London Bridge was fully opened in January 2018. New Thameslink services start in May 2018 but with the full service in December 2019.

A large new concourse has been created at the lower level amongst a maze of original arches. This is connected to each platform pair by three separate pairs of escalators to aid passenger circulation. It includes new gatelines, new communications systems and, eventually, 82 retail units. In the peak, the station will be used by 170 trains an hour.

Signalling and communications

The track on all the approaches to the newly segregated routes at London Bridge has been relayed, in new locations as necessary, together with all switches and crossings. Bi-directional signalling has been introduced on the entire route between Kentish Town and Blackfriars, together with crossovers placed to make that a reality. This give some flexibility where needed, including engineering reasons.

The signalling is the first application of Level 2 of the European Train Control System (ETCS) in Britain and is overlaid on the conventional signals. This uses a railway version of the Global System for Mobile Communications (GSM-Railway). This is the system mandated as a part of ETCS to communicate continuously between track and train.

A Radio Block Centre calculates a safe 'Movement Authority' for the train, allowing it to proceed for a certain distance ahead. This then passed back to the train by GSM-Railway. Detection of the train is track-based using track circuits, so it is known only to be somewhere within a particular fixed block.

Trains will also use Automatic Train Operation (ATO) to get them to perform as near as possible to their maximum capability. With the service frequencies envisaged, there will be little scope for underperformance and station stop times will be very tight.

A Traffic Management System (TMS) is being supplied by Hitachi; this is the main means of train regulation; the busier the system, the more important it is to keep the trains in a specific order and at the required frequencies.

ATO/ETCS is being applied over the core section between Elephant & Castle/Bermondsey diveunder and Kentish Town. This will provide a robust 24tph through the core.

The AC line overhead line equipment has to be reconfigured and the power supply strengthened for 12-car

This is a traditional Power Signal Box panel display depicting Norwood Junction. The row of white lights indicates a route set up for a train; the red lights are the train itself if it is on the section displayed. Thus train 2L40 is approaching the station, the route is set as far as is visible and the signal at the platform end displays a proceed aspect. Notable about the station is that Platforms 1 and 2 are each side of the up slow line, but that Platform 2 is not now in normal use. In the days of slam door trains, this decision was up to the passenger. *John Glover*

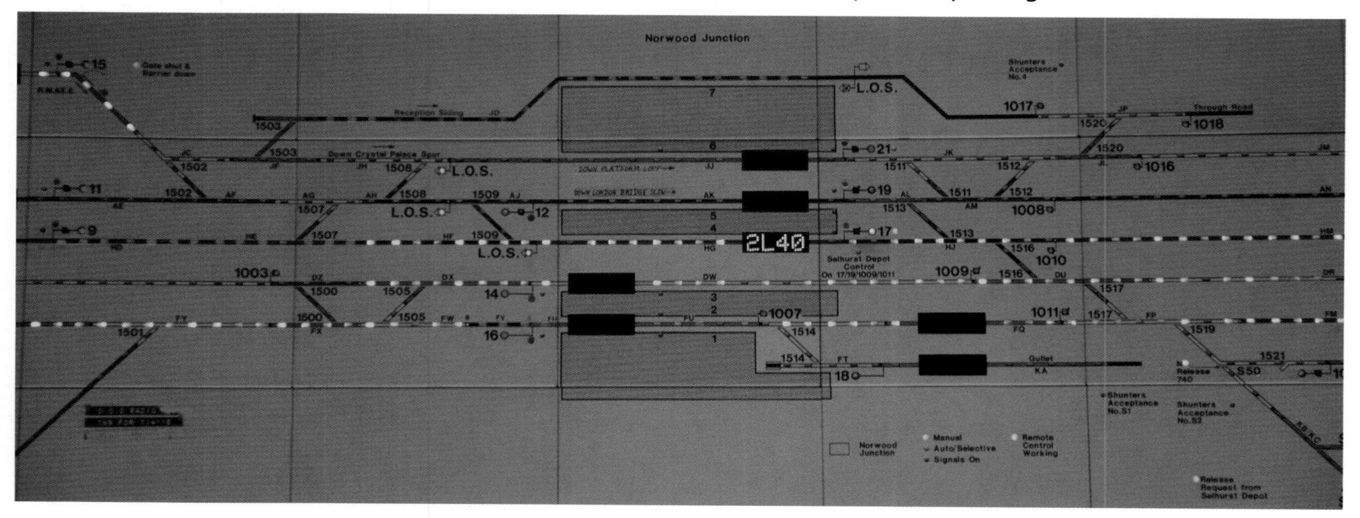

Passenger information systems have been upgraded and this display at Farringdon (northbound) shows the next two trains and an outline of several beyond that. It also indicates the length of the train, which is of added importance when this can vary from four cars to 12 cars. Also shown is whether or not the train is deemed to have first class accommodation. *John Glover*

trains. The existing substations at Elstree & Borehamwood and Ludgate Cellars (near Blackfriars) have been significantly upgraded. South of Elstree, the AC is now distributed via that Auto-transformer system, which provides much more power to the trains.

There is an integrated station control at London Bridge. Southeastern runs the train control system, under contract from others as appropriate. This is the station operator's eyes and ears; all duty managers sit together.

Information provision for passengers is designed to spread the load and to keep people moving wherever possible. The aim is to try not to give them cause to stop, since this is likely to obstruct others. More than half the London Bridge concourse is within the paid area.

Four fifths of users are regulars, who will come to their own conclusions as to the best route to follow, but the remaining fifth need some help.

New style passenger information displays are being used on the platforms of the stations St Pancras, Farringdon, City Thameslink and Blackfriars. These are designed to give more train calling pattern information for the next two trains, 30 minutes worth of future departure times, and the time each of those trains is expected to arrive. Together with aids to help passengers position themselves along the platform, the aims are to increase boarding time efficiency, to reduce on and off-train congestion, and reduce platform crowding generally.

A test of all such displays and their back up systems is how well they cope with out-of-course events. In these locations, with reversible signalling, this could result in some wrong line running.

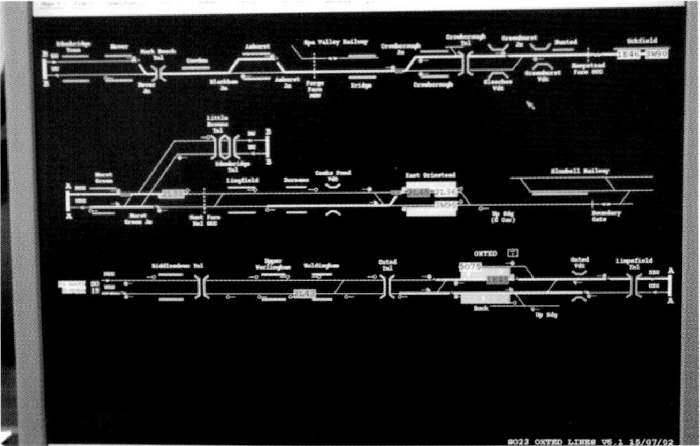

The Oxted panel shown here is in Three Bridges Area Operations Centre. This covers the whole of the branch from Riddlesdown to both East Grinstead and Uckfield. The effect of track singling on the Uckfield line is particularly noticeable. The physical connection to the Bluebell Railway at East Grinstead is also shown. Services on 23 November 2016 when this photograph was taken were reduced due to industrial action. *John Glover*

Blackfriars station

Blackfriars station, like London Bridge, is situated above ground level. This station underwent a large-scale rebuild, in which the three terminating platforms originally on the east side of the station now became two through lines (Nos 1, 2 to/from Farringdon), and the two platforms on the west side (now Nos 3, 4) became terminating lines from the south.

This aim was to enable Thameslink trains approaching from or routed towards London Bridge to be kept separate from Blackfriars-only services to minimise the number of conflicting junction movements.. The incorporation of the Wimbledon loop operations into Thameslink (south of Blackfriars, these run out via Sutton and back via Wimbledon, and vice versa) was due to the lack of any real alternatives, and the trains have been extended north of the river. All such trains approach Blackfriars via Elephant & Castle.

The proposal was that they should terminate permanently at Blackfriars. Campaigners, however, would have none of this, and these trains (at 4tph but of eight-car Class 700 length maximum) will all run to Midland main line destinations in the final timetable.

Separation of terminating and through traffic was however only part of the scheme. The platforms needed to be extended to 12-car lengths. This was achieved by lengthening the platforms onto the railway bridge over the Thames, from which passengers can enjoy perhaps the best views from any station platform in Britain. This enabled a secondary station entrance to be built at Bankside, on the south side of the river. Blackfriars has thus become the first station to have an entrance on both banks of the River Thames, one in the City of London and the other in the London Borough of Southwark.

Former Great Northern unit No 313121 has been heavily modified and now belongs to Network Rail. It has been used for ERTMS testing on the Hertford branch and is based at Willesden Train Care where it was photographed on 9 June 2014. It is unique within the class, as it now contains a toilet. *John Glover*

Left: The former British Rail logo is very widely recognised and here it graces the new Bankside entrance to Blackfriars station on 30 June 2016. *John Glover*

Below: Southeastern's 16:55 to Dover Priory formed of 375307 is leaving the terminal Platform 3 at Blackfriars on 30 June 2016. On Platform 4 to the left is 465193. Stations with four very long platforms on a bridge over a major river are, to put it mildly, unusual. *John Glover*

The spacious layout of Blackfriars station gives unprecedented views of the Thames from all platforms – as long as those pesky trains don't get in the way! This is Platform 1 for the southbound Thameslink trains on 30 June 2016. This, and the adjacent Platform 2, will each be occupied for around 20 minutes in each hour when the full 24tph timetable is in operation. *John Glover*

Looking north from Blackfriars Platform 3 is the decidedly steep and curved down gradient. Over about 300 yards this leads to the 770 yards Snow Hill tunnel, which itself includes the City Thameslink station platforms. It is to be fervently hoped that this does not cause adhesion problems on southbound (ie approaching) trains during inclement weather. *John Glover*

Having two station entrances, roundly 300 yards apart, does have its down sides. Liberally placed around the Bankside entrance are notices instructing those who look at them to 'walk across Blackfriars Bridge for the Underground'. The road bridge is on the west side of the railway and adjacent, but that can be a wet and windy route.

The District/Circle lines station is of course wholly on the north bank and while it is possible to reach it via the enclosed National Rail station platforms, it does mean touching in with one's Oystercard, then up the escalators/steps/lift to the selected platform, walking its length, and down again on reaching the far side and touching out. But do people even look at those notices? The long-suffering station staff on south bank barrier duties still receive a stream of enquiries as to where the Underground station might be.

Farringdon

Farringdon was an inoffensive wayside station with four platforms, owned by London Underground, under an overall roof. It has long been served by the Hammersmith & City, Circle and Metropolitan line trains (Platforms 1 and 2), to which was added what is now the Thameslink service on the former Widened Lines (Platforms 3 and 4). At deep level, there will shortly also be the Elizabeth line (presumably Platforms 5 and 6).

Farringdon is becoming a focal point through the provision of a number of rail services and a key interchange for passengers changing trains between them. The Thameslink platforms had already been lengthened to accommodate eight-car Class 317s/319s, but a further expansion has been necessary to take the 12-car Class 700s. This spelt the end of the Moorgate branch of the Widened Lines beyond Farringdon, as the space was needed to enable the southbound Thameslink station platform (No 3) to be extended. Closure took place on 20 March 2009.

The station platforms at Farringdon have always been on a gentle curve, but the two separate lengthening exercises have turned them into reverse curves. The 20m coach length of the Class 700s ensure that the platform to train gaps that curvature brings are not excessive.

A new footbridge between the platforms has been built for those interchanging between Thameslink and the Underground. Rather incongruously, on the (pedestrianised) Cowcross Street, a new station entrance has been placed opposite the existing one. This entrance is principally for Thameslink and the forthcoming Elizabeth line services; Underground passengers enter by the original.

This has long been the station at which Thameslink trains paused to raise/lower the pantograph and move between 25kV AC from the overhead and 750v DC electricity from the third rail. This is a slick operation, and station stop times

On the Widened Lines at Farringdon, the branch to Blackfriars didn't even wait to get to the end of the platform before it diverged, as can be seen here with 319432 disappearing into the tunnel. The line to Moorgate continued to the left, or rather it did so on 22 April 2009 when this picture was taken. The need to cater for Thameslink trains of up to 240 metres in length made a platform extension to the tunnel mouth inevitable. The closure of the line to Moorgate thus became a necessity. *John Glover*

The Moorgate end of the Widened Lines was closed for good. This was the view from Barbican station looking east towards Farringdon on 3 June 2013. The eastern entrance to that Crossrail 1 station reaches nearly as far as these platform ends. ***John Glover***

of one minute here are no longer than those at other central London stations served by Thameslink.

Overhead wires have now been extended to City Thameslink, which becomes a second point at which changeover can be made. Normally, AC to DC cutover remains at Farringdon southbound, with a second chance at City Thameslink. Any following trains are held at Farringdon. Should that attempt fail too, the train is emptied of passengers and sent back to Farringdon via the crossover newly installed at City Thameslink to return on the AC.

Going north, the change from DC to AC is normally at City Thameslink. Similarly, another chance is offered at Farringdon, but if not possible the train is returned on DC via the crossover.

There are also two north facing sidings north of City Thameslink into which DC trains can be diverted, but these can accommodate eight car sets only.

King's Cross Thameslink

This Widened Lines station had long suffered from inadequate platform widths and platform lengths and there were inherent difficulties of rectifying these matters in a very confined space. In view of the closeness of the new St Pancras International Thameslink platforms, closure took place on 9 December 2007, and the new underground St Pancras platforms were opened on the same day.

Fitting out this new Thameslink station at St Pancras was part of the works for HS1, the Channel Tunnel Rail Link. This is of a functional design, notable for its platform lengths which presage those of the Elizabeth line when that opens.

Govia Thameslink Railway

The Thameslink, Southern and Great Northern (TSGN) franchise was awarded to Govia Thameslink Railway (GTR). It is planned to last seven years from September 2014 until September 2021. As such, it includes the Thameslink/Great Northern franchise previously operated by First Capital Connect and the South Central franchise operated by Southern, which by then included the Gatwick Express operation. It also covered some services operated previously by Southeastern.

The GTR franchise has been let as a management contract, in which fare box revenues are passed to the Government rather than retained by the train operator. Similarly, all performance income payable by Network Rail is passed to the Department for Transport (DfT).

GTR receives a payment from DfT for running the franchise. This payment varies and depends on performance against Service Delivery, Customer Experience and Ticketless Travel benchmarks. The DfT funds all payments against Delay Repay claims, but GTR funds the administration costs.

The management contract approach was taken as franchise bids received by those letting contracts will build in safeguards in their pricing to reflect the risks involved in carrying out the work. In this case, the scale and complexity of the physical and technical works, the changes in service provision as those works advanced, and the difficulty in estimating future revenues, all pointed to a need to limit such risks to the TOC.

It was felt also that the operator would need to focus on delivering the changes and managing their impact on passengers.

What was the (then) Coalition Government seeking in letting what has become the single largest rail franchise in Britain? The following is sourced from a Department of Transport document of September 2013[42]. Thus:

- 'The new franchise will facilitate the Government's major investment in infrastructure, through the Thameslink Programme of works, and in rolling stock, through the introduction of 1,140 new Thameslink vehicles built by Siemens.'
- 'It will build upon the peak rail capacity increases into and out of London set out in the Government's Rail Investment Strategy[43], and the 286 additional vehicles procured by Southern from Bombardier ... for use before the new Thameslink trains are delivered.'
- 'The new franchise will deliver the Thameslink Programme, bring the Class 700 vehicles into service, and improve the customer experience throughout the franchise period.'

There is much more in the way of detailed requirements, but as discussed above, the practical issues as they emerge cannot be dismissed.

Thameslink trains

The Thameslink project, large as it is, is resulting in the extensive rebuilding of existing routes and linking them and the services provided together. There is very little completely new construction.

A northbound Thameslink service arrives at Kentish Town formed of a single four-car unit No 319006 on 4 March 2017, where it passes a Class 700 unit on the southbound. The overall grey appearance of these two trains does not seem to show them off well. ***John Glover***

The build of Class 377/5s has helped Thameslink out. Here 377520 stands at Kentish Town with a southbound service on 4 March 2017. This is one of a batch of 23 units built in 2008–09 to Bombardier's 'Electrostar' design; of necessity, these are dual voltage units. *John Glover*

The Class 700s for Thameslink services have been introduced to service as they became available. 700014 is seen here entering Three Bridges with a Brighton service on 23 November 2016. *John Glover*

It follows that all component parts of new Thameslink have been operated by various train types over the years, and also by a selection of Train Operating Companies (TOCs). The key requirement of trains for Thameslink services was and is the dual voltage capability.

The Class 319s which performed these services have been progressively phased out and reconditioned for use in the north of England, their place being taken by increasing numbers of Class 377/2, Class 377/5 and Class 387/1 units from Bombardier of Derby, totalling 46 sets. These in turn have been replaced with the large new purpose-built fleet of Class 700 vehicles. The £1.6 billion contract to finance, supply and maintain the train fleet was awarded in 2013 to a consortium of Siemens and Cross London Trains, comprising Siemens Project Ventures GmbH, Innisfree Ltd and 3i Infrastructure plc.

That Siemens won the contract caused some anguish in industry circles in Britain.

Desiro City

The Siemens 'Desiro City' Class 700s are built in Krefeld, Germany, with deliveries to the new Three Bridges depot (south of Gatwick) from 2015 onwards. The first train to enter public service did so on 20 June 2016. They were ordered by the Department for Transport.

There are basically two types, the Class 700/0 of eight-cars (60 constructed) and the Class 700/1 of 12-cars (55 constructed). That gives a total fleet of 1,140 vehicles. The Class 700s are maintained at the new Three Bridges depot and an expanded Hornsey depot on the Great Northern.

Neither the eight-car nor 12-car formations have an intermediate cab, thus avoiding the cost of additional equipment and the space it takes up when compared with two or three four-car units. The resulting lack of flexibility does though limit the matching of the formation to the density of the traffic on offer.

All trains are constructed as two single half units bolted together, gangwayed from end to end within. Should one fail from a traction point of view, the other can carry on unaided.

Each vehicle is around 20 metres long, giving train lengths of 243m (12-car) or 162m (eight-car). There is no intention of running what would be a minimum of a 16-car train with 2xeight-car sets. They are equipped with tread brakes as well as disc and regenerative braking and are air conditioned. Maximum speed is 100mph.

The manufacturers are proud to tell enquiring minds about the energy efficiency. This is such that each train saves enough energy to boil over 3,000 kettles per day, should anybody wish to do so.

Each of these aluminium-bodied and hence relatively lightweight vehicles has two sets of wide external double sliding doors. These are placed at the one third and two thirds positions. Internally, these trains have an open interior throughout; the only internal doors are those separating Standard and First Class passengers. An earlier intention to have different internal layouts for those units intended for Metro-type operation as opposed to outer suburban was discarded.

Their somewhat utilitarian internal design and décor has not been well received, giving the impression that price has been a more important factor than quality.

Seating arrangement is 2+2 each side of a central gangway in both classes, with the gangway being a little narrower in First Class as a result of wider seats. There are wide through walkways for the length of the train.

Seating in the 12-car Class 700/1s consists of 52 First Class and 601 Standard class, plus 14 tip ups and two wheelchair spaces. This totals 669 seats. They are said to be able to accommodate 1,750 passengers or more, with space for over 1,000 standing.

An interesting twist is that the First Class seats are equally divided between the two Driving Motor vehicles, so such passengers are faced with a very long walk if, on boarding, their selected end of the train is already full. This assumes that neither has been downgraded to Standard Class for the journey concerned.

The Class 700/1 eight-car trains have the same number of First Class seats, so the ratio of First to Standard is that much higher.

There are five controlled emission toilets, reduced to three in the eight-car versions, of which one is for the disabled.

New stabling sidings where light maintenance can be carried out have been established at the five sites of Brighton, Cambridge, Cricklewood, Horsham and Peterborough, plus of course the major depots at Hornsey and Three Bridges. Heavy maintenance is undertaken by Siemens.

Reliability has been disappointing. After a disastrous start in terms of the frequency of technical failures, GTR described the situation in November 2017 as 'improved in recent months, but still not where it should be.' It was hoped that the rolling out to all units of the latest software would result in a rapid improvement in performance.

In addition to new trains, GTR are running the biggest ever driver recruitment programme. It takes between 12 and 14 months to train a new driver, while familiarisation for the existing staff is also necessary.

Ultimate destinations, North

The assessed capacity of the central section of Thameslink, that between Kentish Town and Blackfriars, is 24tph. But in which direction should these trains proceed, both north and south?

There is a basic problem in that the route through central London is defined very precisely, and of the two main lines north the Midland to Bedford (50 miles from St Pancras) has no branches. Not running the whole length of the line and/or omitting some station calls are the only variations possible. The Great Northern line to be reached via the Canal Tunnels does divide at Hitchin for Peterborough (76 miles from King's Cross) or Cambridge (58 miles) at the new grade-separated junction, but that is really all the choice there is here. Essentially, Thameslink trains here have to be part of the outer suburban operation; all the inner suburban services are part of the Moorgate inner-suburban operation, as now.

That will still leave some Great Northern outer-suburban operations to run to and from King's Cross; notably this includes all trains to King's Lynn. Will this result in some passengers making quick dashes between St Pancras and King's Cross, to catch the next available train?

A new point for operational conflicts will be the at grade Belle Isle Junction, where the Canal Tunnels tracks join the Great Northern main line and meet other services which remain operating from King's Cross. Any 12-car services into King's Cross will need to use the main station, as the Great Northern hotel has long prevented the suburban platforms with their eight-car limits from being extended.

While the Midland line is four-tracked throughout to Bedford, the Great Northern main line reduces to double-track for the 2 miles 50 chains between Digswell and Woolmer Green. This is for the Welwyn viaduct, through Welwyn North station and the two ensuing tunnels. This may provide some pathing problems. Intermediate terminating points see little use at present.

All services mentioned form part of the GTR franchise. Main line long-distance services are run respectively by East Midlands Trains and Virgin Trains East Coast. There is also some open access operation on the Great Northern line.

The long-standing plan for the 24tph peak service is to run 16 trains to and from the Midland Main Line, and 8 trains to and from the East Coast Main Line. In the south, 16 trains are to run via London Bridge and 8 trains via Elephant & Castle.

Is 24tph the most that can be expected when the system has settled down? Or might (say) 30tph be achievable, in time?

Always to be borne in mind here is that operationally Thameslink could never be described as a simple railway. A notable constraint is that the busiest section, that between Canal Junction in the north (where the Great Northern and Midland routes separate) and Blackfriars Junction in the south (divergence for London Bridge and Elephant & Castle) is plain double track, with no passing loops. All that can be offered are two dead-end platforms at Blackfriars when approaching from the south.

Ultimate destinations, South

The situation south of the river is much more complicated. It is an exaggeration to say that trains running south from Blackfriars could in theory reach just about everywhere on the old Southern Railway system, but the choice of routes and hence ultimate destinations is in theory huge.

Given a short list of destinations, this needed to be followed up on the grounds of practicality, the assessment of traffic levels, looking after existing customers, and how

The Southern Railway reconstructed many stations during the inter-war years, Horsham being one of them. This coincided with electrification and work was completed in 1938. It has been substantially modernised in recent times, but care has been taken with the Grade II listed building by Network Rail to retain the ambience of the original. This external view was taken on 19 April 2014. *John Glover*

From time to time stations need reconstruction for a variety of reasons. Today, trains from East Grinstead proceed only northwards; lines to east and west from the high-level tracks closed in 1967, while that to the south is now part of the Bluebell preserved railway. From British Railways point of view, it was closed (on the second attempt) in 1958. The recently rebuilt station building is seen on 23 March 2014. *John Glover*

A two-car 171724 looks rather lost in the vastness of East Croydon, with the 14:34 from Uckfield to London Bridge. The running of short trains is unlikely to make the best use of scarce track capacity; on the other hand, is it sufficient for the traffic on offer …? The date is 13 June 2016. *John Glover*

the whole would (or would not) slot together. This quickly gets into the arcane fields of platform lengths, signal spacing, junction capability, adequacy of power supplies, and so on, though they are of no less importance for that. What frequencies will you need or be able to offer, both in the short and the longer term?

How long a train did the likely patronage on each of the various routes suggest? Was that more or less constant throughout the end-to-end journeys, or does the patronage expected north of London vary greatly from that in the south? There was also the problem of what to do with the lines which were not selected.

The answers will exert a strong influence on how many trains and of what configuration are needed. By the way, where will all the trains be based and maintained?

Perhaps the long-standing Thameslink commitment for services via London Bridge of trains routed via East Croydon and Gatwick Airport to Brighton was always likely to remain and, as has been seen, the Wimbledon loop services via Elephant. But what of the rest? A typical feature of the area to be served is the large number of towns, but very few of them of more than medium size. Apart from Greater London itself, which includes East Croydon, large cities with their associated traffic generating powers are few.

Proposals for services via Croydon have had to be curtailed. This followed concerns about the number of Thameslink trains using Windmill Bridge Junctions (north of Croydon) as well as those of Southern and Gatwick Express, and the net effect on the overall line capacity.

Other concerns have been the condition of the infrastructure on what is the most congested railway in Britain. The £300m Network Rail Improvement Fund is to include work relating to track, signalling, key junctions, drainage, cuttings and embankments, and reducing trespass. This, say GTR confidently, will bring a reduction in delay minutes of up to 15%.

Timetable 2019

The proposals put forward by GTR for Thameslink service patterns were as follows; only those in the south to north direction are shown here in Table 9.3. The new Cambridge North station opened in mid-2017 and is intended to serve the Science Park.

Great Northern

Great Northern Inner Suburban services are little affected by the major Thameslink upgrades, but new trains are to be provided. Siemens have an order for 25 Class 717 dual voltage units for Great Northern services from Moorgate. They are expected to enter service in 2018.

These are six-car sets, as a result of the platform length limitations imposed by the below ground stations over the 2¾-mile section south of Drayton Park acquired from London Underground in 1975. Here, the DC/AC changeover takes place.

From May 2018 peak service frequencies at Moorgate are planned to rise from 12tph to 14tph and off peak frequencies will rise generally.

London St Pancras International

It may be mentioned here that during the period of Thameslink development the main St Pancras station has been completely rebuilt. It now houses:

East Midlands trains long distance services	Platforms 1–4
Eurostar international services	Platforms 5–10
Southeastern services from Kent	Platforms 11–13
Thameslink (at low level)	Platforms A, B

The original station had only seven platforms (one of which was latterly disused), and these major works thus required a doubling of platform numbers overall.

Given also the length of Eurostar trains at around 400 metres, this led to substantial platform extension works

Table 9.3 Proposed Thameslink services from December 2019

All services operate at 2tph frequency

Service	Days
Services via London Bridge	
Bedford, fast from St Albans City, to Brighton, fast via Gatwick Airport	Daily
Bedford, fast from St Albans City, to Gatwick Airport, semi-fast via Redhill	Daily
Bedford, fast from St Albans City, to East Grinstead	Mon-Fri, peaks
Bedford, fast from St Albans City, to Littlehampton via Hove	Mon-Fri, peaks
Peterborough, semi-fast, to Horsham, semi-fast via Redhill	Daily
Cambridge North, semi-fast, to Brighton, fast via Gatwick Airport	Daily
Cambridge, stopping, to Maidstone East	Mon-Sat
Luton, semi-fast, to Medway Towns via Greenwich	Daily
Services via Elephant & Castle	
Welwyn Garden City, semi fast to Sevenoaks via Catford loop	Mon-Fri, peaks
revised to start at Blackfriars	Daily, all other times
Luton, semi-fast to Orpington via Catford loop	Mon-Fri, peaks
revised to start at Kentish Town	Daily, all other times
St Albans City, stopping, to Sutton, then Wimbledon via Streatham	Daily
St Albans City, stopping, to Wimbledon, then Sutton via Streatham	Daily

One unusual feature of London St Pancras International is the variety of destinations which can be reached directly from the station. On 17 December 2015, you could travel on successive trains to Leeds, Bruxelles Midi, Bedford and Sutton. *John Glover*

Shopping mall in the pre-Christmas build up, or a railway station? The answer is both, being a view of a main pedestrian route into London St Pancras International station, complete with Christmas tree, on 15 December 2015. The problem here is that if the shopping gets too popular, those who have no interest in catching a train might obstruct genuine passengers. *John Glover*

outside the existing train shed, while those platforms for both Midland main line and Southeastern services are effectively of new build throughout.

Prior to the completion of HS1, Eurostar services terminated at London Waterloo from their introduction in 1994. They transferred to St Pancras on 14 November 2007.

The Southeastern services call at the newly established Stratford International station on High Speed 1, with further stops at Ebbsfleet where the North Kent services diverge or Ashford to services to Thanet. International services do not and as yet have not called at Stratford International, despite its name.

East Midlands Trains services to Nottingham or Sheffield may call at Luton or Luton Airport Parkway as well as Bedford on sections of the route which are shared with Thameslink.

The platforms for all these services are at the same level as they were beforehand, but the main passenger circulating areas, including shops, HM Customs and other matters associated with international travel, are at the level below. This is more or less at street level. The Thameslink station platforms A and B are underground, at a level below that, with access from roughly the area beneath the buffer stop ends of the East Midlands Trains platforms.

Similarly rebuilt has been the access to the six lines of London Underground at King's Cross St Pancras, which include extensive new low-level passageways, escalators and lifts, and new entrances. These can be somewhat tortuous to follow, as the signage does not always seem to suggest the most direct route.

Future work

The whole of the Thameslink Programme takes place against the background of a Brighton Main Line which has serious capacity constraints. Of these, the Croydon area is perhaps the most difficult, but far from the only one. Network Rail's proposed work in the area includes two additional platforms at East Croydon station with a much expanded high-level concourse, grade separation of virtually all the flat junctions in the Norwood Junction, Selhurst, West Croydon and East Croydon area, and two additional tracks between East Croydon and Windmill Bridge Junction, immediately to the north. This will need extra land, which in turn needs to be protected from other development.

There has been considerable and more immediate concern about the condition of the infrastructure The £300m Network Rail Improvement Fund (£200 million on the southern section, £100 million on the north) is to include work relating to track, signalling, key junctions, drainage, cuttings and embankments, and reducing trespass. This, say GTR confidently, will bring a reduction in delay minutes of up to 15%.

Work on upgrading the Brighton Main Line needs, if at all possible, to be carried out in conjunction with capacity relief work at other locations, the upgrading of power supplies and the resignalling which becomes due in the early 2020s. The whole will become part of the so-called digital railway.

Such work also needs to be aware of the aspirations of the owners of Gatwick Airport, now competitive with rather than complementary to Heathrow, and their expansion plans. Also to be considered are the wishes of Transport for London on the future shape of the inner-suburban services, and those of local authorities in matters such as housing provision and future employment levels almost anywhere.

South London Metro

Is a South London Metro a longer term possibility? Could it stand alone as a franchise or concession? This is an exceedingly complex group of lines, not the least of the problems being the need to serve both West End and City destinations.

A major operational difficulty is the plethora of flat junctions. These are serious inhibitions to getting the maximum capacity out of the lines concerned. How would the service boundaries of such a Metro be defined sensibly?

Junctions are not the only limitations; others are the availability and length of station platforms, turnback arrangements and what the signalling can or could offer. Perhaps crucially, how possible might it be to keep the inner-suburban trains separated from the outer-suburban operations, but without material disadvantage to either group? What freight presence might there be?

How well understood is the present service offering, by the public at large? Would higher frequencies using a simplified pattern of operation offer better value in all its senses? The answer here is probably yes, but major disruptive and expensive works would be needed and there will always be those who lose out in such circumstances. The imposition of a change of train to reach one's destination, where today there is a through service, is never welcomed.

Another consideration here is the Greater London boundary. Suburban services from Croydon enter Surrey beyond Riddlesdown (Oxted line), Kenley (Caterham branch), Coulsdon South (Brighton line), Woodmansterne (Tattenham Corner branch), Belmont (Epsom Downs branch) and Cheam (Epsom line). The administrative boundaries are no tidier than those of the railway!

There is a tenable proposition here for the whole concept to be examined in depth.

How likely are any of these potential developments to become a reality, and in what timescale? Even then, how can the resulting effects on the railway be quantified, planned for and funded?

One of the least desirable mixtures of traffic on any railway is high speed passenger and all stations suburban. In the case of conflict, which one should be given precedence by the signaller? This is the scene at Beckenham Junction on 16 October 1987 with unit 3218, when Eurostar services were routed over South Eastern metals before HS1 was completed to Waterloo. This is a double-track section of line; the second train is in a bay platform. *John Glover*

10

Building the Elizabeth Line

Crossrail is unusual for Britain, but it isn't a Schwebebahn (the suspension monorail in Wuppertal). The nearest comparisons are the RER in Paris, or a German S-Bahn.
Howard Smith, Director of Operations, Crossrail

After lying dormant for several years, what had become Cross London Rail Links Ltd (CLRL) was relaunched in 2002. Later known as Crossrail Ltd, the business case for the 'new' Crossrail was set out as follows in 2003. The term Crossrail or Crossrail 1 is used generally here; the Elizabeth line name applies from the opening of the central tunnel section in December 2018.

The sSRA's consideration of the Chelsea–Hackney corridor is discussed later.

'The purpose of Crossrail is to provide a significant increase in the capacity of the present rail networks into and across London to relieve congestion and overcrowding, to cater for the expected substantial growth in demand for travel into and across the capital over the coming decades, and to increase accessibility.'

CLRL's proposed route option, then known as the benchmark scheme, was a central tunnel following the protected alignment across London, from Paddington to Liverpool Street and then Whitechapel. At the eastern end the route would divide; one branch would proceed to Stratford (and over Great Eastern lines) to Shenfield. The second branch would continue to the Isle of Dogs and the Royal Docks, then under the Thames to join the North Kent lines at Abbey Wood. Some services would continue to Ebbsfleet.

To the west of Paddington, Crossrail would join the Great Western main line before dividing into two branches. One would join up with the North London line, providing services to Richmond and Kingston. The other would be via Ealing Broadway and Hayes & Harlington and thence to Heathrow, subject to the Crossrail promoters coming to a satisfactory agreement with Heathrow Airport, which owns the access rights to this branch.

Montague Report

This all came with a £10 billion bill at 2002 prices, but was it affordable and would it represent good value for money? The Government was supportive but decided to appoint an independent assessment team headed by their business adviser, Adrian Montague. It reported in 2004.

The benchmark scheme was the base from which comparisons were made; one of the concerns was the looseness of the proposals for what happened west of Paddington. Should, indeed, Crossrail terminate there? Montague considered six additional options:

1. Paddington to Shenfield and to the Isle of Dogs
2. Paddington to Shenfield and to Abbey Wood
3. Paddington to Shenfield and to Ebbsfleet
4. Heathrow, Maidenhead and Paddington to Shenfield and to Ebbsfleet
5. Heathrow, Maidenhead, Kingston and Paddington to Shenfield and to Ebbsfleet
6. Heathrow, Maidenhead and Paddington to Shenfield and to the Isle of Dogs (variant of Option 4).

A key finding was that the central section of Crossrail was by far the most costly, and this would be the situation even if such costs were reduced to a minimum. Curtailed options serving destinations to the east of London only would reduce value for money, since the costs of the central section would be spread over a smaller network.

Notably, the Review was uncertain as to whether the planned potential throughput of 24 trains per hour at peak was achievable, given also the need for service reliability. There was particular concern on dwell times at stations if trains were to have only two sets of doors on each side of a car. This would impede people's ability to get on and off quickly. (It may be noted here that the Class 345 trains as built and described later have three sets of double doors.) To this was added how well the innovative signalling systems might cope.

The route to Kingston had a second iteration; Montague showed it in tunnel from west of Paddington and rising to the surface short of Gunnersbury, with an intermediate station below ground at Turnham Green. The Kingston option was however discarded, the Review noting that 'this is also the aspect of the current route design that has attracted most public opposition'.

Some of the route options looked better than others and the Review was especially keen on those linking the central spine with Heathrow and growth areas to the east of London.

CLRL was jointly owned by the Strategic Rail Authority (the Department for Transport after the abolition of the SRA in 2005) and Transport for London. The Review commented that such arrangements 'do not promote decisive, robust governance. 'This would be essential as the scheme approached Parliamentary scrutiny, and beyond.'

Overall though, Montague gave the Crossrail scheme a clean bill of health. But this was not the only group suggesting in which direction the future lay.

SUPERLINK

The independent Superlink organisation emerged in 2005 with rather different proposals for uses of the central Crossrail tunnels, should they be built. Crossrail, they claimed, was designed as a Metro scheme, not a Regional scheme. As such, it did not serve new markets, with its additional usage revenues hardly covering the operating costs.

Superlink would operate on a wider canvas altogether, much more on the lines of linking existing railways from a medium or even longer distance to central London (as represented by the Crossrail central area tunnels). The station at Whitechapel was omitted.

This would remove the need for many passengers to change to the Underground, at various locations. An outline of what was suggested is shown below.

The promotors also claimed that Superlink would some divert existing services away from their present routes (notably the South Western main line from Weybridge eastwards, the Lea Valley line south of Harlow, or Tilbury loop services west of Barking). That would release capacity for more Metro-type services within Greater London.

It turned out that this was not to be. Where Superlink did seem to have a valid criticism was that running only 10tph west of Paddington out of the 24tph arriving there from the east looked like a waste of resources. This still rankled. The extension of at least some of those trains via a new construction in the Old Oak Common/Willesden Junction area to continue to Watford Junction and beyond has its good points, while some at least of the various schemes to take a railway south from Heathrow Terminal 5 remain live.

Other potential Superlink beneficiaries such as Cambridge will get new services courtesy Thameslink, while Stansted Airport and local services will benefit from the widening of part of the Lea Valley line and, potentially, Crossrail 2.

CROSSRAIL AS BUILT

The idea of through running from the north to the south of the capital, as with Thameslink, using railways that largely existed previously, took hold of the public imagination. The Crossrail 1 scheme eventually approved was designed to run between Shenfield and Abbey Wood in the east and Heathrow Airport and Maidenhead in the west.

Like its predecessor, this was to use new underground construction in central London.

The new Crossrail programme involved:

- building a new underground railway across central London, improving existing tracks on the western and eastern branches, building 10 new stations and improving 30 existing stations
- buying a fleet of new trains and a maintenance depot
- appointing a company to operate the service.

The Department for Transport jointly sponsored the Crossrail programme with Transport for London. The programme is being delivered by Crossrail Ltd, a subsidiary of TfL, with Network Rail undertaking the surface infrastructure work necessary on the existing railway.

The decision to invest was based on the forecast growth in the population in London and the South East and the resulting increase in demand for public transport. The business case estimated that Crossrail would produce £1.97 worth of benefit for every £1.00 of cost, through reduced journey times, reduced crowding and quicker interchange between services. The benefit:cost ratio increased to 3:1 when wider economic benefits were included.

A Hybrid Bill to promote the scheme was introduced into Parliament in February 2005. Authorisation was achieved, with the Bill becoming the Crossrail Act 2008.

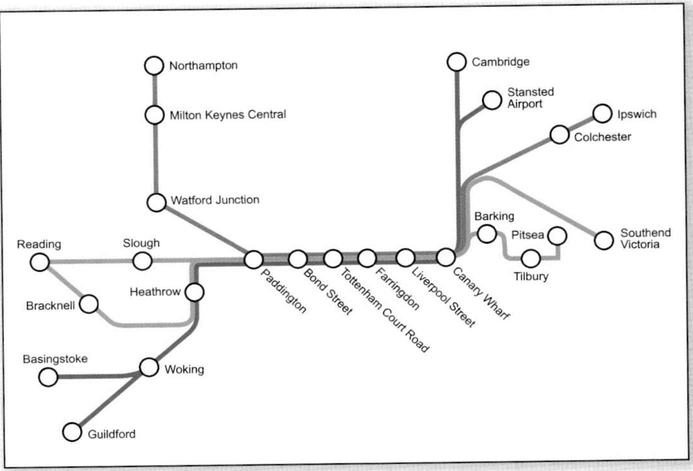

The Superlink cross-London proposal, 2005.

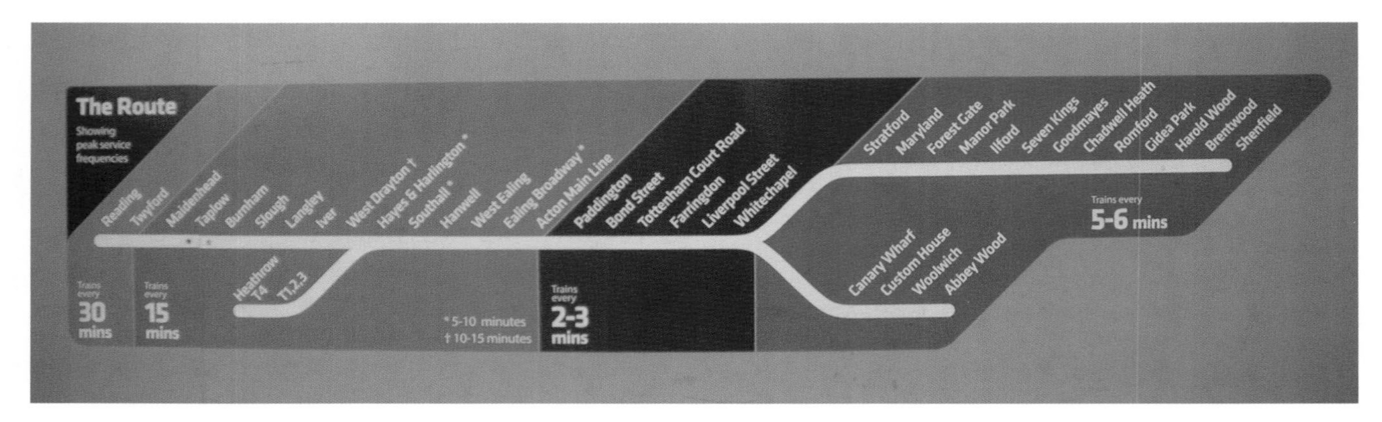

With its opening still a matter of years away, the street hoardings surrounding the construction work at Hayes & Harlington station on 12 April 2016 advertise the forthcoming extent of the Crossrail network and even the service frequencies. How many local stations provide such easily accessible information on what they offer for the price of a rail ticket? Come to that, how many of the passing public have much idea of what is possible? *John Glover*

The Act gave deemed planning permission and the necessary powers for the railway to be built, operated and maintained. The original budget of £16 billion was reduced by £1 billion in the subsequent Capital Spending Review, which also added a year to the timescale.

Crossrail Ltd became wholly owned by Transport for London in December 2008, following Royal Assent to the Crossrail Bill.

Reading, 11¾ miles beyond Maidenhead, was substituted as the western terminus, but this did not happen until 2014.

Construction

For just over three years from 4 May 2012 to 26 May 2015, eight Tunnel Boring Machines (TBMs) were used to construct 42km of new rail tunnels. Each of the TBMs weighed 1,000 tonnes, was 150 metres long, and worked with a crew of 20 tunnel gangs. These teams worked in shifts around the clock, producing around 100 metres of tunnel per week. A Tunnelling and Underground Construction Academy (TUCA) was established at Ilford in 2011, with the aim of providing the necessary numbers of skilled underground workers.

These are large tunnels, too. In comparison, those for the Victoria line (1960s) have an internal diameter of 3.81m, which was increased to 4.35m to include a side walkway for the Jubilee line extension (1990s). Those, though are tube lines; the Crossrail tunnels are for full-sized rolling stock in the National Rail sense, with an internal diameter of 6.0m. That requires the shifting of a lot more spoil during construction and it also constitutes a limit on the routes that it is practicable to follow. This can be due to the foundations of large buildings, let alone obstructions such as the Underground and sewers.

The cutting edge of the tunnel boring machines used consisted of a head which loosened the earth, following which a screw conveyor moved the material away. A rotating arm placed the tunnel lining segments precisely, to form a ring of eight segments. Each ring weighs 22 tonnes. Hydraulic cylinders braced themselves on the completed rings to push the machine forward.

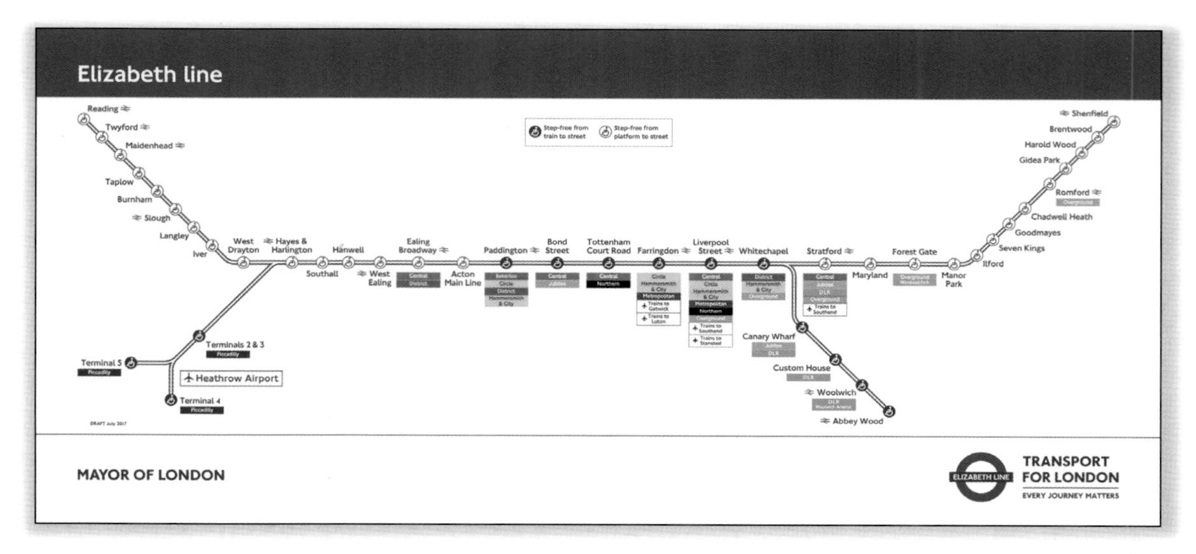

Crossrail1/ Elizabeth line diagram, July 2017

Anglia Railways No 170202 takes a break at Stratford in between journeys on the Cross-Link service which operated from 2000 to 2002. It ran from various origins on the Great Eastern main line to the South Western at Basingstoke. At six unevenly spaced trains a day each way (five on Sundays), with varying stopping patterns, it demonstrated the problems of securing train paths on a busy network. The use of the North London line to cross London meant that this too was a peripheral service, with little opportunity to carry passengers to or from central London. ***John Glover***

A belt conveyor system moved the excavated earth from the rear of the machine to the tunnel portal. In the other direction, pre-cast concrete segments were delivered to the segment feeder. They differed in shape to enable the tunnel to curve.

Tunnelling is a very high risk occupation and in this project consumed 250,000 concrete tunnel segments, employing over 10,000 people. Five twin-bore tunnels were driven, as follows. Traditionally TBMs are named, and as can be seen carried those of females:

- Royal Oak to Farringdon west (Drive X). Two 6.8km rail tunnels, constructed by TBMs *Phyllis* and *Ada*, were completed in May 2012 and January 2014 respectively.
- Limmo (Canning Town) to Farringdon east (Drive Y). Two 8.3km tunnels constructed by TBMs *Elizabeth* and *Ada*, completed in May 2015.
- Pudding Mill Lane to Stepney Green (Drive Z). TBMs *Jessica* and *Ellie* completed their 2.7km tunnel drives in February and June 2014 respectively.
- Limmo to Victoria Dock Portal (Drive G). TBMs *Jessica* and *Ada* completed a second drive of 900 metres.
- Plumstead to North Woolwich (Drive H). TBMs *Sophia* and *Mary* completed their 2.9km drives.

Of the seven million tonnes of excavated material removed as a result of the tunnelling, more than three million tonnes was transported by rail and barge to Wallasea Island in the Thames estuary. This created a new 1,500-acre nature reserve for the Royal Society for the Protection of Birds. Of the rest of the seven million tonnes total, 98% was said to the reused beneficially.

Tunnelling can be exacting work and may need to be very precise. At Tottenham Court Road, clearances over the existing Northern line tunnel and beneath an escalator tunnel were so tight that there was less than a metre clearance both top and bottom.

The tunnel drives finished at Farringdon, an event attended by the then Prime Minister, David Cameron. Particularly notable is the cavern at Stepney Green, where the two eastern branches diverge. The tunnelling was now complete.

That however was only a first stage as the tunnels then had to be fitted out. The key here is the integration achieved. This involved bringing together the many different programme activities, which together delivered the end-to-end railway. Making sure the interfaces between the various groups works, and works well, is of prime importance.

Crossrail 1 was the biggest engineering project in Europe.

Above: Abbey Wood is being upgraded from a two side platformed station to a full-blown terminus for the Elizabeth line while retaining its facility for Southeastern. Bombardier 'Electrostar' 376032 leaves in the down direction on 18 July 2016 when work was in full progress. *John Glover*

Left: This is the Royal Victoria portal of Crossrail 1 on 18 July 2016 as the double-track line approaches the surface station of Custom House. The Docklands Light Railway is on the left. The stations of each here are to be interlinked. *John Glover*

Fitting out

Fitting out can be a complex and time consuming process. There is also an order in which many of the activities must be carried out. Thus the provision of platform doors in the central area has to await the platforms themselves being ready to receive them. In a more general sense, part of the design aim is to provide some common thread in the appearance of both trains and stations.

Tunnel systems

The tunnels as constructed are empty; from top to bottom the following services need to be installed and commissioned as necessary. Right at the top is the overhead line equipment (OHLE). Many of the services on the tunnel walls are represented by cables or pipes. Before these can be installed, though, the walls have had to be drilled with holes by a rig, to support the brackets which will hold them.

- Signalling systems
- Tunnel lighting
- Radio systems
- Communication and control systems
- Power cables
- Fire Main
- Side walkway at train floor level.

At the base are the tracks and, very necessary, the drainage.

In station areas there is also the need for escalators and lifts to reach surface level and the associated passageways and exits to the street.

In the majority of cases, there is access to and from other lines using that same station to be accommodated. To what extent can facilities be shared?

Track

Initially, tracklaying took place from east to west, starting at Plumstead where the engineering depot is situated.

During the day a wheeled gantry was used to carry the sleepers at measured intervals, following which it placed sections of rail into position on the top. Following it was the concreting train. This was a self-contained concrete batching factory. Each night it was entering the tunnels to pour up to 250 metres of concrete, thus setting the sleepers and rail into place.

A more basic track and concreting shuttle operated from the western end working from the portal eastwards towards the complex in situ constructed slab track.

Slab track accounts for about 80% of standard construction; the remaining 20% is for specialised requirements. Thus floating track slabs are used to reduce noise and vibration where such matters may be sensitive, and existing structures such as the Connaught Tunnel require special treatment.

The Plumstead railhead is the main base for the infrastructure installation in the Crossrail tunnels generally. Subsequently, it becomes the site of the permanent infrastructure depot, with around 250 employees. This will perform all maintenance functions on that part of the railway that isn't owned by Network Rail.

On the left is Prince Regent DLR station, to the right is Crossrail 1 as it descends to the Connaught Tunnel beneath the link between what was once three docks. The use of slab track will be noted. It is 18 July 2016. ***John Glover***

Ventilation

Ventilation is an important issue for the central London stations. Ventilation dynamics are altered by the provision of full-height platform doors, which will in effect remove the rush of air felt by waiting passenger from an approaching train. There is a new challenge, represented by the trains being air-conditioned and the unwelcome ability of the system to suck in hot air if the tunnel is not cooled sufficiently. That becomes more of a problem if signal checks mean that trains become stationary in the tunnel for any length of time. This all produces a need for ventilation fans and shafts.

The ventilation and intervention strategy for Crossrail as a whole is the subject of an agreement with the London Fire and Emergency Planning Authority.

Power

Traction power feeds for the central section are located at Pudding Mill Lane (eastern portal onto the Great Eastern) and Kensal Green. Either source is sufficiently powerful to supply the whole of the section single handed, if necessary.

Signalling

The Crossrail route has three signalling systems, which have to work seamlessly, both individually and the transition for trains between one and the next:

- East of the Pudding Mill Lane portal on the line to Shenfield; this is conventional four-aspect colour light signalling, based on the existing Liverpool Street interlocking. This is supported by Network Rail's Automatic Warning System (AWS) and Train Protection Warning System (TPWS).
- On the central section Paddington to Pudding Mill Lane/Abbey Wood, trains are driven and controlled automatically by a Communications-Based Train Control (CBTC) system from Siemens This allows trains to operate at reduced headways and to run with precise speed control and stopping accuracy. In-cab signalling replaces conventional lineside signals. An interlocking system provides train detection, points control and route setting. The trackside signalling communicates with the on-board system and with the Automatic Train Supervision (ATS) systems at the route control centre. The use of axle counters as a secondary means of train detection also covers the use of engineering plant in the central area, and as a standby in case of failure.
- West of Paddington on Network Rail's Great Western line, use is planned of the European Train Control System (ETCS) Level 2. The dynamic switchover from CBTC to ETCS will enable trains to travel into or out of the central section without having to stop.

The signalling and control system stops a platform screen door from opening if the corresponding train door is faulty, or vice versa if a platform door is faulty. It also ensures that the train is stationary and wholly in the platform before the doors will open.

Stations

Stations appear massive to those used to London Underground; for a start the platforms will be 5m wide and of 200m length (with provision for future fit out to 240m). This is roundly twice the length of present Underground platforms; their sheer size is the most striking feature. They are long enough to reach in some cases between two Underground stations and several have two exits. People will need to decide which way they want to turn when they get off the train, and it is a job for the information systems to help them make that decision before they get there.

Of the 41 stations used by Crossrail 1 trains, there are six in the central London batch of Paddington to Whitechapel, common to all train service provision. There are a further four on the Abbey Wood branch and 13 on the line to Shenfield. There are 15 on the route to Reading and three on the Heathrow stub ends. For the time being, the proposed extra station at Old Oak Common is a future consideration.

The North Woolwich branch was never the most photogenic. In the days before electrification it was operated by Cravens Class 105 2-car DMUs, with one seen here at Custom House. The train is heading for Stratford, or perhaps Tottenham Hale, despite displaying Woolwich on the rear blind. This is now a joint station for use by Crossrail 1 and the Docklands Light Railway. No trace of this station, seen here on the very wet day of 1 March 1977, remains. *John Glover*

The remains of the North Woolwich branch Custom House station are seen here on 21 September 2011, long after services had ceased. The Docklands Light Railway was the only railway then left in operation. Crossrail construction has yet to start. *John Glover*

The only completely new above ground station on Crossrail 1 is that at Custom House, seen here under construction on 12 April 2016. This is new from the ground upwards, though the North Woolwich branch station closed in 2006 was on the same land. The Custom House DLR station is out of sight in the foreground, though the track of the eastbound line can just be seen. *John Glover*

Stations served by Crossrall divide by type, as follows. Those below ground level which equate to extensions of existing London Underground managed stations (Bond Street, Tottenham Court Road, Farringdon, Liverpool Street, Whitechapel), those which are also below ground but completely new and free standing (Paddington, Canary Wharf, Woolwich), all to be managed by the operating company. There is the completely new surface station at Custom House (with the DLR station of the same name adjacent), those completely rebuilt and shared with another TOC (Abbey Wood with Southeastern), those on the Great Eastern line (Stratford to Shenfield inclusive) and similarly on the Great Western line (Acton Main Line to Reading inclusive). Finally, there are the three Heathrow stations operated by Heathrow Express.

Operating company

The concession for service operation was let to MTR Crossrail (a subsidiary of the Mass Transit Railway, Hong Kong) by Transport for London, to whom the operator is responsible. Since 31 May 2015, the Liverpool Street–Shenfield route has been operated by the company as TfL Rail. That will continue until the name change to the Elizabeth Line.

The operating contract continues until May 2023 and may be extended by up to 31 months.

Staffing

MTR Crossrail will operate the stations at which it is the only, or the major, service provider.

Some of the existing stations which are served by Crossrail using new low-level platform tunnels are already large in their own right. What do their existing staff know or feel about what is happening and how it will affect them?

It is important to keep the staff at the sharp end briefed and in touch, and how each part of the developing operation does and will impinge on them and others. Thus at Liverpool Street there are the staff of train operators Abellio for East Anglia, Arriva Trains for the Overground (Enfield services etc), MTR for Crossrail (Shenfield services) and London Underground (Central, Metropolitan, Circle and Hammersmith & City lines). Is that all? No, there are also the service providers for London Buses and the British Transport Police to be kept in the loop. Liverpool Street is a Network Rail managed station.

Everybody needs an opportunity to contribute their own points of view and to be informed.

All stations on the Shenfield line are now staffed from first trains to last trains and this will apply to all Crossrail stations. This aids both safety and security. Patrols are made by British Transport Police. Stations are being or have been refurbished, with an emphasis on step free access. That includes the gatelines and ticket machines. Stations also need to be well maintained and clean.

'We aim to build stations worthy of a 21st century, world class but affordable railway,' said Clinton Leeks, Crossrail Corporate Affairs Director, in 2008.

Network Rail works

Network Rail is responsible for the surface sections of the lines east of Pudding Mill Lane portal and west of that at Royal Oak. The company budgeted a total of £2.3 billion for work in the sections both east and west of central London. This includes the upgrading of 70km of track, redeveloping 28 stations and renewing 15 bridges, as well as removing tunnel spoil by rail.

Crossrail 1 uses the Great Western Relief Lines en route to Reading. The existing 25kV AC electrification is extended west from Airport Junction, where the Stockley Flyover has itself been extended to allow parallel working onto the tunnelled spur of the Heathrow branch.

The grade-separated junction at Acton allows Crossrail trains in the up direction to avoid conflicts with freight trains accessing Acton Yard, and a new up side bay at West Ealing station provides for the Greenford branch shuttle. There are new sidings at Maidenhead.

Major enhancements and new station buildings are being provided at Acton Main Line, Ealing Broadway, West Ealing, Southall, Hayes & Harlington, West Drayton, Slough and Maidenhead. Stations generally have undergone platform extension work, though at Hanwell, Langley, Burnham, and Taplow selective door opening was to be used. These stations have undergone minor refurbishment works.

All stations will be step-free from street to platform with lift provision where needed, and the ten central section stations and the Heathrow stations will have level boarding.

Crossrail 1 uses the Great Eastern 'electric' lines to Shenfield, so named as those energised in the original 1949 DC electrification. The main infrastructure changes are remodelled sidings at Gidea Park, Ilford and Shenfield and the provision of a turnback between Chadwell Heath and Goodmayes. Major enhancements were promised with new station buildings at Ilford and Romford, with new footbridges and lifts at Forest Gate, Goodmayes, Gidea Park and Harold Wood. Station platforms here too were extended generally, except at some lesser used station where selective door opening is to suffice. The upgrading of Stratford for the 2012 London Games was sufficient for the needs of Crossrail 1.

Elsewhere at Canary Wharf a new underground station has been built; this is entirely separate from the London Underground station of the same name, which is likewise separate from that of the Docklands Light Railway station, also called Canary Wharf. There is to be no interchange 'within the barrier' between any of them.

Further east, Custom House is a completely new surface station for Crossrail 1. What remained of the former North Woolwich branch station has been obliterated and a connection made to the duly upgraded DLR station of the same name. For a short distance, both lines here run in parallel.

TfL is separately undertaking works to refurbish booking halls at stations such as Chadwell Heath and Manor Park which were not included in Network Rail's

The West Drayton station building seems likely to go back to the date of its construction in 1884, though the inelegant canopy on its frontage does it no favours. It was pictured here on 12 April 2016. *John Glover*

The arrival of the Elizabeth line is seeing a number of stations being upgraded, including here Hayes & Harlington on 12 April 2016. This is the view from the north side of the station looking towards the Relief Lines. *John Glover*

The new up side bay platform at West Ealing sees 165121 on the shuttle service to Greenford. With a single journey time of 10 minutes, a half hourly service can be maintained by one unit. Here it is making a cross platform connection with Great Western 387153 on an up stopping service. The latter will become a Crossrail 1 operation. Connections between the branch and down trains are rather less convenient. It is 3 November 2017. ***John Glover***

works and in 2015 it was agreed that the remaining seven stations, not required to have step free access under the terms of the Crossrail Act, would be made step free as part of a TfL managed programme.

The route then follows that disused alignment through the Connaught Tunnel to the Silvertown area, whereupon it descends into a new twin-bore tunnel under the Thames to a below ground station at Woolwich, where new shafts were needed. Two additional tracks have been constructed alongside the existing North Kent line from Plumstead to Abbey Wood, where Crossrail 1 terminates. This station underwent major remodelling to provide enhanced facilities and interchange with the North Kent line[44].

Class 345 trains

The agreement between Rail for London (a TfL subsidiary) and Bombardier Transportation was let in 2014 for the supply and delivery of (now) 70 sets of Class 345 nine-car 205m trains. There is a purchase option on 14 more trains.

The Class 345s are designed to cater for all services on the Elizabeth line. They are being built at Derby, Litchurch Lane, to the 90mph Aventra design which replaces the 'Electrostar'.

The trains have been purchased outright by TfL rather than through a leasing company.

Each vehicle has three sets of double plug doors per bodyside, as keeping station dwell times down will be critical to the success of the project. This helps to get the maximise use out of the fleet, as well as giving passengers quicker journeys.

Each train is calculated as being able to carry around 1,500 people (seating and standing combined). The end Driver Motor Second vehicles have all longitudinal seating, the rest have two sets of bays of four (total 16 seats) within the otherwise longitudinal layouts, apart from the centre vehicle where four designated wheelchair bays are in effect substituted.

Total seats in the nine vehicles are 454, or around 50 per vehicle on average; the rather shorter 20m vehicles of the Great Eastern Class 315s, which they in part replace, have an average of 79 seats per vehicle. The Class 315 trains have been used on Liverpool Street services since they were built in 1980.

Internally, the trains feature walk-through connections between all nine vehicles, CCTV, Wi-Fi and real-time information displays. These carry interchange information and service updates for other lines. All trains are air-conditioned and are Standard class only.

The cabs on the Class 345 are TSI (Technical Standards for Interoperability) compliant and incorporate interfaces for the three signalling systems. The trains take their power supply from the 25kV AC overhead only. They are fitted with regenerative braking.

The Class 345 design seeks to balance the needs of short-distance passengers in central London and those of travellers from the suburbs and beyond. Some Crossrail 1 passengers will make relatively long journeys, for instance Reading is 40 miles from Farringdon. Following Metro/London Underground practice there are no lavatories, although toilets will be provided at all the

Class 345s are slowly replacing the Class 315s on the Liverpool Street – Shenfield services and an up service formed of 345008 is arriving at Chadwell Heath on 3 November 2017 with the 13:04 from Shenfield. For the time being, these trains are being stabled and maintained at Ilford. *John Glover*

345008 arrives at Seven Kings with the 14:10 Liverpool Street to Shenfield on 3 November 2017. End to end journey times for the 20¼ miles with 12 intermediate station stops are 43 minutes. *John Glover*

A pair of Class 345s in passenger service cross at Seven Kings on 3 November 2017. On the left is 345008 with the 14:10 Liverpool Street to Shenfield service, to the right 345009 with the 14:04 up service from Shenfield to Liverpool Street. *John Glover*

surface stations as well as several of those in the central section. The Crossrail journey between Paddington and Heathrow will take 22 minutes.

The first sets of Class 345s began to enter service in June 2017 on the Liverpool Street–Shenfield service. They have been delivered initially as shortened seven-car trains, which are the longest that the high-numbered platforms at Liverpool Street can take. In their truncated form, they are based at Ilford depot, though the stabling sidings here have been substantially altered to allow nine-car operation.

The two extra cars to make nine-car sets are being added in 2019 when the Shenfield services start running through the central tunnels. The complete fleet will be based at the new dedicated maintenance depot at Old Oak Common, commissioned in late 2017.

The first nine-car Class 345s are being deployed on the Heathrow Connect services between Paddington (main line) and Heathrow Airport T4, from May 2018. It will be noted that these nine car trains have cabs at each end only; they are not divisible in service. There is thus no possibility of running short trains at quieter times.

Around 450 drivers are being recruited and they need training. MTR will have many other new staff too, whose uniforms will be branded with the familiar roundel. At first this is as TfL Rail, later as the Elizabeth line.

Depot

The trains are to be stabled, maintained and serviced by Bombardier for the term of the agreement, which continues until 2046, at a depot which it has been the company's responsibility to build at Old Oak Common. The assets will be handed back to Rail for London at the term of the agreement. It is a functional and performance based agreement; technical risk is owned by Bombardier.

The depot is being fully signalled.

Bombardier are using their Automatic Vehicle Inspection System, where cameras and optical sensors collect and analyse data and monitor vehicle condition. Train maintenance includes light overhaul, exchange of bogies, wheelsets, motors and other principal on-train equipment for the full Crossrail fleet of up to 84 units.

The depot will be capable of extension to cater for 11-car (245m) trains, should more vehicles be added to the trains at a later date. This is certainly seen as a possibility.

Operation

Three objectives behind the Elizabeth line network upgrades are connectivity, capacity and reliability. Might it be possible to increase the throughput from 24tph to 30tph if so needed in the future, without compromising such aims? If capacity is short of requirements, the choice is to increase the total number of trains, or to lengthen each one. Given sufficient incentive, one might even be able to do both!

Of the original fleet of 66 trains, 59 were expected to be in daily use.

There are no sidings on the central section, but there are a number of crossovers. A potential difficulty is the termination of a substantial proportion of the westbound

Empty stone traffic wagons head west through Ealing Broadway behind 66136 on 18 July 2016. The mixture of local passenger and freight traffic both on the Great Western Relief Lines and on the North London (in particular) offers operating problems for both. Bringing freight trains to a complete stop is to be avoided wherever possible, as it can take a lot of time to get them started again. ***John Glover***

service in the sidings beyond Paddington at Westbourne Park. It takes time to ensure a train is empty before closing the doors, and it will only be able to move relatively slowly into the turnback sidings. Furthermore, access here can be limited by conflict with another train departing eastbound.

Outside the direct Crossrail interests, electric trains operated by Great Western Railway carried passengers for the first time on 5 September 2016. These were the Class 387 'Electrostar' units built by Bombardier and were at this stage running between Paddington and Hayes & Harlington only.

These were the first of a fleet which extends to 45 four-car units. The service operated was extended successively to Maidenhead and then Reading. They can run in four-car, eight-car or 12-car formations on GWR, displacing the Class 165 'Turbostar' diesel units.

Timetable 2019

There are a lot of conflicting requirements in setting the future timetable, not the least of which is the likely volume of demand where Crossrail is providing an entirely new service. Yes, these things can be modelled, but it is in the end the operators who have to cope.

The central section of Crossrail which all trains have to negotiate is that between Paddington and Whitechapel, a distance of around 9km. This includes the four intermediate stations of Bond Street, Tottenham Court Road, Farringdon and Liverpool Street. The end-to-end running time for this section is calculated to be a sprightly 12 minutes. This compares with the 23 minutes needed if the journey is made on the Hammersmith & City line of London Underground, which has 11 intermediate stations. That alone is an indication of how Crossrail will speed up the journeys of many people.

Services will operate at broadly the same times as London Underground, with first trains arriving at Tottenham Court Road station around 05:30 and the last departing at about 00:30. Future night services are not ruled out, but they would require 'significant changes to the maintenance practices of Network Rail on the surface sections of the route'.

The services described here are those proposed as at late 2017, but full details were yet to be made available.

At peak, the central section will see 24tph. Going east, the service divides at Whitechapel into 12tph to Abbey Wood and 12tph to Shenfield. That will not be enough to cater for the volume of passengers using stations on the Great Eastern section to Shenfield, and an additional 4tph will operate in the peak direction only between Liverpool Street main line and Gidea Park.

Going west from Paddington, the districts to be served are rather less densely populated than those in the east. More than half the trains were anticipated to terminate here, but something nearer 16tph is now expected to continue. Of these, provisionally, 6tph are likely to take the branch to Heathrow Terminals 2, 3, with 4tph continuing to Terminal 4 and 2tph (possibly 4tph) to Terminal 5.

For those continuing on the main line, 4tph are likely to terminate at Reading with a further 2tph terminating at Maidenhead. The balance seems most likely to terminate at West Drayton.

Peak service frequencies are shown here, but it should not be assumed that all Crossrail trains will call at all stations, especially west of London. All stations from Reading to Paddington would be a tedious journey and in any case there are the services of an outer-suburban nature that Great Western Railway may continue to provide at reduced levels at stations like Twyford, Maidenhead, Slough and Ealing Broadway to be taken into account. Similarly, track access possibilities need to take into account of Heathrow Express services,

Off peak services will be at reduced frequencies, with 20tph now intended over the central section. They will offer 10tph in the east to each branch. In the west the situation is not known, though not all the services on the central section are likely to continue west of Paddington.

Smaller stations will generally have a minimum of 4tph.

The resulting timetable sees an unbalanced service between the east and the west. The earlier but defeated Crossrail Bill saw this as a problem and promoted the additional line to Aylesbury in the west, but included only Shenfield in the east.

However, the present system will add around 10% to total rail capacity in central London.

The branches

There are five railways that branch off Crossrail. From the east, Romford–Upminster is a self-contained single-line operation, with a system connection only from the Romford end. Operation is by a single unit shuttling up and down and no change is anticipated. The line was electrified in 1986 and is operated by London Overground.

The service from West Ealing to Drayton Green, Castle Bar Park, South Greenford and Greenford has run from Paddington or Ealing Broadway, but has been cut back to a self-contained service operating from a newly installed bay platform at West Ealing. Operation of this double-track line and the other single-track branches west to Henley-on-Thames is by Great Western Railway.

The Slough to Windsor & Eton Central stub end branch (no intermediate station) has the disadvantage that it diverges from the south side of the formation at the west end of Slough station. It is thus adjacent to the fast lines and the running of through trains to and from the Relief Lines (on the north side) is not really practicable. So this too will remain as a shuttle service.

Further west, the line from Maidenhead runs to Furze Platt, Cookham and Bourne End, where a trailing branch comes in from the final station, Marlow. Any train travelling the whole branch must reverse at Bourne End. (The principal line used to continue to High Wycombe, but that section was closed in 1970.) The net result in this constricted location is that the maximum train length that can be accommodated beyond Bourne End is two cars, although five cars can be used between Bourne End and Maidenhead. This can result in the two parts of the branch being operated separately, with an enforced change for passengers at Bourne End.

That leaves the line from Twyford, to Wargrave, Shiplake and Henley-on-Thames, another single track branch with a bay platform at Twyford. Both these branches had a residual peak only through service to Paddington, but these ceased at the end of 2017.

These three branches (not that to Greenford) were at one time proposed for electrification, though that now seems very unlikely. Given the single fleet of nine-car Class 345s and the lack of any short electric units suitable for branch use, together with the Bourne End problem, retaining operation by Great Western Railway diesel units looks probable.

A related branch problem is how connections at their respective junction stations will be maintained, and what part each operator and Network Rail will play in achieving a satisfactory result.

Windsor Castle stands guard over the branch train of a Class 117 unit as it progresses towards Slough (left of picture) on 4 September 1977. The Windsor Viaducts with their 255 arches ensure that the Thames Bridge is of sufficient height above the river for navigational purposes. *John Glover*

The Maidenhead–Marlow service features this reversal at Bourne End. In July 1978 a Class 117 approaches from Marlow, arriving in the platform which can only accommodate two coach lengths. It will then reverse to continue to Maidenhead. The curvature here is dictated by the River Thames (out of sight in the background) and the need for the train to cross it on a bridge. *John Glover*

At Bourne End on 6 November 1998, the Marlow branch train formed of 165001 waits in what appears to be an ordinary wayside station, until one notices that the line is truncated at the far end. This was the former continuation to High Wycombe, but there is a road beyond the stops and housing beyond that. The platform on the right can take five cars, but it is not possible to proceed from there towards Marlow. *John Glover*

Staged Operations Plan

The inauguration of Crossrail services is being staggered over a four-and-a-half-year period, as shown below.

- May 2015. Liverpool St (main line) to Shenfield services introduced as TfL Rail, replacing the Abellio Greater Anglia operation and using refurbished Class 315 trains. Their reliability has been much improved through various modifications. (Stage 0)
- June 2017. Introduction of first new Crossrail Class 345 trains (seven cars only to fit Liverpool Street station platforms), then progressive withdrawal of Class 315s on Shenfield services. (Stage 1)
- May 2018. The Crossrail line opens between Paddington (main line) and Heathrow T4 using Class 345 full-length trains at 4tph. This replaces the Heathrow Connect service and part of the Great Western Railway inner suburban services. (Stage 2)
- December 2018. The key Central Operating Section opens. This allows the commencement of through operation between Paddington and Abbey Wood (only). Crossrail 1 is renamed the Elizabeth line, with the kind permission of Her Majesty. (Stage 3)
- May 2019. Eastern interface commissioned, providing through services between Paddington and Shenfield. (Stage 4)
- December 2019. Western interface commissioned, with through services extended from Hayes & Harlington to Reading and hopefully Heathrow Terminal 5. The Elizabeth line is now complete. (Stage 5)

These dates are related to the changes in the National Rail Timetable. It may be noted that the nature of the type of operating contract used by TfL, termed a Concession, means there is no revenue risk for the operating company; the risk money is on the company's performance, which includes that of Network Rail and others.

Funding

The major part of the £14.8 billion funding needed comes from the Department for Transport, Transport for London, the Greater London Authority (supported also from the proceeds of supplementary business rates) and the City of London. Other contributors include the Canary Wharf Group (design and construct the Canary Wharf station and contribute to its cost), Berkeley Homes (funding the station box at Woolwich), and Heathrow Airport Ltd as successors to the British Airports Authority.

Future Crossrail

Crossrail Ltd is charged with delivering the end-to-end railway, including necessary alterations to the existing rail network owned by Network Rail, through to final completion. The company hands over elements of the new infrastructure to TfL in the summer of 2018, in advance of the start of services in the central tunnel in December 2018.

After that handover, Crossrail Ltd retains responsibility for the commercial and technical close out of the construction contracts and for delivery of the final stages, which will see services operating throughout the complete network in December 2019.

What sort of growth will the Elizabeth line engender over time? The infrastructure is designed to take 11-car trains at 30tph; will this be needed, and if so when? How feasible and/or desirable might future West Coast Main Line destinations be? Could earlier ideas for other west London destinations be revived?

There are several further events in the offing affecting Crossrail 1, all of which are in one way or another to do with Heathrow Airport.

With Phase 1 of HS2 now in possession of its authorising Act, a new station is to be built at Old Oak Common as part of that scheme, with the specific intention of encouraging interchange to and from Crossrail 1 (which will also need the provision of new platforms). This site also has the potential to provide interchange with new stations which it is intended to provide on the West London line (Hythe Road) and North London (Old Oak Common Lane) line via, it must be said, rather lengthy walkways.

A further possibility is new platforms on the Great Western fast lines, though this is a mere three miles from Paddington. Given the negative effect on track capacity and journey times, how many trains would it be sensible to stop there?

Old Oak Common would also be a useful interchange point for those using HS2 to or from the north of England. From here they would be able to take a Crossrail 1 or (possibly) a Heathrow Express train to the airport. The long-term future of Heathrow Express is perhaps less certain.

Then there is the proposed new rail route from Reading to Heathrow Airport, replacing the long-established Rail-Air coach link. This would diverge from the main line at a junction in the area of Langley, with new construction taking it to Terminal 5.

How and by whom might that be operated, whether as part of another service or independently? As a stopping service, limited stop, or what? A route via Heathrow from Reading to Paddington is not going to be time competitive with trains on the main line via West Drayton. Would fares for passengers whose journeys happened to take them via Heathrow carry a hefty airport surcharge, too?

There is also the question of plans for another runway at Heathrow. This would permit substantial further expansion of the airport's usage and the consequential higher demand levels for surface access by both airline passengers and airport/airline staff. Present indications are that travel by public transport will need to be promoted strongly, though initial plans for railways refer only to the direct link from Reading and the long talked about southern route towards Staines-upon-Thames and thence to Woking and/or Waterloo.

11

Further Development

Confucius, he say, may you live in interesting times. Anon

Where, then, do we now stand? When the aftermath of World War 2 had subsided, the railway had many difficult years. Few anticipated the growth in road transport, especially with the private car and freight, which had the added advantage of many Forces-trained drivers. They could make use of surplus road vehicles owned by the state.

On the passenger side, this was the era of New Towns, though little attention was given to the proximity of the railway and the possibility of stations to serve them. The Motorway era began and its routes were expanded.

The net result was that railway traffic levels did well to maintain their previous volumes, while many traffics slowly ebbed away. The railways were still seen primarily as commercial enterprises, with passenger fares and freight charges both controlled by public bodies.

Railways Act 1993

The Railways Act 1993, the privatisation Act, was seen by many as the then government hoping to pass the problem to the private sector, which could run the railways more efficiently anyway, couldn't they? What actually happened took virtually everybody by surprise.

The years of trying to show how the railways benefited society had slowly borne fruit. The Victoria line of London Underground was funded on the basis of community gains, while the Transport Act 1968 introduced the concept of government grants for socially necessary services.

But there was no whole-heartedness about developments of this nature, and there were many negative views too. Beneath it all, one felt, there was a feeling that railways as a mode of transport, had largely had their day.

At some stage, all this changed. Politicians were beginning to doubt whether road building or widening, unpopular as it often was, could answer the growing congestion problems. The quality of what the railways could offer passengers, whether long distance, suburban or rural, improved noticeably. The railway managed to become what many people saw as the answer to transport problems, rather than a problem in itself.

Result? Passenger volumes grew markedly, and kept growing. Politicians joined the general enthusiasm for the railway that everybody now wanted. High Speed 1 and High Speed 2 became accepted as the way forward (except by a few voluble dissenters). This was less because of their speed benefits, real as these are, but for their ability to free up the existing system and add greatly to the overall capacity available.

Similarly, a number of well-chosen urban rail schemes, for instance in Merseyside, Greater Manchester and Strathclyde, demonstrated what could be achieved in cities. The latter included state-of-the-art fares schemes, which in London were led by Travelcard and later with the Oystercard.

One of the most public and effective collection of schemes to be delivered, on a large scale and for a considerable period, was the provision of quality transport for the London 2012 Games. It was a very public demonstration of what a well organised transport system could do; after exhaustive preparations, it worked almost without fault.

It has thus become increasingly obvious that the railway in its many guises, including light rail systems, has much to offer. Meanwhile, the continuing growth of usage brought its own problems.

Systems need to be expanded, not only to cater for today's traffic levels, but also to anticipate what was likely to happen in the next 10, 20 or 30 years. This will never be an easy task, since it also needs to take account of population changes which all suggest growth, the locations of where people will have their homes, where the jobs will be created and how access will be achieved.

In the mega-scheme category already described are Thameslink and Crossrail 1, the Elizabeth line, both to be completed in 2019. Will these be enough? All the indications are no, and to follow these is likely to be Crossrail 2, but that will not be before the 2030s at the earliest. By then, more than a decade of further growth will have taken place.

Seating is often described as 2+2 or 3+2 to give some idea of both capacity and comfort. However, as this view shows, 2+2 can still give the effect of 'tight pack'. There are no spacers between each pair of seats, and while that increases the gangway width and thus the standing capacity, it seems to offer a rather undesirable compromise. This is 317122, with a body width of 2,820mm (9ft 2in) on 17 September 2014. *John Glover*

Use maximisation

Another approach which is also being pursued is to make the very best use of what is already there. Thus the main line suburban tracks out of Waterloo are presently signalled (with four-aspect colour lights) to accommodate 18tph, or one train every 3min 20sec. This railway has the advantage of a whole series of grade separated junctions for the lines diverging to Epsom and Chessington South (at Raynes Park), to Shepperton and Twickenham (at New Malden) and to Hampton Court and, separately, Guildford via Cobham (both at Surbiton).

What further can be done? The first approach is to lengthen all trains from eight cars to 10 cars; this was achieved in 2017 (a 25% increase in capacity). Could this be 12 cars? There are really difficult engineering considerations relating to platform lengths, particularly but not only at Waterloo, but where there's a will there's usually a way. That would add another 25% capacity.

Can service frequency be increased by reducing headways? Practical limitations to this are platform dwell time generally and the throat layout at Waterloo. The 15mph restriction over the latter means that it takes over 90 seconds for an up train to get from the home signals to the buffer stops.

Would the introduction of ETCS Level 2 be a way of reducing headways between trains? Network Rail have suggested that this might enable the present 24tph limitation of the South Western main line tracks to be raised to 30tph, but that this would need Automatic Train Operation (ATO) to achieve the full benefit.

Collectively, there might be a way here of substantially increasing the present service volumes in terms of carrying capacity. Not the least of the problems is that ETCS Level 2 has yet to be deployed on the scale suggested. The signalling system needs to provide the age-old but essential standard of no more than one train on any one section of track at any one time. That way, collisions cannot happen. Where novel approaches such as ETCS vary from traditional systems is by replacing the predetermined sections of track (those between fixed signals) with a flexible block of space, which moves with the train.

This is the interior of the West Japan Railway's Shinkansen 'Bullet Train' on show at the National Railway Museum, York. The use of (unidirectional) 3+2 seating looks comfortably spaced, but so it should with a body width of 3,383mm (11ft 1 in). This Series 0 vehicle was built in 1976 and withdrawn from service in 2000. ***John Glover***

It is of interest to note that London Underground's Victoria line is now offering a peak service of 36tph, albeit with 134m long trains rather than 240m and much less restrictive track layouts, which allow greater rates of accelerations and braking.

There will need to be a greater consistency in driving standards. Common observation will show that different motor car drivers will drive the same car in a rather different manner, and much the same can be said of train drivers. Automated driving, possible with advanced systems, is a way of effectively eliminating the variables which are inevitable with manual operation; the result is (hopefully) a capacity-optimised system. This extends to decisions of when to accelerate and by how much, when to apply power and when to coast, and when to start braking and again by how much.

Important though it is, train frequency is only part of the equation which has to be solved. If each train holds half as many passengers again as now, are the platforms going to be wide enough? Is access by bridge, subway, passageways, stairs/lifts/escalators and entrances/exits capacious enough to be able to cope? What happens in the street outside, when passengers either converge on or disperse from the stations?

If train frequencies increase, the platforms still have to be largely cleared of the passengers alighting from the previous train and refilled with passengers to join the next before it actually arrives.

A further complication arises when trains for a number of destinations leave from the same platform, since not all passengers will board the first train to arrive. This is particularly problematic on National Rail, where the same platform may perhaps be used for trains to (say) six different destinations, each at relatively infrequent intervals. Even then, they may have different stopping patterns, or not all run the whole length of the route.

Such situations are particularly likely to arise on Thameslink trains proceeding south from central London, but this is far from a unique situation. The Underground's subsurface lines have similar problems; for example from Tower Hill westbound, successive trains may be proceeding to Edgware Road (Circle line), Wimbledon, Richmond, or Ealing Broadway (all District line destinations).

Depending on the line or route concerned, grade separated junctions which will resolve many conflicting movements between trains, can be a rarity.

Southern 'Electrostar' 377137 calls at Clapham Junction with an up service on 25 July 2014. The substantial construction to the left provides escalator access between the bridge and the platforms. With its 17 platforms, this station is the busiest interchange to be found anywhere on National Rail but platforms, though adequate, are not as wide as might be wished. *John Glover*

Metroisation?

It is for reasons such as these that Sir Peter Hendy, Chairman of Network Rail, has suggested that the national network needs to be Metroised. The term Metroisation is defined as the process of gradual change to dedicated and clearer routes, with simplified and more consistent stopping patterns, a more frequent service, and new interchanges. This approach seems to have originated in Australia, on the Melbourne Metro.

In a speech at Infrarail in 2016, Sir Peter outlined his thoughts for National Rail as follows:

> 'If we are going to fit in the trains that we need, we're going to have to run it as the Tube is run – so that the trains are very frequent, they'll all be packed, and they'll go into and out of terminal stations very quickly.
>
> 'Practically, it's going to be the only way that we are actually able to fit in enough trains to carry people around. If assets can be run like the Tube, we could make Britain a model for the rest of the world.
>
> 'We've got to do it faster than anybody currently supposes; it can't be like previous signalling schemes, which is a 50-year programme of which only the first 10 years are ever delivered.
>
> 'This also means running stations like the Bakerloo line terminus at Elephant & Castle, where trains arrive at peak hours, a driver gets out at one end and another gets in at the other end.
>
> 'In 20 years, every London terminus will be like that, because it will be the only way we can get more trains in and out of it – and I can't see any other way of operating, which is why I think Metroisation is the right answer. Having trains hanging around a London terminal for 20–30 minutes at peak hours can't be an effective utilisation of platforms.
>
> 'But we need the signalling system to allow us to do it, we need franchises to mandate that to happen, and we'll need enough staff and enough rolling stock to allow the railway to cope with that capacity.'[45]

So what might Metroisation imply? In general, for the Network SouthEast type services, we might see a gradual development of more dedicated lines with lessened interaction between them, simplified and more consistent stopping patterns between trains to even out running times, with the aim of operating more frequent services.

Coping with prolonged growth

The strategic options fall into three broad categories:

- Reduce demand for the services
- Improve the productivity of the assets and other resources
- Increase the supply of trains and/or the infrastructure on which they run.

Of these, reducing demand given the more mobile and growing population can perhaps be dismissed as not worth general consideration. Raising fares by one or more percentage points above the Retail Price Index is a time-honoured way of doing it gradually, but the Mayor of London, Sadiq Khan, has already said that he wants to keep the fares over which he has control basically unchanged during his term of office. This will, if anything, result in further demand growth to be accommodated, but reduced income for the operator.

However, analysis and action in terms of planning policies on housing and where people are likely to be employed is perhaps desirable, though this is essentially a long-term approach.

One of the wider gaps to be found between train and platform is that at Clapham Junction's Platform 17. It is used by trains between the South Central and West London Lines. 'Mind the Gap', indeed. This is a direct result of track curvature. Could it be lessened? The main problem here is the use of this route by mixed traffic, especially freight, and the clearances have to allow for all comers. It is 25 July 2014. *John Glover*

Gains in productivity are also important from wherever they may be sourced. 'Doing more with less' is the way to keep ahead and stay ahead of one's competitors. New methods, new technology, new equipment can all feature in this, though there can be problems. The 1980s change to Driver Only Operation (as a result of the Midland Suburban Electrification) resulted in prolonged labour stoppages, with the whole project seriously delayed as a result.

Sadly there have been more recent problems of this nature, albeit not on London Underground, where the last passenger service to be operated with both a Motorman and a Guard ran in 2000.

Sign of the times? A large cycle park has been created here at Paddington station, used primarily perhaps by those who commute into the capital and then cycle to their place of work. This is Park and Ride with a difference; the date is 18 July 2016. *John Glover*

More trains, more infrastructure?

The last 20 years have seen a relentless growth in rail traffic throughout Britain, in London at least as much as anywhere else. Table 11.1 shows the volume of morning peak passengers arriving at each of the London 'cordon points', and again for the rest of the day.

The cordon points are defined as the first Zone 1 station that a service calls at or passes through on its way to the city centre terminal. The aim is to count all passengers, but once only. Thus 'London Bridge' includes Charing Cross, Waterloo East and Cannon Street, 'Vauxhall' includes Waterloo, 'St Pancras' includes Farringdon and City Thameslink and 'Old Street' includes Moorgate.

Passengers on the non-franchised operations such as Eurostar, Grand Central, Heathrow Express and Hull Trains are excluded.

Table 11.1: Passenger Arrivals in Central London by National Rail services, excluding London Underground, typical autumn weekday, 2016

Cordon points	AM peak	Rest of day	Arrival totals, all day
Vauxhall	113,600	106,100	219,700
London Bridge	133,000	68,100	201,100
Victoria	65,800	68,100	133,900
Liverpool Street	71,800	39,500	111,300
Euston	30,600	50,000	80,600
St Pancras	36,200	38.000	74,200
Paddington	26,500	35,600	62,100
Blackfriars (via Elephant)	30,700	21,500	52,200
King's Cross	22,800	27,500	50,300
Fenchurch Street	25,400	9,600	35,000
Marylebone	14,000	11,600	25,600
Old Street	13,000	4,200	17,200
Totals	**583,400**	**479,800**	**1,063,200**

Source: Rail Passenger Numbers, DfT, 28 July 2017

A modern staircase leads to a new footbridge and way out at East Croydon. There are also lifts available. It is 13 June 2016. *John Glover*

Below: Major works took place at Waterloo in August 2017 to allow platform lengthening on the south (main line locals) side. Eight cars was the limit as shown here; the challenge was how to increase this to 10 cars. This is the view of the station throat from island Platforms 1 and 2 showing just how tight the curvature was. 456855 is leaving on 21 January 2016. The work required the reprofiling of all platforms 1 to 6. *John Glover*

Results are shown in the descending order of the all-day totals. The wide disparity in volumes can be seen, with the 'Southern' routes still coming out top of the list. Also to be seen is how City stations (Liverpool Street, Fenchurch Street and Old Street) do a much greater proportion of their total business during the am peak. The Intercity stations of Euston, Paddington and King's Cross see most of their arriving passengers during the rest of the day. Both Victoria and St Pancras are evenly balanced.

These totals are increasing and a key issue is capacity and how it can be enhanced.

Basically, the available tools with the existing railway are:

- to increase service frequency
- to lengthen each train to carry more people
- design issues, such as more standing room and fewer seats
- the number and positioning of doors to minimise station dwell times
- new signalling.

It also needs to be remembered that more trains mean strengthened power supplies, more depot accommodation, more maintenance facilities and more staff.

The place, if any, of double-deck trains is also of relevance, though accommodating them on anything other than completely new railway construction in Britain (such as HS2) is highly unlikely. For commuter-type

At Willesden Green, a southbound S8 Metropolitan line train to Baker Street on the non-stop section to Finchley Road passes a Jubilee line train of 1996 stock in the turnback siding on 2 January 2015. *John Glover*

What might the interior of future Underground tube stock look like? This is the Siemens Inspiro mock up, which was on display in East London during 2013. This too features wide, open gangways between cars. ***John Glover***

operations they also suffer from slow passenger loading and unloading. This is due to few doors, the need for passengers to negotiate stairs to the upper and lower saloons (up, down or both), and their basic unsuitability for many people with disabilities.

There is also the matter of freight services and how they can be accommodated on what is becoming a largely passenger network. This needs to be achieved in a way that meets freight customers' needs and hence those of the freight operators. The traditional approach that would relegate freight to movement at night is just not good enough in today's competitive environment.

In any event, time has to be set aside for the railway infrastructure to be both inspected and maintained.

More new lines?

But adjustments to the existing network can only go so far, and all the indications are that new lines will need to be developed to keep up with volume growth. The primary new scheme at the moment is Crossrail 2 (to be discussed), which is likely to run on a northeast to southwest axis through central London.

In what may well turn out to be a prelude to Crossrail 2, there is a need to come to grips with housing expansion in the Lea Valley. Meridian Water are to build around 10,000 new homes in the area south of the present Angel Road station. This is to be resited rather nearer the existing Northumberland Park station and renamed Meridian Water.

This will entail the building of an additional track (and platforms) on the eastern side of the existing railway, resulting at first in a three-tracked railway between Lea Bridge and the new station. A 4tph all stations service from Stratford is anticipated, with operations commencing in 2018.

This is to be built so as to be compatible with the proposed Crossrail 2 scheme, which envisages quadrupling the Lea Valley line and is discussed below.

CHELSEA–HACKNEY, OR CROSSRAIL 2?

If cross-London schemes are to be the answer for the future, what other scope might there be after the completion of Thameslink and the Elizabeth line?

The 1989 Central London Rail Study proposed the Chelsea–Hackney line. The original intention was that existing railways both north and south of central London would be linked by a new underground railway between them, thus offering a new series of cross-London links. In some ways this was a further development of the 1935–40 New Works Programme, which saw the Underground acquiring some National Railways lines, notably those of what became the Northern line extension from East Finchley to High Barnet and Mill Hill East, also the Central line from Stratford to Epping and North Acton to West Ruislip.

The proposal as seen in 1996[46] was for a tube type line running from Wimbledon in the south west to Epping in the north east, offering a service of 30tph in central London. This would take over the District line between Wimbledon and Parsons Green, where District line trains from the Earl's Court direction would terminate.

There would be a new underground station built at King's Road, Chelsea and subsequently at Sloane Square, Victoria, Piccadilly Circus, Tottenham Court Road, King's Cross St Pancras, Angel, Essex Road, Dalston, Hackney Central and Homerton, thence to Leytonstone.

By taking over the Epping branch north of Leytonstone (rather than that to Hainault), the Central line service would then be simplified to run only on the Hainault branch.

The Chelsea–Hackney line was aimed at solving three principal issues:

- Relief of crowding on the Victoria line, in particular the cross-London link between Victoria and King's Cross St Pancras, but also the Piccadilly, Northern, Central and District lines.
- Improving rail access to Hackney, which traditionally has had poor Underground links to central London.
- Similarly for Chelsea, which is not well served by the existing tube network.

The Chelsea–Hackney route was safeguarded from conflicting developments, originally in 1991.

A reassessment in 2011 produced three route options. These were the safeguarded route from Epping to Wimbledon, as previously, a London-focussed Metro scheme, or a Regional scheme.

The Metro scheme would be a self-contained scheme without directly involving services on Network Rail. The presently favoured Regional scheme takes a similar in-town alignment but would be extended over Network Rail infrastructure at each end.

A Liverpool Street to Cambridge train consisting of smartly turned out 317668 is seen here routed via Stratford on 19 May 2001. This is always an alternative to the normal route via Hackney Downs and no stations at which such trains normally call are omitted in the process. ***John Glover***

Crossrail 2 route (autumn 2015)

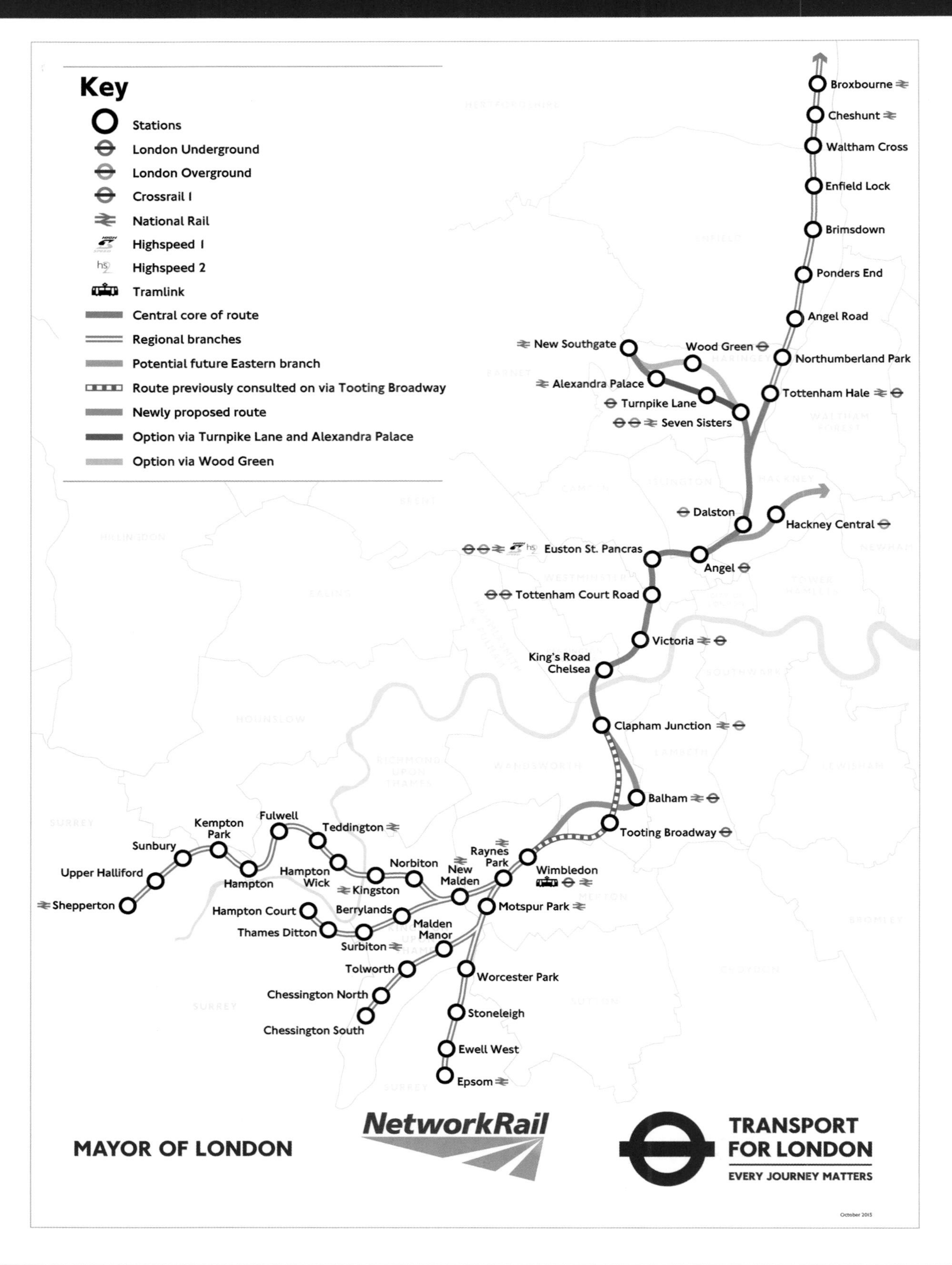

Crossrail 2

Chelsea–Hackney was to be a tube-style operation, although the use of trains to (at least) sub-surface dimensions was contemplated. This was the key to having the northern terminus at Epping, where the former Great Eastern branch was built to main line clearances. The Crossrail 2 project as its successor is also aimed at filling a northeast-southwest gap in public transport infrastructure, thereby supporting population, housing and employment growth and relieving overcrowding on the existing network.

It would help address London's housing shortage by making sites such as the Lea Valley more attractive to developers, though much of this is on flat, low-lying ground. It would also help to relieve capacity constraints on the South Western Main Line, relieve congestion on the Victoria line and the Morden branch of the Northern line and cater for the dispersal of passengers to/from HS2 at Euston.

Meanwhile, the eastern end of the Central line would be left to its own devices.

The central section of the now proposed route is from a combined Euston St Pancras (with passenger access from the platforms to both main line stations), Tottenham Court Road, Victoria, King's Road Chelsea, Clapham Junction, Balham (or Tooting Broadway, to be decided) and a subsurface (but not tunnelled) four platformed station at Wimbledon. This would be around four metres deep and situated on the south eastern side of the existing station. The latter would remain as is, with the exception of the London Tramlink Platform 10. This would be abolished and the trams would in future terminate on street in the vicinity of Wimbledon Bridge House.

The centre two Crossrail 2 platforms would be used for trains terminating at Wimbledon, with access to the maintenance depot and sidings.

Crossrail 2 trains would then rise to the surface, one each side of the existing Network Rail formation, and continue alongside to New Malden, with a rebuilt junction at Raynes Park to reach Epsom and Chessington South.

At New Malden, Crossrail 2 trains would join the existing slow lines to continue towards Kingston and Shepperton, or to Surbiton and Hampton Court.

The final destinations on all these branches except Chessington South are all in Surrey.

North of Euston St Pancras, trains would serve Angel (after which there could possibly be a future branch to Hackney Central), Dalston, and then there would be two branches. One would take Crossrail 2 trains to Seven Sisters, then Turnpike Lane and Alexandra Palace (or possibly on an alternative route with a station at Wood Green), to a surface terminal adjacent to New Southgate Great Northern line station.

The other branch would come to the surface at Coppermill Junction, south of Tottenham Hale, and Crossrail 2 trains would then run over the existing Network Rail Lea Valley tracks via Enfield Lock, to terminate at Broxbourne (Herts).

Without further infrastructure work, that would result in acute congestion problems on the Lea Valley line, though a third track to the new Meridian Water station is already in hand. The intention is that this be incorporated in the Crossrail 2 works. This would result in the present double-track to Broxbourne being quadrupled all the way from Coppermill Junction to Broxbourne Junction (for the Hertford East branch).

The proposal is for the new tracks on the eastern side of the existing formation to be used by outer suburban trains and those serving Stansted Airport. There would be new platforms on these tracks at Tottenham Hale, Cheshunt and Broxbourne only (the single platforms at Northumberland Park and Meridian Water becoming redundant).

Crossrail 2 services would use the existing lines and terminate at Broxbourne, where the present station consists of two island platforms. Separation of Crossrail 2 from other railway operations in North East London would thus be all but complete.

Service patterns

A peak throughput of 30tph in the central area is proposed, reducing to 24tph/20tph off peak. Of these, 10tph in the south would terminate at Wimbledon (as described earlier) with 20tph proceeding beyond. It is intended that 6tph will continue to Epsom (though not beyond), 4tph to Chessington South, 4tph to Hampton Court and 4tph to Shepperton. The remaining 2tph would be short workings to Hampton Wick, only.

In the north, there would be 15tph to New Southgate and 15tph to the Lea Valley, of which 3tph would terminate in a new platform at Tottenham Hale, making this a five-platformed station. Other turnbacks would be provided at Enfield Lock and, in the south, at Hampton Wick.

It is intended that Hertford East would be served by trains from Liverpool Street as now and possibly Stratford, but with fewer stops than an all-stations Crossrail 2 service, which would be too slow. A similar situation would arise if the Crossrail 2 service was extended north of Broxbourne; Stansted Airport may be an attractive destination, but it is still nearly 20 miles further on.

The same sort of challenges might occur at the Surrey end, though the continuation of some services from

Opposite: This map shows the extent of the Crossrail 2 Regional network, as proposed in 2015. There are two alternative routes of via Balham or via Tooting Broadway, also via Turnpike Lane and Alexandra Palace, or via Wood Green. In each case, the tunnel portals are west of Wimbledon station and on the approaches to Tottenham Hale and New Southgate. Apart from access works for the construction of new underground stations and for ventilation requirements, the surface works concern the necessary adaption of the existing railway plus depot(s) and sidings.

Level crossings are the bane of the railway operator's life, particularly where the land is low lying. They are also a safety hazard, which grows with road traffic volumes, but also rail traffic volumes. This is Enfield Lock station with the crossing immediately beyond the platforms. A route 121 bus is heading for Enfield Island Village, the name indicating the proximity of the River Lee Navigation. It is 17 September 2014. *John Glover*

Waterloo on the line to Epsom is anticipated. This would cater for those living in Leatherhead, Dorking and stations to Guildford via Epsom.

Beneficial results for other traffic would see Waterloo losing substantial volumes of its slow line services via Wimbledon. This would enable a revamp of suburban services generally to take place. Liverpool Street main line would see its Lea Valley stoppers diverted to Crossrail 2, again providing more train paths to the terminus.

Main depot provision would be at Wimbledon on the south side of the existing main line. There would be stabling at Broxbourne, Upper Halliford and Chessington South, with infrastructure maintenance facilities at New Southgate.

Unlike the Elizabeth line, the Crossrail 2 route is presently blessed with nine highway level crossings and a number of footpath crossings. Given the increase in the number of train movements, it is intended that all of these will be closed, with the exception of the level crossings at Summer Road on the Hampton Court branch and at Percy Road, Hampton, on the Shepperton branch. For the others, alternative arrangements will be made for traffic and pedestrians to cross the line. This will be quite a design challenge.

Crossrail 2 would be a National Railways service and it is anticipated that it would be a similar operation to the Elizabeth line with, for example, platform edge doors in the core stations. Signalling would be to ETCS Level 2 standards, with the expectation that trains will be Driver Only Operated with ATO in the core.

Design

As now proposed, Crossrail 2 will have longer trains (much the same as for the Elizabeth line), use 6.4m diameter tunnels, and only a limited number of stations in central London. Platform width would be a generous 6.0m; compare this with the late 1960s Victoria line where, for economy in construction, this was cut to only 7ft 6in (2.2m).

Chessington South was never intended to be a terminus, though it has been so ever since it was built in 1939 due to the creation of the Green Belt. The platform to the left has never been used and the connecting footbridge was never built anyway. The track behind the road bridge on which the photographer is standing would have continued to Leatherhead, but is now likely to be used as a stabling point for Crossrail 2 trains. Here 455910 stands with a Waterloo service in July 2002. ***John Glover***

Other desiderata are straight and level platforms, routes underground that avoid clashes with sewers, parts of London Underground or piled building foundations, and maximising the clearances where such problems are encountered. The minimising of gradients and maximising the radii of track curvature are also desirable, as is low property take and, at the end of it all, a low maintenance railway.

The finding of a viable approach route and site for the Euston-St Pancras station in particular was in the end down to a very few options indeed. It will of necessity have to be at a less than ideal depth of around 25m below ground level. This makes for long surface to platform access routes.

Studies suggest that the Regional option of Crossrail 2 as opposed to the Metro version, which would not encroach on Network Rail tracks, delivers the most benefits. A key element is to integrate with other anticipated Network Rail upgrades. How can these be optimised? Scheme capital cost is estimated at £32 billion. It is capable of being funded by a mixture of public and private investment. London would contribute over half of the capital costs.

The remit of the National Infrastructure Commission, set up in 2015, was to provide an unbiased analysis of the UK's long-term needs. Transport infrastructure is a major example and the Crossrail 2 project was endorsed by the Commission and subsequently by the Government.

It is intended that a Hybrid Bill to authorise construction will at some stage be submitted to Parliament. More immediately, satisfactory outcomes need to be reached on issues such as funding and affordability.

Crossrail 2 is being promoted jointly by Transport for London and Network Rail.

HIGH SPEED 2

The effects of High Speed 2 will extend to local rail services in the London area. A major consideration is the need for additional London Underground capacity to cope with passengers arriving at and departing from Euston on HS2. This will happen from around 2026, which Crossrail 2 would be designed to provide, albeit not initially. How will the needs of Londoners be balanced with London commuters and others living outside the capital? If the available carrying capacity is insufficient to cater for the needs of both groups, who will decide on their relative priorities?

Not all HS2 passengers will use Euston; some will join/alight at Old Oak Common. How can Old Oak Common, as a major interchange with HS2, be best fitted in with the rest of the network? Present schemes show completely new stations on each of the West London line (between Willesden Junction and Shepherd's Bush) and the North London line (between Willesden Junction and Acton Central). The Old Oak Common station on the Great Western main line would have platforms on both the Main and Relief Lines, which hopefully would also provide access to and from the line via Greenford to High Wycombe and beyond.

However, the provision of platforms is not in itself a guarantee of whether any, some, or even all trains passing through will stop. Many Great Western Railway main line passengers from the west will choose to reach Heathrow Airport, for instance, by changing at Reading if the new link from the Iver area to Terminal 5 is built.

BANK REDEVELOPMENT

It is not just new lines which are likely to need to be progressed, exciting though these may be. It is at least as important to upgrade and update the existing system where, in many cases, the strains put on the infrastructure are such that extensive (and thus also expensive) works are required.

Nowhere is this more obvious than at Bank, where the Central line, the Northern line, the Waterloo & City line and the Docklands Light Railway come together, to be joined underground with the District/Circle line platforms at what is still called Monument station.

The principal problem is the very long distances below ground which people may have to walk, which can include the entire length of one of the Northern line platforms. This also makes such people an unwanted hazard for those joining and alighting from Northern line trains. And if that wasn't enough, many will need to add a walk along a long passageway to the Central line or, in a different direction but a similar distance, to the Waterloo & City.

There are also numerous steps, escalators and a Travelator. There are some lifts, but these do not amount to a comprehensive means of disabled access. Entrances and exits to and from the street are also less than ideal, both in terms of where they are and access issues associated with them.

If starting again from scratch, it might have been done differently, but that is of academic interest only. The key problems are the lack of space overall, plus the substantial distances between what, when much of it was built, were entirely separate railways.

Overall, there are 15 entrances and exits, three ticket halls, 2 Travelators, 15 escalators and 6 lifts, plus all the connecting stairways and walkways, which lead to 10 platforms. Its complexity puts it into a class of its own, not only in Britain but also perhaps on a world scale. It is used by around 100,000 people in the morning peak and about 300,000 during the course of a day. This includes those interchanging between lines, as well as those for whom Bank/Monument is the start or finish of their journey.

The Bank/Monument station upgrade is providing:

- A new entrance on Cannon Street, with lift and escalator connections;
- A new passenger concourse with a moving walkway, which will use the existing southbound Northern line platform tunnel;
- A new tunnel and associated platform for the diverted southbound Northern line; and
- New passenger routes between the Northern line, the Central line and the Docklands Light Railway.

Completion of this work is scheduled for 2021.

GOSPEL OAK–BARKING

The Gospel Oak to Barking line, known unofficially as GOBLIN but also as the T&H (Tottenham & Hampstead), was one of the orbital railways, the passenger routes of which were swept up into what became London Overground.

It has a curious history, based on its being an access route for the Midland Railway to the docks at Tilbury. This was for boat trains from St Pancras via a long-severed link north of Kentish Town station to Upper Holloway, but more importantly for freight to and from the Midland Main Line, the West Coast at Willesden Junction, or the Great Western at Acton. Freight traffic continues to the present day and indeed is likely to grow with the establishment of DP World's 'London Gateway' port on the Thameshaven branch. In any event, it is the main rail access route to and from Thames-side industries, and these freight trains also require track access.

The four trains per hour local diesel unit service, latterly operated by a fleet of eight Class 172/0 2-car units, managed to expand the passenger business to the extent of causing severe overcrowding, but the route was never electrified. This was put in hand at the behest of Transport for London and, after a series of blockades, was to be completed in early 2018.

Major works on this 12-mile line included extensive track lowering for a mile through the Walthamstow Queens Road station area. In this section the line passes beneath the Great Eastern Chingford branch, but obstructions include other overbridges and large diameter pipes. A reduction in the

Above: Purchased for the use of London Overground services between Gospel Oak and Barking was a fleet of eight Class 172/0 Turbostars, built by Bombardier. These two-car units have 124 seats between them and were becoming stretched to cater for the traffic on offer. Between 2016 and 2018 this line was electrified, albeit that new electric stock was not immediately available. No 172004 is seen idle in Willesden Train Care on 09 June 2014. *John Glover*

On 27 February 2017, the (first) reopening day, the 10:18 Barking to Gospel Oak formed of 172003 is leaving Walthamstow Queen's Road as a Class 315 passes above with the 10:18 Liverpool Street to Chingford. Both are in London Overground livery. As can be seen, there was still a long way to go with erecting the 25kV AC overhead supplies. *Martin Higginson*

station platform heights here was also needed. Elsewhere, there was a general requirement for track lowering wherever overline obstructions were encountered. There is also a general station improvement programme which includes platform lengthening.

Operation of the electrified services is to be by a fleet of eight four-car Bombardier Class 710 Aventra electrics, part of an order by TfL for 45 such units. Their general layout resembles that of the Class 345s for the Elizabeth line. Delivery in mid-2018 is anticipated.

The result is to be a service in which each electric train will carry roundly twice the number of people as a two-car diesel train.

BARKING RIVERSIDE

This however is not the end of the story. A Transport & Works Act Order has been granted to TfL to extend the Tottenham & Hampstead line from Gospel Oak to Barking line on to Barking Riverside. This means that trains will no longer terminate in the Platform 1 bay at Barking, but be diverted over the 1950s flyovers to the main Tilbury line and platform Nos 7 and 8 (both reversible).

From here they will progress roundly a mile along the Tilbury line to a new facing junction where they turn south towards the new Barking Riverside housing development. This will be a stub-end branch with a terminus 1½ miles distant. There will be no intermediate stations and thus no duplication of c2c services. Passive provision for a future station will however be made at Renwick Road, on the c2c line just short of the junction.

The outer edges of the London suburban area see the 1960s Bletchley flyover across the West Coast Main Line on 30 May 1967. A Class 310 unit stands on the left, with a Class 40 in the distance. It now seems possible that the flyover will be brought back into use as part of East West Rail, or perhaps more importantly as part of a relief freight route which avoids London. *John Glover*

Track capacity on the main line is perhaps another matter, given also the growing needs of freight traffic.

The Barking Riverside branch will be able to accommodate a 4tph service and the station will be built so that an extension under the Thames to Thamesmead and the Elizabeth line terminal at Abbey Wood could be constructed later.

The extension is fully funded, with opening anticipated in 2021.

BATTERSEA EXTENSION

A development at Battersea around the site of the listed former power station will support 25,000 new jobs and more than 20,000 new homes, to be created over the next 20 years.

The southbound Charing Cross branch of the Northern line uses Platform 2 at Kennington. From here, trains may either join the line from Bank and the continuing route to Morden, or use a tunnel which completes a one-way loop under the Morden tracks and returns trains to Platform 1, in the northbound Charing Cross tunnel.

Both tracks of the 3.2km Battersea extension leave the return loop at new step-plate junctions and continue to an intermediate station at Nine Elms and then to the Battersea Power Station terminus. The running tunnels consist of bolted concrete linings, with 5.2m internal diameter to incorporate a metre-wide walkway. There are openings between the two tunnels for escape purposes.

Operation will be by extending present Charing Cross line terminators at Kennington over the extra distance, which will require additional trains to operate the service. It will not be possible to run trains between Battersea Power Station and the Bank branch.

The main tunnelling with TBMs Amy and Helen was completed in November 2017, with line opening expected in 2020.

BAKERLOO LINE EXTENSION

The Bakerloo line's southern terminus at Elephant & Castle has long been a candidate for extension. That might take it to Lewisham and perhaps beyond, and a number of options have been floated.

There is always scope for new stations; this is Imperial Wharf on the north side of the Thames on the West London line. It was opened in 2009 and was photographed on 12 April 2010. Construction of a double-tracked station on an existing viaduct is never cheap, given also the need here for lift access. ***John Glover***

Probably ever since it reached Elephant & Castle in 1906, there have been aspirations to take it further in a general south-easterly direction, but they have all come to naught. This even got as far as including an extension to Camberwell (as a proposal) on the official post war Underground diagram.

This scheme is once again being proposed. After suggestions of extending the Bakerloo tracks over Network Rail to Hayes and/or to central Bromley, partly on new construction, such ideas seem to have been downgraded to 'future potential extension options'.

Instead, the present intention is to take the Bakerloo to Lewisham. The route from Elephant & Castle would be via the Old Kent Road, with two intermediate stations, before reaching New Cross Gate. Here it would offer interchange to Southern Railway and London Overground services, before proceeding to a final stop at Lewisham. This would offer considerable further interchange possibilities with National Rail and the Docklands Light Railway.

In so doing, the line would offer sizeable regeneration possibilities. All the new stations would be located within Opportunity Areas.

There would be no operation over Network Rail lines, which would make it a more straightforward scheme. TfL plans to apply for a Transport & Works Act Order for the line by 2020.

Major new capital investment schemes

The Transport for London Business Plan for the years to 2021/22 was finalised in December 2016, though some of the future rolling stock orders were later postponed. These are the major schemes; it must be noted that the expenditure totals exclude any contributions from third parties:

London Underground	
Modernisation of subsurface railway, resignalling, one third capacity increase	£1,388 million
Crossrail train procurement and other TfL Crossrail expenditure	£893 million
New trains and signalling for Piccadilly, Central, Bakerloo and Waterloo & City lines	£1,237 million
Northern line extension to Battersea	£612 million
Additional trains for Jubilee and Northern lines to enhance capacity by an extra 6tph on each line	£673 million
Major station capacity upgrades already in progress at Victoria, Tottenham Road, Bond Street and Bank	£483 million
Fleet and signalling renewals, accessibility regulations compliance	£419 million
Additional step free station access	£194 million
Camden Town congestion relief, prelude to Northern upgrade 2	£120 million
Holborn congestion relief, prelude to Piccadilly upgrade	£101 million
Energy/carbon reduction schemes	£14 million

(It has turned out that the purchase of 10 new trains for the Jubilee and 6 for the Northern lines was not finalised after all. Both were cancelled in November 2017 following a 2% drop in overall passenger numbers and the associated revenue loss that summer).

Docklands Light Railway	
Asset renewals, capacity enhancements, infrastructure new trains	£30 million
Main line rail	
Barking Riverside extension	£82 million
Gospel Oak–Barking electrification, station investment	£80 million
London Tramlink	
Construction of Dingwall loop (Croydon) for higher frequencies	£12 million
Other operations	
Elephant & Castle station upgrade to support local redevelopment	£53 million
Woolwich Crossrail station equipment fit-out	£24 million

And then? On National Rail as well? Where will the anticipated population growth be accommodated in terms of where they will live, where they will work and how they will get there? What rail services will be needed for access to an expanding Heathrow and/or any other airports and how might they best be fitted into the whole?

12
Conclusions

In 2015, 66% of those who lived in the South East had travelled by National Rail in the last 12 months, the most frequent amongst adults in Great Britain. In London, it was 61%. Rail Passengers Factsheet, Department for Transport, January 2017

So much then for the events of the last 85 years or so, and the present plans which may shape the network in the South East for the next 15. What has been achieved?

It will be clear that the descent of the railway from a profitable private enterprise to one where at least major capital expenditures had to be provided by national government, or by more local organisations, was a difficult transition all round.

The New Works Programme 1935/40 was cut short by World War 2 and only partially recovered afterwards, while various planning interests seemed intent on inflicting major damage to the infrastructure as a consequence of their intense dislike of the Thames railway bridges. Fortunately, their recommendations were unsuccessful, but the aftermath did pave the way for the creation, many years later, of heavy rail routes across central London.

More benignly, the Green Belt preserved some of England's green and pleasant land, while the New Towns turned out to be the 1950s equivalent of Metroland. They were not, however, built with the idea that good railway connections were important for their success.

The British Railways Modernisation Plan of 1955 was well intentioned, but sadly lacking in forward vision. In the succeeding decade, it did however result in the electrification of more of the system in London and the dieselisation of the rest. But the main line railway and the Underground alike were still in urgent need of more upgrading.

The problems were the damage that the private car was wreaking on passenger volumes, falling populations in inner London and less than buoyant employment levels in central London. The Victoria line did eventually get built on the grounds of the social benefit it would produce; it was never a commercial proposition. Dr Beeching's 'Reshaping' of 1963 did much in some circles to harden attitudes against the railway as an outdated anachronism, though services in the London area remained remarkably intact.

The 1970s introduced the concept of 'grant aid' for those services which needed it, but value for money became a mounting obsession of government. Various bodies would have had railways turned into roads, or the system reduced to its rather small profitable core. Politicians became ever more active, with Ken Livingstone as Leader of the Greater London Council introducing his ultimately disastrous 'Fares Fair' policy for the Underground and buses in 1981.

Managerial reorganisation within British Rail, as the organisation had retitled itself, split the passenger business into InterCity, Network SouthEast and Regional Railways in the late 1980s. This resulted in a more focussed and accountable approach, which extended on Network SouthEast to much more than painting every station lamp post bright red! The railway was getting better at drawing attention to itself. Services benefitted generally and further electrification filled many gaps.

On the Underground, the Jubilee line extension to Stratford got under way, following earlier successful efforts towards rejuvenating Docklands with the Docklands Light Railway.

Where we are now?

But with the national system, the Railways Act 1993 meant privatisation of it all and, notably, the separation of operations from infrastructure and the introduction of franchising. Not all went well, with the infrastructure company, Railtrack, lasting only until 2002 when it was replaced by Network Rail.

Slowly, the railway was becoming seen as part of the answer to urban transport problems, as opposed to part of the problem itself. The outstanding event of the early 2000 period was perhaps the introduction of London Overground

Southeastern's 375808 approaches St Mary Cray on the up Chatham slow line on 16 October 2007. With the aid of the Chislehurst Junction connections, there is a range of possible London destinations. The building of the junctions was a direct result of the Kent Coast electrification of the late 1950s. ***John Glover***

as part of Transport for London which, with a very considerable level of public expenditure, produced a worthwhile orbital rail network around the capital. Most of this meant a total reconstruction of lines already in existence, with some new work elsewhere, but the results have certainly paid off in terms of increasing passenger volumes.

Another success story was the continuous upgrading of the Chiltern line, which started in the British Rail era, but was pursued vigorously under private ownership.

As always, the performance of the dozen or so franchises providing National Rail services in the London area has been patchy. Governmental infatuation with statistics has continued; whether or not this is the best way of judging what is being achieved may be open to doubt.

Should the Department for Transport separate out the longer distance and shorter distance franchises, or keep them as an integrated whole? Both approaches have been tried and rejected as in Great Western and Thames, or perpetuated as with Virgin West Coast and London Northwestern. The position of Network Rail has also come under fire; to what extent should it get into bed, metaphorically speaking, with one or more Train Operating Companies? Should Network Rail itself be split up?

Meanwhile the day-to-day work has to go on, with what has amounted to unending passenger growth. Seemingly, the numbers have been little affected by the economic gloom of recent times. Major projects soon coming to fruition are Thameslink and Crossrail 1, the Elizabeth line, (2019). They don't come much more major than these two. Having said that, Crossrail 2 will run them close if it progresses as hoped.

There are a large number of other schemes, notably on the Underground, as detailed in the preceding Chapter. With growth continuing, it is a task in itself to try and ensure that the capacity of the infrastructure and the quality of the operation both attain and keep high levels of performance.

Where we go next?

Railway performance has slipped a little in recent times. To what extent is this due to trying to carry ever more passengers on a system which in many cases is largely fixed? More passengers getting on and off trains mean longer dwell times, and so on.

Is the Operations, Maintenance and Renewals budget sufficient? (If it isn't, that spells nothing but trouble in the years to come.)

Station staffing can be an emotive issue; someone in a ticket office is not the same as a person with operational responsibilities on the platform. This ticket office was installed at street level at Walthamstow Queen's Road station on the Tottenham & Hampstead, following the TfL takeover; it is 13 April 2010. *John Glover*

Are the railway organisations squeaky clean? Or could they do better? It was interesting to hear a representative of the Rail Delivery Group say that the public believed that 21p in every pound of TOC revenue was profit. This compared with the reality of 3p. It is what people *think* that is the difficulty, not whatever the real situation may be.

Similarly, those who are not rail users have a consistently worse impression of rail travel than the users. To some extent this will be their way of justifying their actions, as using the railway may not even cross their minds. Typically this might be expressed as: 'Oh, the car's more convenient'.

Attitudes to fares are another such area; the range of prices for a given journey in what in all essence is a very similar product can be breathtaking.

So, there is work to do here.

Politics

The railway has perhaps gained a few steps up the political priority list in more recent years, but that can never be taken for granted. As the former Prime Minister Harold Wilson famously said, 'a week is a long time in politics'. An inherent industry problem is that the time taken for major projects to come to fruition will frequently outlive the electoral cycle. Investment in railway upgrading does not necessarily come high up the list of MPs' wants, however well disposed towards it that they may be.

It may also be argued too that the five-year Control Periods are not of sufficient length where major schemes are envisaged.

How might financial sponsors be rewarded? For instance, if an outside body invests in work that provides additional train paths, to what extent can they, or should they, be able to specify how that new capacity is used? Does that imply that franchise commitments should be flexible? What is the politics of it all?

Such questions are becoming ever more relevant, since the effects on each of Intercity, local services and freight operations are all part of the planning process and capacity allocation programme.

That planning has to take into account short, medium and long-term aspirations. Network Rail are looking to devolve planning to the components of their emerging Route structure, but it is recognised that the timetabling needs to be managed on a nationwide basis.

Mayor to control local lines?

On organisational matters, it has long been an ambition of the Greater London Authority (established in 2000) and earlier the Greater London Council (abolished in 1986), to have more of a say in the operation of main line rail services.

This was achieved in the creation of London Overground, to which a second group of lines, those from Liverpool Street to Chingford, Enfield Town and Cheshunt (via Southbury), was added in 2015, as was the Romford–Upminster branch. These are now marketed as part of London Overground.

At the same time, the Liverpool Street–Shenfield services passed to TfL Rail, but this was in effect an early manifestation of the changes which are being brought about by the introduction of Crossrail.

Will such transfers continue, as the Mayor Sadiq Khan, elected in 2016, clearly hopes that they will? Under the Mayor's plan, metro type services would all be run by Transport for London on a concession basis, leaving only the longer distance services on Network Rail to be operated as part of the DfT's franchises.

Unfortunately for him, few rail services actually run entirely within Greater London. The effective termini of what are often called the inner suburban services will usually be several miles beyond the GLA boundary, with destinations such as Shenfield, Bishop's Stortford, Hertford East, Welwyn Garden City, Luton, High Wycombe, Windsor, Guildford, Caterham, Tonbridge and Gillingham.

The present Secretary of State, Chris Grayling MP, was however having none of it. Speaking in Parliament on 6 December 2016, he said 'We can deliver improvements through partnerships, but we must remember that partnerships are not just about London'. A source close to Mr Grayling reaffirmed his position that handing over control of suburban rail lines to TfL would make operators unaccountable to passengers from outside London[47].

The taking of a controlling interest by TfL in part(s) of the South Eastern franchise which is due for renewal in December 2018 was thus ruled out and the same would seem to apply for the Thameslink, Southern & Great Northern (GTR) franchise due in September 2021. That franchise, though, may have some more fundamental problems.

The question of who should have control of what the various transport undertakings should or should not be doing, the setting of fares, and who should contribute what moneys towards it in investment terms or otherwise, remains unresolved.

This story seems unlikely to end here.

Assets

Is the rolling stock product right? How do people rate the maximising of seat provision with minimal elbow or leg room, compared with more standing room and fewer but more comfortable seats? A major consideration is the time taken for their journey, but given multi-purpose operations such as the Elizabeth line and especially Thameslink, how does one strike a reasonable balance?

Reliability appears to be a number one priority amongst most users, much of which is down to the engineering fraternity. Why are some types of rolling stock far less reliable in terms of time/distance between failures than others used on similar duties? The poor performers need to be rooted out.

Right time arrival is another wish list component. At considerable expense, do we need a purge on getting rid of flat junctions, which can cause much delay? Or is it more important to simplify operating patterns, which might mean more passengers having to change trains during their journeys? Or both?

Operational safety has been much improved, which focusses increased attention on the level crossing. More trains and more road traffic means more potential conflicts. How serious does the industry need to be on further reducing the number of crossings? This has been a notable component in the planning of Crossrail 2.

Guards on Underground passenger services were no longer needed after the withdrawal of the 1959 tube stock on the Northern line. Seen here at Borough station at the end of such operations in January 2000, a smartly turned out individual performs the traditional task of closing the doors. ***John Glover***

Marylebone is now the only London terminus which has no electrification, though this has been proposed from time to time. The existing 23km of fourth-rail on the Aylesbury line doesn't help the case. On 24 June 2008, 168219 will shortly be forming a train to Birmingham Moor Street, while on the right a train of the now defunct Wrexham & Shropshire undertaking is about to leave as the 06:45 to Wrexham. 67001 is at the tail end. ***John Glover***

Is the use of assets, which includes the use of the staff, as efficient as it might be? One person operation of buses is nowadays almost universal, but it was not always so. This meant that the driver had to collect the fares or inspect tickets/passes, open and shut the doors while being alert to the needs of passengers, including those with wheelchairs, pushchairs and heavy luggage, drive the bus and supervise what went on inside it. That was not achieved without some worker resistance, but achieved it was.

What staff presence do we need on stations, to carry out what duties?

The continuous reduction of unit costs is a key component of the long term well-being of the industry.

References

1. *Railways and Victorian Cities*. John R. Kellett, Routledge & Kogan Paul, London, 1979

2. London Passenger Transport Act, 1933, s3

3. Lord Ashfield, House of Lords Debate 02 March 1933, vol 86, cc 973-1031

4. London Passenger Transport Board, Annual Report and Accounts, 1935

5. *Sir Herbert Walker's Southern Railway*, C. F. Klapper, Ian Allan 1975, pages 263-275

6. *For Starters: The Business of Life*, Sir Peter Parker (autobiography). Jonathan Cape, London, 1989, page 182

7. Modernisation and Re-equipment of British Railways. British Transport Commission, London, December 1954

8. Op cit, para 124

9. 'Great British Railway Journeys': Darlington to Dunbar. Michael Portillo, first broadcast 5 January 2017 on BBC2

10. London Transport, Report from the Select Committee on Nationalised Industries, Vol 1 Report and Proceedings. paras 445-462, 593. HMSO 313, August 1965

11. The Financial and Economic Obligations of the Nationalised Industries. Cmnd 1337. HMSO April 1961, para 5 et seq

12. A Railway Plan for London. Preliminary Report by a Working Party. British Railways Board & London Transport, March 1965

13. London Transport, Report from the Select Committee on Nationalised Industries, Vol 1 Report and Proceedings. paras 461-2, HMSO 313, August 1965

14. Railway Policy, Cmnd 3439. HMSO, November 1967

15. Railway Finances, The Serpell Committee, Department of Transport, London, HMSO, 1983. Para 1.4 et seq

16. Proposed Increases by British Railways Board In Certain Country-Wide Fares and Charges. National Board for Prices & Incomes, Report no 72. Cmnd 3656, HMSO, May 1968

17. The Future of London Transport, a paper for discussion. Greater London Council, October 1970

18. Report of a study of Rail Links with Heathrow Airport, Part 1. Ministry of Transport, HMSO, May 1970.

19. Transport (London) Act, 1969

20. London Rail Study, Part 1. Greater London Council & Department of the Environment, 1974, paras 1.12-1.13.

21. Modernisation and Re-equipment of British Railways. British Transport Commission, London, December 1954

22. Op cit, para 36

23. Great Northern Electrics in Hertfordshire. A Case Study on the Role of Railway Modernisation in Suburban Development. Hertfordshire County Council Transport Co-ordination Unit, April 1980

24. British Railways Board: London and South East Commuter Services. Monopolies & Mergers Commission, Cmnd 8046, HMSO, October 1980. Ch 8, also Appx 2 part 3

25. Op cit, Appx 11

26. British Railways Board: Network SouthEast. Monopolies and Mergers Commission, Cm 204 HMSO, September 1987

27. Transport Policy, a Consultation Document, Vol 1. HMSO, 1976, para 7.47 et seq

28. Transport (London) Act, 1969, s1, 3.

29. British Railways Board: London and South East Commuter Services. Monopolies & Mergers Commission, Cmnd 8046, HMSO, October 1980

30. Op cit, para 4.11

31. Op cit, para 13.8

32. See for instance the Fifth Report of the House of Commons Transport Committee, Session 1981-82, Transport in London. HMSO, 127-1, July 1982

33. Public Transport in London, the next 10 years. Greater London Council, 1985

34. Light Rail for London? A Report for the BR/LRT Liaison Group, Autumn 1986

35. Transport in London, Department of Transport, 1989

36. Central London Rail Study, Department of Transport, British Rail Network South East, London Regional Transport, London Underground Ltd. January 1989

37. Central London Rail Study – A Report on Further Work, 1990. A working paper by officials from the Department of Transport, HM Treasury, British Rail, London Regional Transport and London Underground Ltd.

38. Department of Transport East London Rail Study, Summary Report, Halcrow Fox and Associates, London, undated c1989

39. A Rail Hub for Britain; an analysis of the effect of building a single interchange point for London on passenger demand. Dr Peter Gordon, an unpublished thesis submitted in partial fulfilment of the requirements of the University of Westminster for the degree of Master of Philosophy, 2000.

40. London East–West Study, Shadow Strategic Rail Authority, November 2000

41. The contents of this section have been based on the Approval of Passenger Track Access Contract by ORR (undated) and may not take fully into account later amendments such as the extension of Crossrail 1 beyond Maidenhead to Reading.

42. Thameslink 2000 closures, Statement of Reasons, Shadow Strategic Rail Authority, 23 September 1999.

43. The Combined Thameslink, Southern and Great Northern Franchise. Stakeholder Briefing Document and Consultation Response, Department for Transport, September 2013.

44. *Rail Technology Magazine*, April/May 2016

45. The Impact of New Rail Schemes, London Transport, September 1996

47. *Epsom Guardian*, 08 December 2016.

Bibliography and Acknowledgements

Bibliography

A Very Political Railway – The Rescue of the North London Line. Wayne Asher, Capital Transport Publishing Ltd, 2014. ISBN 978-1-85414-378-5. A detailed history of the fight for the future of this line which, at its worst, had been 'Shabby, Unsafe and Overcrowded'.

British Railways Locomotives & Coaching Stock 2016. Robert Pritchard & Peter Hall. Platform 5 Publishing Ltd, Sheffield, 2016. ISBN 978 1 909431 27 0. Comprehensive publication which includes much technical detail.

Great Northern Suburban. John N. Young, David & Charles, Newton Abbot 1977. ISBN 0 7153 7477 X. A useful history of the network as it was up to 40 years ago.

London and its Passenger Transport System. F. A. A. Menzler, Chief Development and Research Officer, London Transport Executive. Paper to the Royal Statistical Society, 1950, supported by 33 tables.

London Railway Atlas, 4th Edition. Joe Brown, Ian Allan Publishing Ltd, Hersham, 2015. ISBN 978 0 7110 3819 6. Detailed present day geographical railway mapping of an area rather larger than Greater London, showing individual tracks and with much historical detail as well. Includes opening (and closing) dates of each station and sections of track.

London's Overground. John Glover, Ian Allan Publishing Ltd, Hersham, 2012. ISBN 978 0 7110 3524 9. A detailed look at London Overground, the history of the lines and how the whole was brought together as a single operation.

London's Underground, 12th edition. John Glover, Ian Allan Publishing Ltd, Addlestone, 2015. ISBN 978 0 7110 3826 4. General history including all aspects of its development.

Long Term Planning Process: London and South East Market Study. Network Rail, October 2013.

Planning London's Transport, To Win as a World City. London Transport, November 1996.

Railway Passenger Stations in England, Scotland and Wales, A Chronology. 3rd edition. M. E. Quick, Railway & Canal Historical Society, 2005. Highly detailed reference source of approximately 440 pages.

Railway Track Diagrams: Vol 2 Eastern, Vol 3 Western, Vol 4 Midlands & North West, Vol 5 Southern and TfL. TRACKmaps, Frome, various dates. Very detailed diagrammatic representations of all the lines in the area covered showing normal direction of travel, system of electrification (if any), controlling signalling centre, official distances, platform capacities, level crossings, etc.

The London Underground, A Diagrammatic History. Douglas Rose. 8th edition, 2007. Map of system showing opening and closing dates for stations, and sections of route, station renamings, site relocations and much else.

Turning South London Orange: Reforming Suburban Rail to Support London's Next Wave of Growth. Sam Sims, Jonathan Roberts, Brett Wilson. Centre for London, January 2016.

To this list must be added the railway periodicals, notably but far from exclusively, *Modern Railways* and *Rail News*.

The scope for website interrogation is endless, but for present purposes those of the Department for Transport (and indeed Government generally), Crossrail, Network Rail, Thameslink, the various Train Operating Companies and Transport for London are particularly valuable.

For historical matters, the Railway Archive contains much useful material.

Acknowledgements

I am very grateful to Dr Martin Higginson and Mike Lamport, both of whom pored over early versions of the whole manuscript and made a number of helpful suggestions. I would also wish to acknowledge and thank Guy Brigden, Chris Curtis, Larry Heyman, Adrian Shooter and Howard Smith for the many useful suggestions they have made. All gave their help freely, with comments related to their specialist knowledge.

My thanks are due also to Dr Peter Gordon for permission to include parts of his PhD thesis.

Index

Stations and locations are generally listed under their current names.
Schemes that did not progress beyond the planning stage are only lightly indexed.

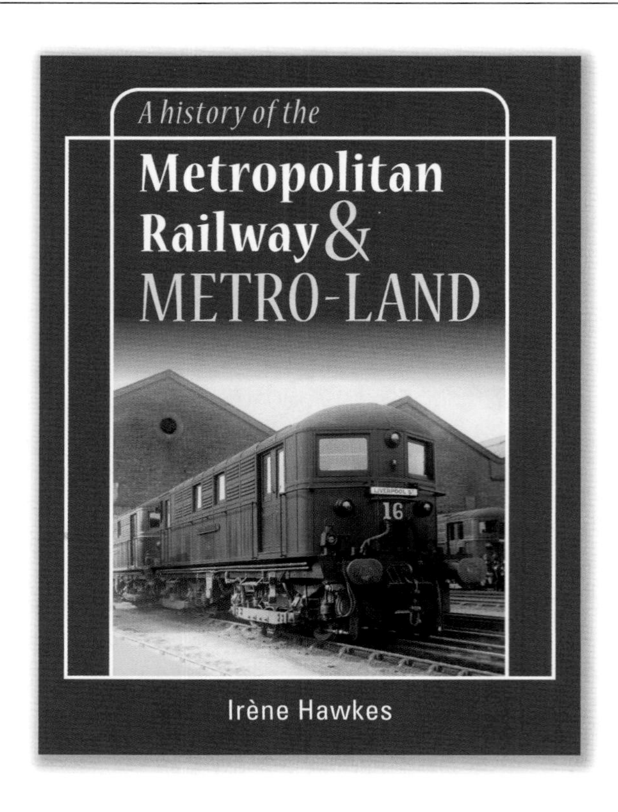

A History of the Metropolitan Railway & Metro-land

Irene Hawkes

Opened as the first underground passenger-carrying railway in the world in 1863, for the next 40 years the Metropolitan Railway expanded far beyond London's boundaries into the countryside of Middlesex, Buckinghamshire and Hertfordshire. It also bought land and developed housing along its tracks, fostering the British suburban dream of an affordable home in lovely garden suburbs linked by a fast train service to the city. In 1915 the term Metro-land was coined, summing up this very British semi-detached idyll.

This new history of the Metropolitan Railway shows how property development was as much a part of its business plan as its railway activities. Packed with a wealth of detail and illustrated with photographs, illustrations and contemporary advertising throughout, this superb book is both the story of an innovative and successful railway company and a social history of the suburbs.

ISBN: 9780860936749
Binding: hardback
Dimensions: 280 mm x 210mm
Pages: 160
Photos: over 150 photographs and illustrations
Price: £30

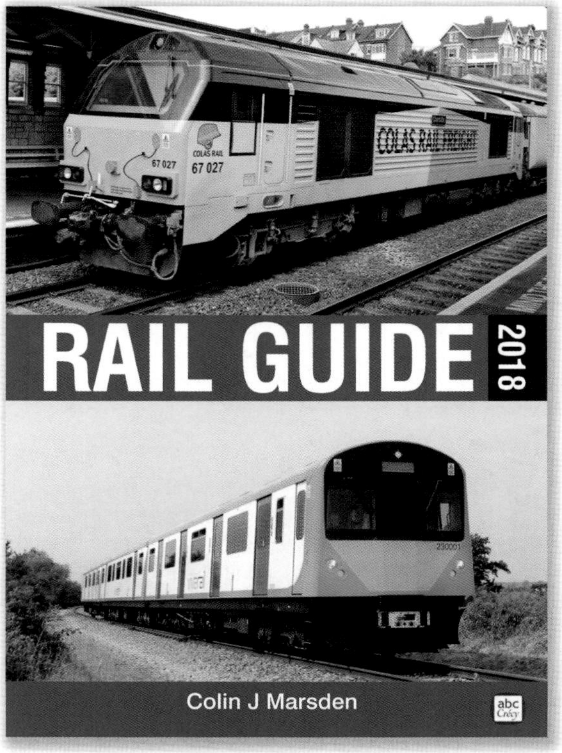

abc Rail Guide 2018

Colin J Marsden

The new edition of this best-selling annual publication has been thoroughly revised and updated to provide the most accurate listings, in operator order, of the locomotives, multiple units and stock used on the railways of Britain, the Isle of Man and Ireland. Entries are also separately cross-referenced to their operators.

There are many additional sections including those dealing with stock used by infrastructure companies, private train operators, tramways and Metro systems. Among other topics covered are coupling codes, TOPS numbers allocated to heritage traction and off-lease stock.

abc Rail Guide 2018 is simply the most comprehensive and accurate single volume reference source on the contemporary railway scene, the essential guide for all railway enthusiasts seeking to keep up to speed with the dynamic and rapidly changing railway landscape in these islands.

ISBN: 9781910809518
Binding: hardback
Dimensions: 210mm x 150mm
Pages: 304
Photos: around 500 including colour
Price: £22.50

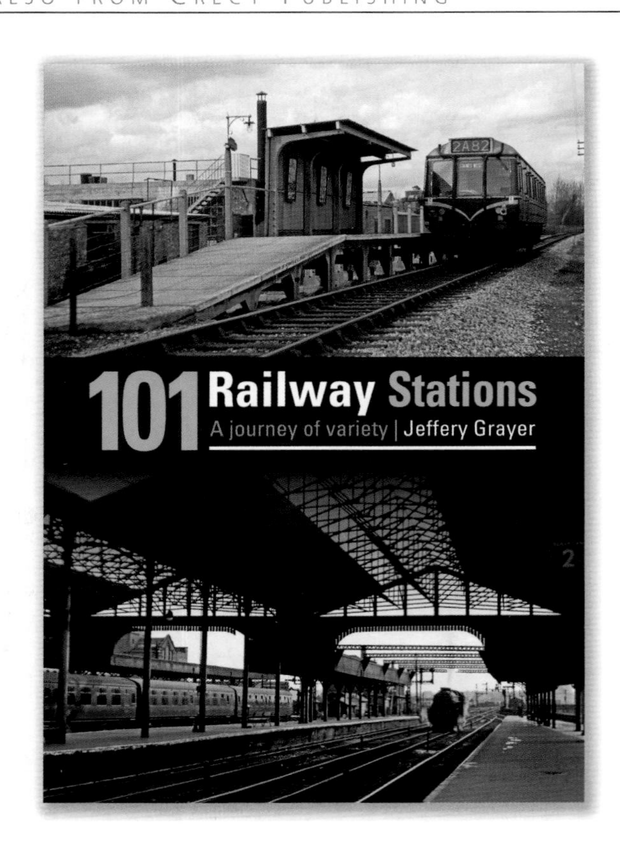

101 Railway Stations
A journey of variety

Jeffrey Grayer

In 1948 British Railway passenger trains called at just under 7,000 railway stations. Today that number has been reduced to around 2,500. Despite the substantial cuts to the size of the national network and the number of stations over the last 70 years, this book is a celebration of the remarkable variety of the stations that still exist. These range from some of the great city-centre termini, which in their scale and grandeur can be viewed as the Victorian equivalent of the medieval cathedrals, to stations serving small towns and remote basic halts deep in the heart of the countryside.

The author has selected 101 examples of the most interesting stations from across the network to show the diversity that still exists among Britain's stations. The history of each of these is recounted as is what makes it special. There are illustrations of the stations both historic and contemporary, and modern interpretations of what a railway station should look like are also included.

This book is an affectionate and absorbing reflection on a key but often overlooked part of the fabric of British society from the nineteenth century through to the twenty-first that will delight not just railway enthusiasts but also those with a wider interest in our history and heritage.

ISBN: 9780860936929
Binding: hardback
Dimensions: 297mm x 210mm
Pages: 176
Illustrated throughout
Price: £25